SHAME
Confessions of
an Aid Worker in Africa

Jillian Reilly

First published in 2012
Copyright © 2012 by Jillian Reilly
Editing by Roxanne Reid
Cover Art by Yda Walt/www.ydawalt.co.za
Cover Design by Elinore Wrigley de Lisle
Typesetting by Dominique le Roux
Publishing Management by Moonshine Media/
www.moonshinemedia.co.za

ISBN 978-1-4717-6656-5

All rights reserved. No part of this book may be reproduced in any form or by any electronic or mechanical means including information storage and retrieval systems, without permission in writing from the author. The only exception is by a reviewer, who may quote short excerpts in a review.

Visit my website at www.jillianreilly.com

For Luke and Aidan.
May you one day explore the world with eyes wide open.

Contents

Preface 7
1981: When Saving People Was A Ten Dollar Bill 9
October 1993: Setting Off to Save South Africans 14
November 1993: Getting Restless 21
Early 1994: Meet the Parents 28
Early 1994: Officially an Activist? 37
Still Early 1994: Breaking Free in Prison 44
April 1994: Nobody Told Me There Were White Townships 53
May 1994: Everything in South Africa is New Again 63
Middle of 1994: Setting up Stakes 70
Mid to Late 1994: Part-time Lovers 77
Still Mid to Late 1994: I Could See the Future 84
1995-1997: African Renaissance 90
Early 1997: Crashing Off the Monkey Bars 96
Early to Mid 1997: Born Yet Again 101
Early to Mid 1997: Becoming Mrs Reilly 111
Mid to Late 1997: The Singleton who was Never Alone 117

Late 1997: Meeting my Fellow Directors 124
Early 1998: Turning Promise into Paper 135
Early to Mid 1998: Searching for a Future 141
Mid 1998: I Can See Again! 149
Mid 1998: The Salad Kid 158
Mid 1998: Mrs Reilly Tries to Return 166
End of 1998: Bewitched and Bewildered 177
Late 1998 into 1999: Looking for Truth on Tombstones 188
1999: Haunted by the Truth 197
Late 1999: Hunted Because of the Truth 211
End of 1999: Another Unwanted Visitor 218
Early 2000: A Farewell to Mrs Reilly 224
Postscript 231
Thanks 233

Preface

I didn't want to tell this story. Truth is, I've spent the past ten years wishing I had a different story to tell. One where I had developed some groundbreaking development methodology after tireless work under shady trees with African women wrapped head-to-toe in colorful cloth. Where my life's travels, my work, led me to bubble over with accumulated wisdom about saving poor people. Or even one where I had a long-running affair with a Freedom Fighter who had been educated in Edinburgh and was a tender lover. Do I admit to spending many an hour picturing myself on the back of a shiny, muscular horse, legs wrapped around a shiny, muscular Freedom Fighter? Yes, that's the version of my life story I've fantasized about most – clearly for the least wholesome reasons.

Eventually the fantasies fragmented, as they always do, and I had to accept that none of those was my story. The one you're about to read is a story punctuated by everyday humblings, redolent with regret and tinted with a crude combination of arrogance and naïveté. A story, then, about growing up.

Of course, the very act of writing this coming-of-age story forced me to admit that I will never be the wise she-warrior cum world-saver I once believed I would, that I am just another person struggling to make my life "mean something", whatever that means.

You see, for a while, I believed I was somehow special: brave, wise, caring. And for a while I thought I'd found the perfect partner in Africa: poor, needy, mythical. Truth was, I didn't know either myself or Africa, and we never really came to understand each other.

You probably won't put this book down feeling admiration for me – or even pity, as we so often do for dreamers who emerge from Africa defeated. But I hope you might recognize aspects of my story: my longings, my delusions, ultimately, my disillusionment. For these are the universals: the feelings we eventually release when our hungry hopes – either for our own lives or those of souls we deem less fortunate – give way to acceptance of the terribly real lives we are forced to live.

The names of people and organizations in this book have been changed, but the story of what happened is the truth as I remember it, told in the fashion I deemed best.

1

1981: When Saving People Was A Ten Dollar Bill

Growing up, I had a thing for evangelists the way some kids like magic tricks or the circus. I'd discovered another fantastical world, a place where the crippled found legs to stand on, the cancer-ridden would rise up with life. Like magicians who cut women in half, these evangelists had the ability to do things with human beings that seemed otherwise impossible. But unlike the magicians, the evangelists' work was all about putting lives back together. It was about transformation.

When I was ten years old, I spent every Sunday morning in the company of Jerry Falwell. Just after *Tarzan*, just before *Charlie's Angels*, while my father was teeing off at the country club, and my mother and sisters were still asleep, I used to sit on my bedroom floor, legs crossed, nightgown stretched tight over bony knees, face aimed up at the twelve-inch Zenith color television that had been my big-girl birthday present that year. If I reached out, I could touch the screen with my hand, clearing a trail through fine, dusty particles to outline faces with my finger. If my mother had been with me she would have scolded me for sitting too close to the TV and warned of coming blindness. But the prospect of blindness barely troubled me; I was too preoccupied with what was in front of me.

I kept the volume low so the lusty hymns and praise-the-lords wouldn't slip out under the door. And I sat still, reverent like the rest,

SHAME

my eyes fixed and then blinking to hold back the tears. "Give something today," Reverend Falwell pleaded each week. He looked ready to sob. But he was a professional, so instead he just sweated and paced and preached, while everyone in the cavernous West Virginia auditorium sat sniffling and stifling their emotions, the way I did when my teacher read us *Ole Yeller*. I wiped my eyes with my pink sleeve, and wrapped my arms more tightly around my knees.

They were called Boat People, and they were the only ones who weren't crying. They just sat, thin old men and women (even the children looked like age spots) curled over in protective postures or herded in masses into the warehouses that were their temporary homes, waves of confusion and resignation. Even though their eyes were usually cast downwards, I felt they were looking at me. And I couldn't tear my eyes away from them. The Boat People were brownish-yellow with sorry, depleted faces, cheekbones like pegs for hanging coats of skin. My finger travelled over their flat noses and eyes, round and round and again, trying to work out how their faces had all the same parts as mine, but they didn't resemble me at all.

One day during recess at school, while everyone else was out playing kickball, I sneaked inside to find the Boat People's country on the globe. In the corner of my homeroom where the globe stood tilted on its stand, I scanned the patches of countries and oceans, and spoke the syllables slowly in separate whispers – Yemen, Thailand, New Zealand – until I finally found it, Vietnam. I traced the route the Boat People took from there to America, and it was far – at least eight ring finger lengths of ocean. Where did they go to the bathroom? How did they know they were heading in the right direction? The globe didn't provide any answers, only mysterious places that couldn't possibly be part of my world.

"What are you doing, Thunderfoot?" my best friend Cynthia charged into the room. "C'mon, we need you for kickball!"

I started spinning the globe around fast, treating it like any other ball. "Just seeing how fast I can make this thing go," I shouted back. And I could still hear it spinning as I chased Cynthia out the door.

For twelve weeks in that winter of 1981, Reverend Falwell made sweaty appeals on behalf of the Boat People, pleading to his real

1981: WHEN SAVING PEOPLE WAS A TEN DOLLAR BILL

and virtual congregation to give money for food and clothing for these wretched souls.

"My fellow Christians," he paused to wipe away beads of sweat from his forehead with a white handkerchief, "my fellow Americans, if you call the number at the bottom of the screen you can save a life this morning. Ten dollars, that's all it takes to save a life this morning."

Ten dollars? Really? None of this living-off-ten-dollars-stuff made sense to me, but that didn't matter. I could get ten dollars; I knew I could. My heart knocked against my ribs as I squeezed my knees tighter together and rocked back and forth. The Boat People needed me, and with Jerry Falwell's help, I was going to save them.

The problem was that all I had were twelve pennies, four nickels and three dimes (I counted them every week) stashed away in a tiny, beaded purse my mother had given me as an extra birthday gift, just from her. I didn't get an allowance because I didn't do chores, and it was winter so I couldn't wash cars or start a lemonade stand. My only option was to steal, Robin Hood style.

I knew my mother had money. My father gave her an allowance every week because she did lots of chores. I convinced myself that if my mother knew the whole eight-finger-lengths and ten-dollars-to-save-them story, she would want to give it to the Boat People as much as I did. So, on what felt like a particularly hushed Sunday morning, during a commercial for an extra-long, super-absorbent feather mop, I crept downstairs, then over to her purse, which she left on the dining room chair every night, clicking open the wallet – it was starting to feel more like *Charlie's Angels* than Jerry Falwell – rifling through grocery receipts and irrelevant one dollar bills, until I found the bill.

There it was in my hand: Andrew Jackson staring straight at me. He looked so serious, and no wonder, this was serious business. Breathless, back in my room, I pulled my nightgown over my knees and stared into Jackson's face while I imagined their smiling faces. Shiny little Boat People gobbling up Hamburger Helper and buying cold medicine and flipflops, all with the help of my ten dollars. I thought of the thank-you notes I would get from them, as grateful as they could be in stick-figure English. Maybe, just maybe, Reverend Falwell would ask me to come to West Virginia to shake the hands of the people I'd saved. And maybe, just maybe, Amy and Missy and Mom would get up – would Dad actually skip his golf game? – to see me on TV. Because I'd saved somebody – somebodies! – and they hadn't.

For one long week, I held onto that bill. Waiting for Mom to ask if I'd seen ten dollars lying around; shoving the bill into my book bag then checking on it every hour; resisting the temptation to show it to Cynthia and share tales of future savior stardom. My fantasies grew more vivid. Would I take an airplane to West Virginia? Or buy a frilly white dress for the occasion – good people always wear white – just like for Easter?

But as the week wore on I realized I had problems. I didn't have a stamp or an envelope, and I didn't know how to steal them. As Thursday led to Friday, more questions arose. What if the envelope got lost between here and West Virginia? Or worse, what if the postman saw Andrew Jackson staring at him and tore open the envelope over his lunch break? I sat on the monkey bars nervously pulling the crusts off my liver sausage sandwich, considering all the variables, analyzing the risk. How will they know it's my ten dollars? What if it just falls into a big pile of Boat People money, so there will be no thank you notes, no special appearances or free airplane rides?

The next Sunday, I bit my nails while Falwell led a chorus of *Amazing Grace*. I started rocking again, back and forth, heart pounding. During a commercial, a power washer this time, I returned the money to my mother's wallet just as I had taken it out: standing on the tips of my toes. Although I had tears in my eyes, Andrew Jackson never blinked.

Then I went back to my position in front of the TV, and those Boat People went back to staring at me. I covered my eyes. Please stop it; please stop looking at me. Falwell started up again: "Just think about all the things you spend ten dollars on every month …" I couldn't take it anymore. I switched the TV off and waited, waiting and waiting until nine o'clock came and the Boat People had floated out of my mind and I could turn on *Charlie's Angels*. That day it was the one where Jill (I secretly loved that Farrah Fawcett's character had the same name as me) was a racing car driver and her hair looked particularly pretty cascading out of her helmet. I tried to focus on

Farrah's dazzle, tried to forget about the Boat People's wilting faces pleading with me to save their lives. Eventually, it worked.

But I have never forgotten the feeling I had for those glorious seven days, before the doubts crept up the monkey bars. The feelings: the giddiness, the promise, the potential – theirs and mine, the power – oh yes, theirs and mine. The pure sense of rightness, of goodness. The simple, succulent belief that one day soon I would save a life.

I would only release those feelings twenty years later, when I had to let go of many dreamy feelings I'd once held dear; when I fled Zimbabwe in a business-class seat, certain that the only person I could save was myself.

2

October 1993: Setting Off to Save South Africans

"Is it because people are dying in South Africa? Is that why you're going there? To save dying African people?"

"God, Dad, how many times are we going to talk about this?! I'm not going to South Africa because people are *dying*."

"Because you can find dying people here, you know, over in East St Louis. Probably even closer. They'd probably like saving too."

"Are you listening to me? It's not about people dying. In fact, it's the opposite. It's, it's about rebuilding, rebirth! It's about, like, giving birth to a whole new country! And I'm going to be a part of it. I told you; I've got a job working on the elections with one of the country's biggest human rights law firms."

"I thought you said it was an internship"

"Job, internship, same thing."

"You've gotta be shittin' me. They're not paying you, it's not the same thing!"

"Oh, whatever, I'm going to be an *activist*. Nobody pays you be an activist."

"Didn't you get the election stuff out of your system with Clinton? He won. Hillary's doing her health care thing. You got what you wanted."

OCTOBER 1993: SETTING OFF TO SAVE SOUTH AFRICANS

"Um, this is slightly different. They've never even had elections like this before in South Africa, not where everybody voted. Most of the people have never voted, like, in their whole lives. Can you imagine that, never even having the chance to vote?"

"I never have voted."

"Yeah, but that's because you don't want to, not because you're black!"

"So basically it's about working with poor black people. We've got plenty of them here too, East St Louis, the south side of Chicago. They probably haven't voted either."

"Seriously, are you even listening to me?"

"Well, help me understand what the hell is so important that you have to go all the way to South Africa for it."

"To be a part of *history*. To help rebuild an entire society. Nelson Mandela is going to build houses for everyone, and he's promised that equal rights for men and women will be entrenched, embedded, whatever, in the Constitution. There's so much opportunity to bring about real change in South Africa now, to ... to just do *amazing* things there. Why is that so hard for you to understand?"

"I guess because I just can't understand why you can't do amazing things here."

***

Growing up in Chesterfield, Missouri, a suburb of St Louis where St Patrick's Day was the closest thing we had to a claimed ethnic identity, I can't remember the first time I saw a black person. Or anyone else whose skin was darkened by something other than summer sun. But I'm sure it was an event for my young eyes: a happening, like fireworks or a car accident, that made them open wider or focus longer. A realization of something not unthinkable, just never thought of.

Now as I stood in the baggage claim hall of Jan Smuts Airport in Johannesburg, my eyes widened again when I spotted a slumped-over guy in a baggy blue jumpsuit, his hair so closely cropped it looked

SHAME

as if it had been colored-in, his skin clear, his eyes barely open. Of course I knew there would be many black people in South Africa — that was the point of going there. So now my eyes widened in anticipation of my first opportunity to do something amazing in South Africa.

And I thought I knew exactly how the encounter would play out. I would simply say *Sawubona*, I see you, and he would immediately know I was different. Not like the other white people, a good white person. "I see you," the very words I'd never had the chance to say to the Boat People.

***

"*Sawubona*," Ntombenthle had taught me, "is our version of hello, but it literally means 'I see you'. This is how we greet people."

"I see," I'd replied. "I mean, I get it."

"In our culture it's very important to acknowledge someone's presence by saying, I see you." Ntombenthle leaned in to me as she spoke, seemingly unaware of her breasts spilling out of her blouse. And any time Ntombenthle began a sentence with "in our culture," which she did often, I leaned back in to her, lacking any breasts at all but feeling for a moment just as womanly. "You must acknowledge someone as a fundamental sign of respect."

Three months before I'd left for South Africa, I'd decided to make myself a student of Zulu, one of South Africa's eleven official languages. Although I knew English was widely spoken in South Africa, I was determined not to be one of those silly American do-gooders who landed in Africa, only to mouth toothy greetings and kick soccer balls around with children.

No, if I was going to be a real activist, I needed to know how to ask probing questions, to hear sad stories and translate them for the uninitiated. I could have chosen any of the other major languages — Sotho, Xhosa, even Afrikaans. But there was something so essentially African about Zulu, what with Shaka and all. So I'd placed an ad in the Northwestern University newspaper and sat every day for the next week among chattering undergraduates and admired the ad amid prosaic French and Spanish offerings on the page.

OCTOBER 1993: SETTING OFF TO SAVE SOUTH AFRICANS

I placed the cut-out ad in a scrap book, leaving space for my air ticket on the same page.

A week later she phoned, introducing herself in thick, theatrical tones, befitting an African teacher. "Hello Jeel, my name is Ntombenthle, I have seen your ad in the newspaper."

Dom-benth-shle? Nom-ben-tle? I tried three times to say the name, all the while thinking that if this was Zulu I wasn't going to be much of a Zulu student. Two weeks later, Ntombenthle opened the door of her grad student apartment with a blinding smile. "Ah welcome, Jeel, it's so nice to meet you."

Jeel? I'd never heard my name pronounced that way before, and secretly I felt relieved that she couldn't really pronounce my name either. What's more, Jeel sounded suitably foreign, unlike the Jill I'd always known. It was as if walking through that door had transformed me into a new person: Jeel Reilly, Zulu student and soon-to-be doer of amazing things.

Ntombenthle was a PhD student in education and the very picture of an African woman, with a head of cascading braids and a fleshy bosom and bum she had to navigate carefully in her tight apartment. Her whole body shook when she laughed, which was often, and her lips seemed designed for delivering clicky who-knew-those-letters-went-together Zulu expressions.

Sitting down next to her – in the shadow of her – every Monday and Tuesday night at seven o'clock, I believed I had the most perfect Zulu teacher in the world.

Week in and week out, we'd practice the basics. "*Ngingu* Jeel," my name is Jill. "*Ngihlala e-*Evanston," I live in Evanston. All the rote, introductory stuff you repeat endlessly when you're first picking up a language. But this was Zulu, so saying "*Ngingu* Jeel" over and over felt particularly interesting, even important.

Progress was slow because opportunities to practice with other Zulu speakers in Evanston, Illinois, were limited. I spent a lot of time talking to myself, a habit that would come in handy later in Zimbabwe when there was nobody else to talk to. Clicking to myself in the mirror, clicking as I drifted to sleep at night, clicking in the early morning hours that were mine alone.

SHAME

"You do the clicks very well, Jeel," Ntombenthle commented one day, not long before I left for Johannesburg. "You must have some Zulu in your blood." We both giggled, but for hours – okay, days – afterwards I quietly entertained the notion that Ntombenthle might be right, that maybe Jeel was different, special even.

Three months later, we said our last goodbyes at that flimsy apartment door. "*Hamba kahle*, Jeel." "Yes, *sale kahle*, Ntombenthle." Goodbye. Ntombenthle paused. "You are very brave to be going to South Africa at this time, Jeel." Until now she and I had never discussed real life in South Africa, focusing instead on the life imitated on the pages of Zulu text books.

"What, you mean with the elections coming?"

She laughed her breast-jiggling laugh. "Yeeees! I mean with these elections!"

"Well, it's not really a big deal. I mean, I'm sure everything will be fine."

"Ah, you have more faith in my people than I do. Why do you think I am here? Why do you think I have brought my child here? Buthelezi, he's looking for a fight. The Zulus will never agree to being ruled by the Xhosas." Zulus and Xhosas? Ruled? Suddenly it all sounded too Shaka Zulu.

"Well, at least I'll be able to say *sawubona* to the Zulus when they come looking for a fight," I offered, finding refuge in jocularity.

"Ah, that's a good one, Jeel. Yes, you say hello to my brothers and sisters when they come knocking. Go well, my dear, Godspeed."

And I didn't know what to say to Ntombenthle, because Godspeed seemed like something older people said, not students. And standing small in her grown-up doorway, I felt like a very young student.

I didn't practice Zulu on the walk home that night. How could I, when I was occupied by a single, English word: brave. Over and over again. Brave? Brave! I could only remember being called brave once before, when I was seven years old and told my sister Amy I was going to hold my breath as I swam the whole length of the swimming pool. In the end I had to come up for breath half-way across, and Amy stood by the side of the pool laughing.

OCTOBER 1993: SETTING OFF TO SAVE SOUTH AFRICANS

Now I smiled. *Ngingu* Jeel Reilly, and I am brave. I promised myself I wasn't going to come up for air this time.

***

The baggage hall in Jan Smuts Airport was stuffed with frayed travelers vying for spots next to a carousel that showed no sign of movement nearly an hour after arrival. A few people lit cigarettes – you could smoke in airports back then – while others dialed chunky black cell phones with the same hunger as the smokers. The air was hot, not equatorial hot, just airport hot, with too many exasperated people inhabiting one large space. I stared at that slumping guy in his blue jumpsuit, as I clutched the navy blue LL Bean canvas tote that my mother had thought such a good idea because it had plenty of zips and pockets and she imagined zips and pockets might be useful in Africa. With every minute the carousel sat still, I clutched the bag tighter, anxiety and excitement rising in tandem.

My eyes kept darting back and forth between the baggage carousel and the baggage carrier as I searched the creases of his face for his story. I'd spent years at college studying the sad stories, past and present, of South Africa's black people, and I was certain this young man was a lead character in one of them. Has two jobs, I thought, as he rested his body on the carts. He roused himself only when someone approached, lifting himself to pull a cart from the snaking line and push it to them, without pleases, thank yous, or you're welcomes exchanged. I saw how his pants hung loose and long from hips more narrow than mine. God, I wonder how many meals he has every day? Then I glanced back at the carousel, more sluggish than the black man himself.

Finally the baggage carousel started moving, and a guy who looked like one of the white hunters on *Tarzan* – chunky boots and legs, khaki shorts – shouted out, "Oh hurrah, the monkeys who run this place actually figured out how to get us our bags!" The room shared an uncomfortable giggle, and I heard a voice behind me.

"Madam, here is a trolley for your bags." I spun around. He was there. The first black person I could potentially help in South Africa was there!

"Excuse me?" I blurted out. Oh shit, shit, shit I didn't say *sawubona*.

"I'm asking do you want a trolley for your bags, madam," he mumbled, halfheartedly extending the trolley towards me.

"Oh, yes, yes, thank you, thank you so much. That's very kind of you, really very, very nice of you." I reached out to accept the trolley as though it were a gift. "*Sawubona!*" I said at last.

His face was as still as his body. "You need help with your bags, madam?"

"Huh? Sorry, I mean, excuse me?"

"Madam ..." he carried on.

"Jill my name is Jill! Uh, *Ngingu* Jeel!"

Now the first twitch of an emotion appeared on the man's face: annoyance. "You need help with your bags, madam?" he repeated

"Ah, yes, of course. No, I mean, no I don't need help. I can carry these all on my own." I waited for a sign of relief, maybe even admiration for brave, strong Jeel, so different from all the other whites, but the man's eyes stayed fixed on a spot on the floor for a moment before he slouched off.

"Thank you, though, thanks very much," I said, trying to grab him back. "That's very kind of you. *Ngiyabonga kakhulu*," I shouted, thank you! But he just returned to his post, splayed over the carts, until the white hunter man signaled for his help and he quickly grabbed the man's luggage from the carousel. I watched as the two worked together silently, collecting the bags and stacking them on the trolley, before walking out with the white man leading the way. My new friend almost skipped along, his eyes focused, maybe even a little smile on his face.

I stared as they disappeared through the door. And then it dawned on me: you fucking idiot, all the trolley guy wanted was money. How could the white hunter guy get it and you didn't? For a few moments I imagined a different scenario, one where I'd ably reached into my tote and pulled out some money and been that kind of good white person, even if I'd wanted to be a different kind, with conversations rather than donations. I took a deep breath and saw my bag circling. Okay, so the *amazing* work would have to start tomorrow.

3

November 1993: Getting Restless

I woke the next morning to the sound of drums beating. Not headbanging rock band drums, but heart-thumping warrior drums. *Shaka Zulu* style drums. *Ngingu* Jeel Reilly, and I am brave, I repeated to myself, pulling the sheet up to my neck. The drumming didn't stop. I remembered weekend mornings with *Tarzan*, when a faraway rhythmic drumbeat signaled that natives were either planning to attack or preparing for the wedding of the chief's chubby daughter. Tarzan would have been concerned; he knew that these kinds of drums – the kind vigorous dark men banged with coarse hands – rarely meant celebration.

I sat up, still holding the sheet high and tight. *Ngingu* Jeel Reilly, and I *am* brave, I reminded myself. I'm going to walk outside and find Jerry and Maria Campbell, my hosts in South Africa, rigging a tape recorder with drumming just to make me feel like I've truly arrived in darkest Africa. This had to be a joke, right?

The drumming seemed to grow louder. I glanced at the panic button next to the door, like a doorbell, except it was for you to ring when unwanted visitors arrived. When they'd showed me around the day before, Jerry and Maria had pointed out the panic button the way most hosts show you the bathroom or the heating system. They explained that if I pushed it, five guys with AK47s and attack dogs would show up in less than five minutes. I think it was supposed to make me feel better.

"They get pretty pissed off if they just come out for a scare," Jerry added, "so make sure you really need help if you push this thing." I nodded, trying to decide where the fine line might be between fear and imminent danger, panic and paranoia.

Now, considering the merits of the panic button anew, I got out of bed and dressed, certain that flimsy pajamas were a liability in any situation involving rhythmic drumming or armed guards. I looked out the kitchen window and saw Jerry's sons, Brendon and Michael, seven and five, weaving pieces of kikuyu grass through the spokes of their bikes. So I walked into the back garden to join them, in a Northwestern T-shirt and sweatpants which at that moment possessed all the protective feel of body armor.

"Hi Jill," they said in bored unison. If they heard the drums, they weren't bothered, too concerned with seeing who could find the world's longest piece of grass.

I looked towards the *koppies* or hills where the drumming seemed to be coming from, half expecting to see smoke pouring into the air. I could barely see over the high wall that circled Jerry and Maria's property with a lethal coil of razor wire. I'd heard about South Africa's heavy security, but somehow hadn't expected it from academic liberals like Jerry and Maria. Surely they weren't afraid of black people? Wasn't that barbarians-at-the-gate stuff rife only among the white Tarzan-guy community? I noticed a sign informing me that the fence was electrified at about the same time that I first heard singing accompanying the drumming.

"They're the Zionists," Jerry said, coming up behind me and handing me a cup of coffee. He stood shading his eyes, staring off into the hills. Jerry Caldwell was an African history professor at Northwestern University and my academic advisor there. After my first class with him, I'd told my girlfriends he was a dork, and they said all history professors were dorks and I should switch to political science where at least there was a chance they'd be sexy. Jerry wore a grey cardigan sweater, had a mild case of dandruff and was one of the few professors who repeatedly showed up for lunch at the professor– student table at our dorm, willing, it seemed, to eat the lentils au

NOVEMBER 1993: GETTING RESTLESS

gratin, willing to make small talk with a pack of twenty-year-olds who tried alternatively to ignore and impress him.

I'd taken his class – An Overview of the History of Southern Africa – because one African history class was a requirement for all history majors. I hadn't expected that Southern Africa would appear as troubled and mysterious as Vietnam had seemed years earlier, that it would have the same head-reeling, globe-spinning effect on me. Soon enough I'd signed up to be an African history major, then written an honors thesis, then decided I *had* to go to South Africa for the elections because the new South Africa might produce a new Jeel Reilly. And the man I once called a dork encouraged me at every step, making me feel smart if not brave. Soon enough, I was inviting him out for lunch. Soon enough, he was introducing me to his family and offering to let me stay with them while they were on sabbatical in Johannesburg. Now here I was in his backyard, wondering which version of Africa I had landed in.

"I thought Zionists were in Israel?" I replied, trying to appear casual.

"Different kinds of Zionists these," Jerry chuckled. "They're evangelicals, born-again Christians. "

"Seriously? God, I thought I'd left those behind in the States." A picture of Falwell flashed into my mind.

"No way, evangelical churches are huge here. Fastest- growing churches in South Africa, across all of Africa, actually."

"I didn't realize South Africans were that religious."

"Not religious, really, just desperate. When people don't have much, these kinds of ideologies are very appealing. Gives people something to believe in, some hope. Why do you think the missionaries were so successful across Africa?"

"Makes sense." I paused and looked back towards the where the beating sounds were coming from. "So are they running around with snakes up there? Dipping people in water?"

"No, just dancing and singing. Someone's being born again, going through this whole sort of induction ceremony. It's pretty amazing to see, they dance in circles, play the drums for hours, sometimes into the night. You should go up there and watch."

23

It sounded fascinating, if only in a *National Geographic* way. "I don't know, I think the only birth I'm interested in is the New South Africa."

"Well then, you'll be interested in this." Jerry picked up a newspaper from the dusty patio table and handed it to me with its front-page headline: "Future Hangs in the Balance". I scanned the story, which focused on the Inkatha Freedom Party's (Ntombenthle's Zulus) resistance to the elections.

"Journalistic hyperbole," I said, resorting to a university habit honed over too many professor-student lunches of brandishing academic words when I felt the most uncertain. "Makes a good headline, but is it ...?"

"It's reality," Jerry interrupted. "Terre'Blanche is threatening to form a breakaway Afrikaans state, the IFP says there'll be civil war. The whole place could blow up, you know."

"Obviously you're not too worried. You're here with your family."

Jerry paused and scratched his head, another dorky thing he did when considering something. "My in-laws own lots of guns," he deadpanned.

"The only thing we have to fear is fear itself," I offered. Quoting was another of my bad habits.

"That and a country going up in flames," Jerry sniggered. He usually won these little sparring contests and I was ready to end it.

"Yeah well, I guess I'm going to head out today, look around your neighborhood, Melville, that's what it's called, right? Before it all goes up in flames."

Jerry winked, making me wonder how afraid he really was. How brave I really was. How afraid I should be.

***

Jerry and Maria's gate closed behind me. A band was playing in my head, one of those choruses of big black ladies in robes belting out a hallelujah-type song, and my heart beat in time with their celebratory rhythm. The black ladies were celebrating my arrival in South Africa, the very act of me stepping out alone, one foot after the other on Johannesburg's streets, filled with poor black people just waiting for nice white people to do amazing things on their behalf. By the time I set off to explore Melville, the Zionists' drums had stopped beating, though Jerry's comments about his gun-toting relatives still echoed. I promised myself I wasn't going to be afraid. How could I fear the very people I'd come here to help? I took a deep breath of Joburg's warm, dry air and kept walking.

I learned a lot on that first trip out of Jerry's house. I would learn a lot on every trip around South Africa, but this short trip up five blocks was a revelation.

I learned that Melville didn't have sidewalks. Most of South Africa's streets didn't have them, which made pedestrians feel like forlorn hitchhikers or sloping dogs. And as with so many things in South Africa, it left you wondering if this kind of everyday danger was exciting or just, well, dangerous.

I learned that large South African birds made *haw, haw, haw* noises that sounded just like the pterodactyls on *The Flintstones*. I smiled because it seemed so African, ancient and almost mystical. I learned that there were no friendly dogs in South Africa, only snarling ones that went from rabid to bored in the time it took me to pass the gates they patrolled.

I learned that white people didn't walk around neighborhoods. Maybe they were waiting for sidewalks or maybe it was some apartheid injunction against strolling that I hadn't heard about. I learned that black workers felt free to enjoy peaceful naps in the front yards of white people's houses, flopping about in an un-orderly, un-apartheid way. I couldn't help but stare, but they didn't stare back. Not one of them would look at me or anywhere in my white person direction. How could I say *Sawubona* when they seemed determined not to see me?

Never mind, I had months to break through years of apartheid ignorance. I would keep trying to make that all-important connection, starting with actually seeing each other, before saying to each other *I see you*. So I hit Melville's streets, lined with restaurants, cafés and second-hand bookstores, every day for the next week. I left behind the razor wire surrounding that quiet din of threats and warnings that comprised so much of everyday South African conversation. The constant threat of "them" shared like the weather forecast. Fractured stories of muggings, hijackings and rapes swirling like a funnel cloud. Swirling the way that don't-sit-too-close-to-the-television had so many years earlier – the threat apparently so real and yet so abstract.

And every day I faced the challenge to make a connection, staring into blank stares, trying to catch averted eyes, armed with one simple weapon: a smile, sometimes toothy, sometimes tight, ever present. I can't say when it started, but at a certain point during that first week the smile became strategic, or at least deliberate. An alternative to *Sawubona*, not a conversation, but at least the offer an interaction, a smile being the obvious entreaty of a very, very nice white person. One, two, three black people, smile, smile, smile. Hello! Hi! I said with my smile, I'm acknowledging you. When I passed, people shifted almost imperceptibly, certain not to touch. Smiling to the woman in the red sweater and braided hair standing at the bus stop: Hello, Hi, I see you! Smiling to the gardener, barefoot in a blue jumpsuit, bent over to trim a hedge. I see you too! Smiling at any, every black person who passed. Smiling so much, I forgot I was smiling. But that was good, right? We had a whole history of isolation, theirs and mine, to overcome. With enough persistent smiling, I believed they would let me into their world. And then the real conversation would begin.

I thought I was quietly going about business on my smiling safari, making Johannesburg a happier and therefore safer place. Until Jerry decided to join me on one of my outings.

"You don't have to smile at them, you know," he said as we returned home from picking up milk. He didn't look at me as we spoke.

"What do you mean?"

"You're not going to make their day by smiling at them." He spoke quietly, looking up to follow the path of one of those *Flintstones* birds.

"No, I ..." I protested, but Jerry wasn't interested.

"Their lives are pretty bad, and you can't change it with a smile."

"I don't think I can change their lives with a smile. I just want to be a decent person."

"Do you feel the need to smile at white people all the time to be decent?" he countered.

"Of course not."

"Then don't be patronizing with blacks. Treat them like you would anyone else. You have to accept that you can't make everybody's life better simply by behaving differently."

"What a depressing thought. You really believe none of us can change anything by role modeling the right kinds of behavior?"

"Maybe Nelson Mandela can, but you and me, no. And you might actually make things worse without knowing it."

"Worse? How can I possibly make things worse by being kind?"

"By confusing them."

"You make them sound like children, Jerry."

"Not children, just people who have experienced a certain system and understand how it works."

"Isn't that the very system that's changing with the elections?"

Jerry looked up at the circling birds again. "Not everything's going to change with these elections, Jill, you know that. Some things are pretty entrenched."

"Okay, then, whatever, I'll practice scowling, then maybe I'll fit in better with the other whites here."

"Just make sure it isn't about you more than them." Jerry didn't take his eyes off the sky as he spoke. "Make sure it isn't more about making you feel good than them."

Can't it be both? I wanted to ask. What's so wrong with me feeling good because they feel good? Instead, I just admired the birds with him. Because, of course, Jerry won these everyday jousts, which had seemed perfectly obvious over lentils, but was becoming annoying over *biltong*. Now I could imagine that it was Jerry using the word "dork" as he described me to Maria in bed at night.

4

Early 1994: Meet the Parents

Before I booked my flight to Johannesburg with South African Airways, I had enjoyed a satisfying fantasy moment that saw me trawling gritty downtown Johannesburg streets with my head high, wearing a stern but friendly look on my face; me with dreadlocked black friends sweating it out in bouncy racially mixed nightclubs; enjoying exotic char-grilled meats at trendy restaurants with up-and-coming anti-apartheid activists; knocking on the doors of shacks while gathering testimony with my human rights worker friends. You get the idea.

In my fantasies, Joburg was like one large inner-city high school, and I was the instantly popular new girl. Maybe it was because I was never popular in my own high school that I was willing Jeel into a sort of minor stardom in her new African life.

So I decided to arrive in Joburg two weeks before my internship was scheduled to begin, to allow myself time to develop this actively earnest social life. After ten days of smiling my way through the streets of Melville, sometimes riding with Jerry and Maria to suburbs further afield, I hadn't met a single white person Jerry or Maria hadn't introduced me to or who didn't hand me a receipt at the end of our conversation. Not a single person my age. And I hadn't exchanged a single word with any black person, other than a mumbled thank you to the guy who sold me a "bunny chow" – a strange street food consisting of a hollowed out half-loaf of bread filled with curry.

The sad truth, I was coming to realize, was that the only people who seemed interested, even desperate, to talk to me were the very whites I thought I'd come to help depose: Jerry's gun-toting relatives, who perhaps thought they'd found in me someone more fearful than themselves. Even though I'd walked out from behind the white walls, I found myself cosseted in a curious and hot-housed white world; a hot-house that at that moment in South Africa's history was suffocating rather than growing things.

Maria's family, the Van Rooyens, orbited around Jerry and Maria's house during the week and descended upon it at the weekends, when stopping by became staying over.

I had no idea how to react to them at first. They were, after all, Afrikaners: the inventors of apartheid, thieves and rapists who had claimed South Africa's wealth as their own. If the villains in South Africa's story were white, the Afrikaners were the arch villains.

I'd never encountered such gracious villains. "Welcome to South Africa," each one of them said. They were so pleased I'd come. I must be so tired. I kept smiling and saying thank you and waiting for someone to do or say something that would reveal the evil within. Instead I got tea and *koeksisters*, a type of twisted donut.

There were so many brothers and sisters that I had to keep repeating their Afrikaans names, like Elsie and Riaan, to remember them. The women were housewives or office managers who knitted lace doilies over strong coffee or weak tea. The men were police officers or small business owners who smoked unfiltered cigarettes and usually topped their glasses of Coke with a tot of brandy, all sweet and strong and befitting a people whose lives seemed either cloying or corrosive.

Maria's aging mother, Anneline, gambled every Saturday afternoon, prayed every Sunday morning and packed a gun every day just in case one of those *"kaffirs"* got in her way. "God help the silly bugger who tries," she said, the pistol shaking in a hand palsied by age and sherry. When I told her I was going to work in Johannesburg, she offered me the gun. "You don't even have to know how to aim straight," she said, pushing it towards me like an ice cream cone for a child, "down there I'm sure they'll be plenty of naughty *kaffirs* we'd be better off without." Her children rolled their eyes, embarrassed. They were quiet just to quiet her.

Maria's father, Eric, was a teetotaler who'd been a police captain at the height of apartheid in the 1970s and 80s, and refused to talk about what he'd seen, much less done. It left him a gentle man, the most removed and reflective of them all. He spoke to his wife in calming whispers, and when Jerry or Maria would mention South Africa's "reconstruction" after the elections or the need for "reconciliation" he'd just nod his head without saying anything. The family knew Jerry and Maria's politics, but I never heard them arguing about it. Family was too important to be strained by something like politics.

"So Jerry told us you're going to work here, Jill," one of the sisters, Andrea, said in a sing-song tone.

"Yes, yes, I'm going to work at a human rights law firm, on, well, uh, human rights!" I beamed.

"Okay, that's nice," the women chorused.

"I've never understood this concept," the youngest brother, Kobus, offered with a twisted smile. "What are rights exactly and why should everyone have them?" His wife, also Maria, swatted him. Some form of swatting seemed to be common among Afrikaans wives.

I took a sip of sweet white wine and put down my knife and fork. "Well, I, uh, think it's about respecting each individual's basic human needs, as well as their potential for growth and development, and recognizing the need to provide the most basic requirements for that development. Housing, food, education." Kobus's face looked blank, but the women continued their generous nodding.

"The term 'human rights' has been common in international parlance since the Second World War," Jerry proclaimed. Everyone turned their gaze on him and I was grateful. "Since the Holocaust, the UN has pioneered the basic principles of human rights in an attempt to prevent a repeat of the Nazis' fundamental denial of the Jews' humanity."

"*Ja*, well, then I guess that's necessary," Kobus conceded, then asked Maria for another beer.

"Some of our blacks, they don't really understand how to live properly, do they?" eldest sister Elsie offered in a sweet, almost hushed voice. She must have been the family's conciliator. "They need to be taught, as you say, how to develop properly."

"Well, I didn't really mean to suggest that that it was about teaching them something, not really," I said as I took another sip of wine. "It's more about ensuring that other people ... that systems ..., I guess it's really more about government systems, respecting and, uh, recognizing their needs. Their basic, um, human needs. I already said that, didn't I?"

"Are you sure the blacks are actually human?" the old lady cackled. The table practically rolled their eyes in unison, and Maria glanced at me in apology. The old lady kept sniggering into her sherry, relishing her own mischief.

"Good for you, Jill, working on these human rights things," Maria's father said. "I think I've spent all my life working on human wrongs!" And with that he offered me a gracious exit to the conversation. I sensed that he was accustomed to ending conversations one way or another.

The Van Rooyens never talked to me about my work again. Instead, they chose to educate me about their country and their customs.

"Okay, let's try it again, Jill, *boh byu tee*," they'd say, trying to get me to pronounce the name of a minced beef casserole. I'd try again, *bah-boo-tee*, and fail, and everyone would giggle on cue.

They shared with me their love of their land, smiling when they talked about the bush, the constancy of the seasons and the behavior of the animals, untamed and yet somehow predictable. When nature produced storms and droughts, they forgave her, figuring God or Mother Nature had a bigger plan they didn't know about. They kept a copy of *Newman's Guide to Birds* permanently splayed open and ready on a coffee table in case of a sighting in the lemon tree in their back yard.

But the Van Rooyens also talked about their plans: to get money offshore, to have extra fuel, to teach the children how to use guns. That conversation usually started long after lunch, when the bounce of the booze had turned to depression. The women couldn't believe it had come to that; the men kept warning how much worse it was going to get. The women's eyes seemed just ready to tear; the men's upper lips grew stiffer. Sentences ended with a sigh and the favorite South African rejoinder, *Ag shame*, a catchall phrase meaning something like "oh what a pity".

They began weighing their options for the immediate future under a black-led government in a democratic South Africa, returning reluctantly to the reality that they had no options. There was no other place in the world where they belonged and they knew that. Their singular sense of place began to feel less like a tie and more like a tether.

The Van Rooyens weren't the only ones making back-up plans. Some white South Africans had set to work building bunkers under their houses, where they could escape when the bombs exploded and the blacks became too restless. They created the ultimate hiding places, within the earth, underground, away from Africans but still in their beloved Africa. They stocked up on canned goods and candles, in anticipation of electricity and water systems breaking down or being vandalized within moments of the handing over of power. Pick n Pay supermarkets were reporting shortages of creamed corn and baked beans, and rumors snaked through the streets about hordes of angry blacks that would knock down doors, demanding houses and cars. *They're going to come, and they'll take whatever they want, jewelry, cars, whatever they can get their hands on.* For many, impending chaos felt an absolute certainty.

One day, about a month before the elections, Elsie and her husband Thys invited me for Sunday lunch. Elsie had become attached to me because her daughter had left that year for Stellenbosch University outside Cape Town and so Elsie's nest was more gaping than empty. She and Thys lived in Vereeniging, a middle-to-working-class Afrikaans neighborhood south of Johannesburg, in a sprawling ranch home with a white wrought iron fence that had three "Beware of the Dog" signs on it. They didn't own a dog.

The afternoon started well, with snacks and sunshine and more silly discussion of South Africa's peculiarities. But after talking about a possible trip to the game reserve one weekend, the conversation stalled uncomfortably, with Elsie and Thys drinking more and speaking less. Maybe it was the attempt to make plans. Maybe it was the absence of the parents, of Jerry and Maria, or the fact that the days till the elections could now be counted down in a single month on the calendar. Suddenly Elsie and Thys wanted to talk politics.

"It's difficult to say what's going to happen here," Elsie said, stubbing out a Stuyvesant that she always promised was the last for that afternoon, maybe even forever. But this wasn't the time for an Afrikaner to stop smoking.

"What do you mean, difficult to say what's going to happen?" Thys snapped. "We know exactly what's going to happen. The ANC is going to win this so-called election and Nelson Mandela will be the President of the so-called New South Africa. All this election rubbish is a bit of performance, really."

I sat like a fly, stiff but twitching, looking at dining room walls covered with watercolors of flowers and the Drakensberg Mountains, another of Jesus Christ looking down over the table. Did these two really want to talk politics? Or was it just a lament, a sad song they needed to sing for each other, with me as an audience.

Back in Chicago, I'd imagined relishing the opportunity to take on these white South Africans, talking them down, disabusing them of all their prejudices and preconceptions. Yet here I was, quiet and observant.

"Of course, man, I know Mandela will win," Elsie replied. "What I mean is that we really don't know what the future will be like for us with him in power." Just then their maid Patience came in and placed a platter with tea and biscuits on the lace-covered table in front of us. "Thank you, Patience," Elsie said and turned to me. "Lovely girl, Patience. She's been with us for twenty years." She leaned in closer, "I don't think we'd survive without her."

"Just take a look over our border, Elsie," Thys continued, "anywhere north of the Limpopo River, that'll tell you what will happen here." He grabbed her pack of cigarettes, tipped one out and lit it from the side of his mouth, then exhaled. "I reckon the history of Africa predicts our future. I know you're one of Jerry's history students, Jill, so I'm sure you'll appreciate what I'm saying." His hand rested on his chin, the cigarette burning inches from his moustache.

A dark bird flew over, the one with the bellowing haw, and I stared up at it hoping someone would lurch for the *Newman's* and the conversation would turn to nature. Nobody moved, so I was forced to reply. "I wouldn't really call myself a historian of Africa, I've just focused on South Africa, really."

"Well, then, I'll give you a quick lesson," Thys offered. "The recent history of Africa hasn't been pretty. 'Liberation'," he said, his fingers forming quotation marks in the air, "hasn't exactly been the big success it was supposed to be. Well, not if your skin's the wrong color or you're not a relative of one of the so-called liberation Presidents." Thys used the phrase "so called" often, as if the whole world was lying and only he knew the truth.

"But we're not like the rest of Africa, you know that, Thys," Elsie pleaded, her hands smoothing the tablecloth. She turned to me, "We're just not like black Africa, really." I half nodded until I realized I wasn't sure what I was agreeing with.

"We'll have to see," Thys replied. "Maybe we're just like the rest of black Africa, and we'll go down the same shit hole once the wrong people are in power." There was silence in the room, while outside neighboring domestic workers nattered over fences.

"Yes, well, clearly there have been a lot of problems across Africa in the past," I said, "but Mandela and the other ANC leaders know they need everyone, all South Africans, to make the new South Africa work."

"I hope you're right," Elsie jumped in, finding comfort in another cigarette. "I just hope that the blacks realize they need us, you know, that we've done good things for this country, made it what it is, really. I'm sure they know that." She looked at me for a comforting nod, but I didn't move. Oh yeah, you've made this country the mess that it is, I thought. But I didn't say a word. I felt as though I was sitting with people whose home was about to be repossessed, and it seemed irrelevant, mean even, to point out that they'd been bad debtors.

"Of course South Africa needs everybody, there's so much work to be done with the Reconstruction and Development Program, to rebuild the country," I finally reassured them.

"Rebuild the country?" Thys exploded. "What do you mean?

It's built. We built it. Roads, dams, power, all of it. We built it!" He downed the remainder of his tea like a shot of whiskey, head thrown back.

"Mandela knows that," I half whispered, putting my cup down. "He's not going to force anyone to leave." What was I doing? Why didn't I tell them to get a life, get a grip, stop all the self pity?

"We'll see what Mr Mandela feels about us leaving when he's actually got the keys to State House." Thys dropped his cigarette on the porch tiles and crushed it with the toe of his boot.

"Thys!" Elsie reprimanded.

"Ag, come on Elsie, stop hassling me, Patience will clean it up." He turned to me, "Might as well enjoy the help while we can get it. We'll be cleaning their toilets soon enough."

***

I continued to visit with Elsie and Thys, on and off, for the next three years, long after I'd learned how to say *bobotie*, long after I'd stopped yearning to say *sawubona*. After Jerry and Maria had returned to Northwestern University and I'd acquired another job, one they still didn't really understand and avoided talking about. I had a small house, though we always met at their grown up, Vereeniging house. Eventually they did buy a dog to go with the sign. "The thing won't kill anyone, but it will at least buy me some time to get ready to kill someone," Thys explained.

Patience kept shuffling in and out of rooms, silently saving lives with the timely production of tea and biscuits. She never seemed to show any sign of change either. I think I tried to say *sawubona* to her once early on, and she sort of laughed through a response of "yeess, *sawubona*" before swiftly getting back to her work. My life and South Africa's events moved on over the course of those three years, yet my encounters with Thys and Elsie remained, sometimes irritatingly, sometimes endearingly, the same.

On my last visit with them, over tea and *koeksisters* on a late Saturday afternoon in August 1997, I told them I was moving to Zimbabwe. To my surprise they were delighted: Zimbabwean blacks were "much nicer", they said, and they dress properly, even look healthier too. "I mean they're not either too skinny or too fat like our blacks," Elsie commented.

Thys nodded, no less enthusiastic, "You'll see, South Africa's going nowhere. No, wait, it is going somewhere, down the toilet. But Zim, it's a good bet. Just make sure you remember us suffering down here while you're sipping your G&T under a *msasa* tree."

Years later, on a particularly bad night, when I'd written one too many donor reports I knew nobody would read, when I'd watched yet another news clip of Comrade Mugabe dispatching his goons to terrorize anyone with an opinion, I thought of phoning Thys. Of finding some sour spoon of pleasure in telling him that actually he didn't know Africa north of the Limpopo at all, that the rest of the world didn't take place inside his quotation marks. But I never did. "Taking on" white racists and "making friends" with black strangers would remain consigned to the 3D world of my African imagination. Turns out history, mine and theirs, was too strong to allow either to happen.

5

Early 1994: Officially an Activist?

I have never forgotten how I felt when the precious offer of an internship in South Africa arrived from Ajay Naidoo, Director of the Legal Aid Support Unit – even later when I got burnt out, when disgust and disbelief at my own futility clouded my ability to see Africa clearly. It was like that feeling up on the monkey bars all those years before – all promise, no pain.

The offer slipped out of my mailbox in a red-trimmed envelope with a *par avion* sticker that I tried unsuccessfully to peel off for my scrapbook. I sat on my futon staring at the envelope, savoring the possibility contained inside, content for several minutes with the mere prospect of lives changing, theirs and mine. This letter seemed to make up for every invitation I'd never received: to prom, to the perfect Ivy League university, to Keith Islington's big party when his parents were in Maui. Because this letter, more than any of the others, confirmed that an important person out there thought I was special. Perhaps Jeel Reilly might be popular after all.

Six months later, I sat for an hour in the Legal Aid Support Unit's crowded waiting room, a chipped coffee table with tattered English and Afrikaans women's magazines nearby. I stared at posters on the wall: "Legal Aid Support Unit is a nongovernmental organization committed to protecting and upholding human rights" or

SHAME

"Women Stand Up For Your Rights!" I admired the gritty authenticity of it all, the flayed pieces of tape on the wall, small tears on the posters' corners. This was real activists' art.

I'd practically run to catch Bus 87 to Commissioner Street that morning, certain it would deliver me from gun-toting whites bearing baked goods, and maids and gardeners with no interest in *sawubona*. "Let real life in South Africa commence!" that black lady chorus in my head sang out as I charged up Eighth Avenue to the bus stop. From the bus window I watched Johannesburg reveal itself.

Like any other large city, there were all the usual urban materials: bricks, concrete, steel and glass. But there the resemblance ended. Below the façade of gleaming windows and shiny chrome, Johannesburg's "informal economy" mushroomed on every corner. After apartheid-era laws that restricted the movement of blacks were scrapped, the black people of Johannesburg had slowly reclaimed their place in the city.

Along the dusty, jammed grid of streets, stalls sold everything from business suits to beef stew. Square old women hunched over pots of roasted meat. Young men in sunglasses hawked handbags and belts draped over each arm as they danced to some groove nobody else could hear. A woman cradled a small baby as she rearranged five pieces of chewing gum and two bananas on a piece of cardboard. People shouted to each other and to passers-by, trying to make a sale or have a conversation above motors and car alarms and vernacular din. They moved along the streets, heads up and purposeful, as if they weren't waiting for someone to call or catch them, as if the streets, the city, were really theirs. As I got off Bus 87 to join them, I shouted goodbye to the driver; it was as though I were shouting it to South Africa's whole white world.

***

"Hi, hi, hi," Ajay Naidoo said when he eventually threw open the door, "come, come in." In that beautiful South African world of my imagination, Ajay had long, thick wavy hair and wore wire-frame glasses. That's what I imagined a sexy human rights worker would look like. Some nights, as I pictured the two of us in court together, I saw a hooked scar on his jowl that would hint at an earlier righteous confrontation. Ajay's entire life had been about confrontation, right? He'd prowl around court rooms arguing the cases of ANC activists, leaving jurors transfixed and transformed, convinced of the black man's innocence. That was the man I'd been planning to spend the next six months of my life with.

The real-life Ajay did wear wire-frame glasses, but his hair looked like it had been cut in the same center-parted, feathered style his entire life. And his manner was more emergency room than court room, hurried and detached rather than passionate and persuasive. I scurried to keep up, following him through his office door, clutching the zipped-up tote-bag filled with a brand new notebook, a grown-up pen that had been a going-away gift from a friend, and a chunky key ring from Maria, whose mother had assured me it could also be used as a weapon. "Aim for the eyes or the nuts," she'd cackled.

Ajay settled at his desk, tossing aside messages, creating what seemed to be random piles of papers, looking for something underneath the new piles. I sat upright and expectant. Finally he looked up.

"Why exactly did we ask you to come here?" he asked. My eyes widened and he added, "Just kidding." I giggled at what I assumed was activist humor. A sense of humor was good, right?

Ajay started shaking his head and muttering, "Nothing at university prepared me for this bloody job. I swear I'd rather deal with judge and jury than manage this lot." I fingered my zippers, straightened my blouse. Ajay picked up the phone. "Do you have this girl's file?" he asked.

The receptionist shuffled in, stood thinking for a moment, and quickly located my file at the bottom of an old stack. "Interns, Ajay, remember it's with all the other interns' files," she said.

"Right, of course," he replied and then focused on my file. It didn't take long; the file comprised nothing more than my application letter and his reply.

"It's uh, not on my resumé, but I, uh, I'm a Zulu speaker," I murmured. He looked up blankly. "Well, I uh, took some Zulu lessons. I would say – no, actually my teacher, she was South African – she said I have a basic grasp of Zulu. Conversational, yes, that's the word I think she used."

"We have a lot of Zulu speakers here," he said, closing my file and setting it aside. He sighed and ran his hands through his hair. "You're American, right? You've been pushing this democracy stuff for years, haven't you?" He stood up and started pacing around the small office. "The Swedes, the Dutch, the Germans, they've flooded us with money. The whole bloody world wants to make sure South Africans know how to vote." And then he swung around to face me. "I need you to teach people to vote. You can do that, can't you? Americans love that voting stuff."

Teach people to vote? Nobody had ever taught me how to vote. I'd only voted once, for Bill Clinton, and nobody had shown me how. My face curled up into a ball of confusion. How do you teach people to vote? Didn't matter, the concept of "teaching" and "Africa" felt right, even if I had no idea what I'd be teaching.

"You don't look very excited," Ajay said.

"No, no. It sounds fine, good, yeah, it sounds good. I, uh, did some work at Northwestern," I tried to sound qualified, "preparing for our last election. I mean, obviously it's different here in a young democracy, there's a, uh, need for civic education. I did some reading on civic education before I came ..."

But Ajay wasn't impressed or even interested. "The thing is," he interrupted, and ran his hands through his hair again, "we need you to do it in prisons." He paused, and then added, "Men's prisons."

"Prisons?" I gasped.

"I know, I know." His pacing grew more urgent. "For God's sake, don't tell your parents, they'll sue us."

"No, no, no, it's okay," I said, clutching my notebook to my chest. I knew it was silly but I swore he could see my heart beating through my blouse. "I mean, I don't mind."

"The ANC wants to make sure all the prisoners can vote." Ajay sat down again and started looking through his mail. "They're going to win anyway. But they want as many votes as possible, so might as well let the murderers have their say." And then he looked back to me, chewing on a fingernail. "You'll have to go every week."

"That ... that would be fine," I said, trying to sound professional.

"I might even have to rope Sarah into going with you. Jesus, am I going to get an earful from her!"

"No, that's fine. I don't mind going with someone else," I replied, pleased to have company from somebody with a nice name like Sarah.

"Good then, great. I'll introduce you to Sarah and she can get you started." Ajay jumped up and moved towards the door. I jumped up behind him, now just as breathless as he was.

"Good, great," I replied, reaching out to shake his hand as though some sort of deal had been clinched.

He looked surprised, "Oh yes, right, handshakes." He shook quickly and skittered off in search of Sarah. After being told she was out for a meeting, he grabbed the receptionist, to hand me over. "Angie! Angie, let me introduce you properly to our new intern. Jill, this is Angie. They call her the receptionist but she's the real director of this place," he joked.

I'd spoken to Angie briefly in the waiting room. She was the quintessential African mama. Her rear end shook from side to side when she walked and the motion shifted the slip under her dress, creating a scratching rustle that was the soundtrack to her movements. Channeling gossip and fielding questions, she spoke with the authority given to women in Africa over the age of fifty and a hundred and fifty pounds.

"*Sawubona,*" I offered brightly.

"*Sawubona, sisi,*" she replied, with a sort of begrudging enthusiasm. "*Kunjani?*"

"*Ngikhona. Unjani wena?*"

She turned to Ajay, "You've got another one who took some language classes. That's nice."

Ajay fidgeted, anxious for the exchange to end. "Jill's going to be working in the prisons, voter education!" He wore enthusiasm for a moment.

"Don't let those men touch you," Angie replied sternly, stretching her top over her belly.

"Angie!" Ajay remonstrated, "you're going to scare the girl."

She wagged her finger at Ajay. You got the feeling she did this a lot. "Ajay, you have no idea what kinds of *miggies* and *nunus* those men have on them! Gilbert spends a lot of time at the prison and he's always scratching himself."

"Oh for Christ's sake, she'll be fine. She'll be with Sarah and she scares off everything, even the bugs." Ajay looked down at his watch. "Angie, will you introduce Jill to everyone, show her around, take her to her desk? We've got a desk for her, right?" Angie gave an imperious nod and Ajay hurried off, promising to catch up with me later.

Angie scuffled along, with me trailing at her heels, struggling now to maintain a molasses rather than manic pace. Along with her brief, bored introductions – "Sam, this is the new American, Jill. Jill, this is Sam" – Angie offered insights into what I couldn't see and might have never known about the Legal Aid Support Unit.

Sam, the housing rights expert, was a balding, bearded single man in his forties who wore a scarf even in summer and seemed more preoccupied with his house – the house he was renovating in one of Johannesburg's more leafy suburbs – than anyone else's housing rights. "Don't agree to visit any housing projects with Sam," Angie whispered. "That man's not interested in access to houses. The only things he wants access to are your thighs." I giggled as we ambled towards the tea and coffee.

She surveyed the room, looking for her next story. "See those two over there? Trish, the women's rights lady, and Solomon. I'm not sure what rights he works on. They're together." She leaned in closer, "Having an affair." She tut tutted and tsk tsked as she stirred five spoons of sugar into her tea. "Disgraceful how people flaunt that type of thing these days," as she shook her head.

I tried not to spin my head to left and right as we walked through the open plan office. I tried not to smile too widely. Finally, *finally*, this scene was straight out of my imagination, blacks and whites working side by side at appropriately messy desks, files stacked everywhere, of course, so many people in need, so little time for filing, outdated computers and fax machines that reflected their commitment to pursuing justice on a shoestring budget, more posters with emphatic sayings, and everyone so serious. Nobody smiled my way or even noticed me, but that was okay, they were doing serious work, they had serious responsibilities. And I was seriously among them!

My desk was wedged in a corner and covered with files. "Here you are," Angie announced. "I'll bring you some more background on the prisons work and find out when Sarah's getting in." And then, without enthusiasm, as though it was the last line in her script, she said, "Make yourself at home."

"Good, great, that's great," I said, my eyes blurring over the desk, my desk, at a human rights law firm in South Africa. I took off my jacket and smiled at that room of people who seemed oblivious of me. Didn't matter, I had a desk, a mission, even a dangerous one. I wanted to run back to Melville, to the top of one of the *koppies*, and start dancing in circles.

Sawubona South Africa! It had taken a few weeks, but Jeel Reilly had officially arrived. And she had finally been seen.

6

Still Early 1994: Breaking Free in Prison

"Prisons?!" my father shouted down the phone. He tended to shout through my phone calls from South Africa anyway, but this one was louder than usual.

"Yeah, but they're not like prisons in the States, Dad, I mean a lot of these prisoners shouldn't be there. They're activists, people who haven't done anything wrong, they were just taken off the streets."

"I don't care what country you're in, they don't lock the best and brightest away."

"In South Africa sometimes they do."

"So did they give you this job because you're the new kid in town?"

"No."

"Because nobody else wanted it?"

"No! It's, it's because I'm American, because I understand democracy."

"Yeah, but what the hell do you know about prisons?"

"These aren't normal prisons, how many times do I have to say it? There are a lot of innocent people here, people who just happen to have the wrong color skin!"

"Well, then South Africa must be the only country that doesn't put bad people in prison."

***

I was hurtling along Johannesburg's highways, trying not to hold on too tightly. Sarah Taylor was at the wheel, bullying other cars. She was a tall, sturdy woman in her twenties with a plain, clear face that might have been called fresh if it weren't always so pinched. She drank Jameson whiskey, neat, at the end of the day and told Sam the housing Lothario to fuck off a lot, sometimes in passing. The only time she softened was when she spoke of her two black Labradors, Frieda and Frisky, whom she described as "her life". Every Sunday night she cooked stew for them, an ample brew of bones and broth that many human beings in South Africa would have considered a feast. It was one of the few times during the week when Sarah stood still, stirring and smelling until she was certain the dogs' meal was just right.

"So, you ready to spend the day with the bad guys?" she asked without taking her eyes off the road. "Fine lot these are going to be: murderers, thieves."

"I know there are a lot of prisoners here who've been, you know, wrongfully imprisoned," I mumbled.

Sarah chortled. "We're not going to Robben Island, darling. These guys are thugs."

We were on our way to our first day's work in a prison that had been dubbed "Sun City". The real Sun City was a famous resort carved out of one of South Africa's poorest homelands, with golf courses, casinos, a concert hall, a water park and a bridge that shook every half an hour to simulate an earthquake. Seems South Africans liked the illusion of a threat, even when they were amusing themselves.

Grey, cold and fetid, Sun City prison bore no resemblance to that resort, but it didn't look like the prisons I'd grown up seeing on television either. Whenever my father was out of town, my sisters and I would climb into my parents' bed with my mother and watch *Prisoner Cell Block H*, an Australian TV show set in a women's prison. Although the show was meant to be a drama, we found it amusing, laughing at wrinkled hags like Lizzie and Doreen standing around the laundry smoking fags and waiting to be caught by the "screws". Maybe there was some truth to *Prisoner Cell Block H*, I'd thought that morning as I put on my somber prisoner-educating pants. Maybe behind Sun City's rough exterior might lie a rag-tag family of sorts, washing clothes, bartering cigarettes, watching movies as a reward. Maybe Sun City was just home to a bunch of crazy personalities who'd make me laugh if I watched them on TV every week.

I trailed behind Sarah through the front door of the prison, wearing my serious activist's face. A guard met us, khaki colored and grinning at our good intentions. "*Goeie môre*, ladies," he said.

"Good morning," Sarah replied with a stiff smile.

The guards were all big bellies and booming voices, the women built like swimmers or shot putters. I'd expected them to be rude and brusque, rushing to cover up the evidence of their everyday abuses. Instead they welcomed us like hosts at the Ponderosa – two of you visiting us today? – the women offering us industrially sweetened tea and biscuits while we waited for them to round up our prisoners.

But while we waited, the odor of the place was a reminder that this wasn't television or the Ponderosa. It smelled the way I imagined a morgue might, the air clogged with the stench of bodies locked away and stored.

"*Kom, kom*, ladies!" the biggest belly of them all motioned for us.

"Showtime," said Sarah and stood up to follow. Her flat, worn shoes scuffed on the concrete floor as I followed, wishing I could nudge past and be the one to go in first so someone might think I was the leader. As we walked down an endless corridor of cells, I waited for prisoners to lean out and leer, like they do on TV. But all was silent.

One of the younger guards (whom I'd probably have found handsome if I'd met him in a bar holding a drink rather than a rifle) sidled up next to me. "I'll go in with you," he said in a thick Afrikaans accent.

"I'm fine," I said, hoping it was true.

"You ever been in a prison before, Miss?"

"No," I replied, hoping my clipped answer might make him shut up. Instead it seemed to increase his relish.

"We rounded up the real bad guys for you today, the murderers, rapists. Capital crimes, we call them here in Seth Effrika." He looked at me for a reaction. "These are the guys who kill people." He leaned towards me and whispered, "Who rape ladies." My feet stuttered as we reached the doorway.

***

"One in three people is a victim of violent crime. A woman is raped every twenty-five seconds." The words rolled from my pen into my notebook so quickly I didn't pause to consider them, much less feel them. They were just statistics: combinations of numbers and words that would perhaps prove useful one day. It was September 1st, about a month before I was scheduled to leave for South Africa, on another blustery night in Evanston, and I was in the African Studies Department attending a seminar called "Rising Crime in the Transitional South Africa: A Second Wave of Resistance". It was the third African Studies seminar I'd attended since I'd been offered Ajay's internship and, along with my Zulu lessons, formed part of my preparations to leave.

The seminar was given by a white South African graduate student named Keith Bernstein, a sort of kingpin of the "Africanists": graduate students and aging professors who wore Wrangler jeans and tired sweaters and used the word "fucking" a lot, usually in reference to a government or a university policy. Keith twitched his head to clear fine strands of his bangs from his glasses as he laid out his argument that crime was the single biggest threat to democracy in the New South Africa.

I sat in the fourth row of seats – neither too eager nor too nonchalant – and when the seminar was over I stood and waited for the reception to begin, flipping through my notes. Every twenty-five seconds? I put a star next to that statistic. That couldn't be right, I'd have to ask Keith to confirm it. I looked up to see a small group of undergraduates forming a star-struck circle around Keith, who chain-smoked and drank Chardonnay out of a plastic cup. I lingered just on the outside of the circle, waiting for just the right moment.

"What you were saying in your seminar? We have a similar problem here," I piped up. "Alienation, joblessness, those are the root causes of crime anywhere in the world, aren't they? It's the same story at Cabrini Green." Keith's eager nod sent his bangs fluttering.

"Exactly," he said, stubbing out his cigarette, "America has the same fucking problem. Crime, gangs, it's the only way disenfranchised people feel they can speak up, assert themselves in a society that has so systematically alienated them."

"Dehumanized them even! I think for men especially, crime is a way of asserting their humanity, their male identity."

"Absolutely," Keith said, and we smiled at each other. The undergraduates shifted on their feet and crossed their arms as I moved to the center of the circle, my transformation to popular girl already taking place. Keith continued for the next half an hour to make his case for comparing car-jackings to the Soweto riots. Then he started getting fidgety once there was no more wine to fill his cup. "Hey, should we go down to the Green Mill for some jazz?" he asked. I could have sworn he looked straight at me.

"Yeah, sounds great," I said along with the others, our voices forming a casual chorus.

Keith continued his lecture in the car, tapping his cigarette on the cracked window and bobbing his head to Thelonious Monk. "A genius," he said. I nodded, even though I had no idea who Thelonious Monk was.

I'd claimed the passenger seat, hadn't even had to ask for it, while guys sat silently in the back, catching glimpses of my glossed lips in the rearview mirror. One of them, who kept picking at a pimple on his chin, said something about South Africa's "township jazz", but Keith couldn't hear over his own humming. Another student, who was doing an honors thesis comparing Rio's favelas to Johannesburg's townships, tried to make a point about the role of the arts in a liberation struggle. But Keith just said "uh huh" with a quick glance at the guy in his rearview mirror and lit another cigarette. I considered asking about that ridiculous rape statistic, but it didn't seem like the right time to talk about that most intimate of violent crimes, not with the Gold Coast sparkling in front of us, and Cabrini Green hidden away somewhere in the distance.

"I'm going to South Africa," I shouted when I couldn't keep it in anymore.

"Huh?" said Keith, turning down the radio.

"I'm going to South Africa, for the elections, I've got a job with a human rights organization in Johannesburg."

"Great, great," Keith said, "should be fun." Fun?

"Yeah, I just can't wait to get there. To be really, you know, hands on with the struggle."

"Yeah, my girlfriend's got a wedding here so we can't go back, otherwise you bet we'd be there. Should be a fantastic party."

I fidgeted in my seat thinking, *no, no, not a fucking party, this is serious stuff,* and considered challenging him. But by that time we were at the Green Mill, and Keith was busy herding the youngsters out of the back seat.

***

Sarah went charging into the room full of prisoners, all stern faced and stiff limbed, like an army nurse preparing to inoculate the troops. Every twenty five seconds? That statistic hadn't really haunted me before. Even as all the talk of crime swirled around me, I'd managed to leave those statistics in a classroom, in Chicago, far away from my new, real life. Now I wanted to find that notebook – had I even brought it? – to read through my notes again. Could it really happen every twenty-five seconds?

Head spinning, I pushed forward to face the task ahead. And there that task was, staring me right in the face: hundreds (or so it felt) of men herded into a too-small room. Murderers. Rapists. Maybe an activist thrown in, but how was I going to tell them apart?

I stood frozen while Sarah set up her materials. Was this "them"? Was this the swirling storm I'd managed to avoid until now; had I now chosen to walk into its eye? I noticed the young male guard by the door, his smile now a smirk. Then I heard the words again, "every twenty five seconds", and shook my head to try to forget them. An entire roomful of poor black South Africans were staring at me, every one of them saying *I see you* with their chilly glares. Sarah was glowering at me, anxious for me to take my place, so I cast my eyes slightly downward and half whispered "hello" to everyone and no one.

SHAME

My job was to demonstrate the ballot, holding it high and wide while Sarah talked the men through it. I'd imagined myself so schoolteacher-like in this role, the ballot my blackboard, pointer in hand. But with so many men crowding around and craning to see, it wasn't going to be so orderly. Instead, I just had to pace the floor in front of the curious mob, all of them muttering and whispering, individual conversations gaining the force of one loud one. Sarah's voice boomed and the men went still, standing to attention, the way I'm sure Frieda and Frisky did. I felt suddenly safer, certain the men would sit if Sarah told them to.

"You do not have to belong to any political party in order to vote," Sarah began in her loudest, most pedantic voice. With a ballot in each hand, I started moving, turning to show both sides of ballots that were almost as long as my arms. Big and childlike in their simplicity, the ballots looked as if they should be marked with crayons rather than pens. Next to the name of each political party was the face of its leader, catering for the illiterate masses. I kept walking as Sarah spoke, moving closer in and farther away, equal time to the left and the right. And I made sure the whole room could see each of the candidates' pictures, pointing them out even though Sarah hadn't told me to. "All parties must avoid discrimination based on race, sex, class or religion," Sarah continued.

In most countries I wouldn't have spent more than five minutes parading the ballots in front of that room. But not for these elections, with nineteen political parties in contention, which meant at least a half hour at center stage, turning and twisting, doing everything possible to allow the men to see the ballots that would mark the start of the New South Africa. *Twenty five seconds*, I heard once or twice when I focused on a gnarled face, but I shook my head to force those thoughts back to a Chicago classroom.

About halfway into the process, my mind became surprisingly clear, bathed in adrenaline, unwilling to consider anything but the reality of that moment. I'm in South Africa, in a prison, helping prisoners – jobless, disenfranchised men – to vote. Vote to end one of history's most vicious, racist regimes; vote to prove that social change is possible. No, wait, that social *transformation* is possible. Hallelujah, I thought and almost started giggling, I'm doing something *amazing* today. I offered a satisfied grin to the young, gun-toting guard.

I knew that the Keep it Straight and Simple, or KISS, party was the halfway point of each session. By the time Sarah reached the SOCCER (Sport Organization for Collective Contributions and Equal Rights) party, we were nearing the end, and The Women's Rights Peace Party meant I had to go home. Back to that little house in Melville's *koppies*, behind the wall and the electrified wire, a place strangely more frightening than the prison I spent my days in. I wanted to stay in this black prison, not that white one.

"*Totsiens*," the screws said as we left the room. Goodbye.

I sidled up next to the young guard who'd shown me in. "Make sure you bring more bad guys next time," I whispered. I might have even winked, I was feeling that cocky.

In the car on the way home, I tuned out Sarah grousing about the radio and flirted with the idea of calling Ntombenthle – a letter would be too formal, too Karen Blixen – to tell her I wasn't just in South Africa before the election, I was in South African prisons preparing prisoners for the elections. Ntombenthle would probably howl and jiggle, and then she'd tell me, "Ah, but you are brave, Jeel." And I wouldn't have to say a thing.

"Ah, another day with South Africa's best and brightest," Angie said as I walked into the reception area that evening.

"I've always been attracted to dangerous men," I joked and dropped into a chair.

"You want to save them, don't you? That's what all you little American *nunus* want." She dug a fuchsia-colored fingernail into her nest of hair to scratch her head.

"I might not save anybody, but maybe I can help them."

"Just make sure they're worth helping," she said, looking down at her mail to signal the conversation was over. Angie always decided when our conversations were over.

About two weeks into my work in the prisons, I asked Ajay if I could make daily visits rather than just three times a week.

"Every day?!" he repeated, incredulous. "You Americans really do like your democracy."

"Every day?" Sarah chortled. "You're going to have to find another driver."

"Every day!" Maria's mother howled. "Maybe you can start nicking some guns for us there."

I explained how more frequent visits would mean fewer prisoners in each session and so more effective training. I made my plan sound rational, logical and bereft of emotion. I was a committed activist; that was all.

I couldn't explain to anyone – Jerry, Maria, Ajay, Sarah, even the people back home who had given me diaries and copies of *Out of Africa* – what it felt like to stand in front of a group of South African men and pass on information they needed. Yes, they needed this information about voting, and therefore they needed me. At the end of each session I would hand out small booklets containing simple, pithy messages intended to make people feel comfortable with the voting process: sayings like "this is our election" or "we can make this work." Sometimes I'd whisper, *Sawubona*, before handing them out, eliciting chuckles and smiles. These booklets were their passage to the New South Africa. And I, Jill Reilly, who'd been in South Africa for less than a month, had given them that passage to a better life. Finally, I'd got that ten dollar bill out of my bag, without fear or regret. And it felt *amazing*.

7

April 1994: Nobody Told Me There Were White Townships

By the time the elections took place, Ajay had taken to describing Sarah and me as his "dynamic duo". "You two girls," he'd say, causing Sarah to shoot him her standard-issue glare. "You two women!" he corrected himself. "I'd like you women to work on the elections together. We need monitors on the day, people to help make sure things run smoothly and there's no funny business. Well, the bloody Germans just gave us some money so now we have to figure out how to use it. And I know I could station the two of you anywhere and you'd handle it."

"Ajay, if you send me back to those prisons, I swear to God …," Sarah fumed. "Just because this one," she pointed at me, "has a thing for men in uniforms." I smirked and pointed back at her. We had that kind of relationship by then.

"No, no, it's not prisons," said Ajay. "We've got that covered. It's just, uh, Randfontein. You two women get to work in Randfontein."

"Randfontein, where's that?"

"It's nearby, well, I mean it's not far. So it's convenient, not a lot of driving. It's, uh, just on the other side of Melville."

Sarah's face transformed from confused to horrified, "Oh bollocks, you're talking about that funny little place with all the poor whites."

Ajay feigned a kind of relief. "Yes, that's the one, I'm glad you know it."

"Jesus Christ, Ajay, after all that work in the prisons, you think you'd give us a township, Alex, Soweto, I'd even do Thokoza for God's sake."

"It's a township!" he retorted, defiant, "just a white one. The Germans gave us the money! We have to use it. Even for white people!"

"A white township?" I queried, though no one was listening to me. White people? On election day? My mind reeled back to fantasy images of jubilant blacks dancing in the streets, shaking my hand and offering effusive thank-you-*ngiyabonga-kakhulus* for helping to transform their land. "But don't whites know how to vote?" I muttered "I mean, can't they vote by themselves?"

"Seriously, Ajay, Randfontein?" Sarah repeated, her voice dripping. Ajay held up his hands, as if to say, "What can I do?" He had a way of losing and winning every argument with Sarah, and they both knew it. She marched out of his office and he turned to me.

"Now don't tell me you have a problem with a Randfontein now?" I shook my head. I hadn't been in South Africa long enough to be choosy.

Randfontein stood on the other side of a hill from Melville, stashed away like a family secret. And it was a bit of a secret. Apartheid had been created to ensure the wealth and well-being of whites through the use and abuse of blacks. Those who couldn't take advantage of that system had to be either sick or extremely stupid; the cousins whose names you don't mention. Those cousins lived in Randfontein, a place where kids without shoes ran through the streets and stared at cars they didn't recognize; where women in housecoats went for walks together and shared cigarettes; where stained lace curtains fluttered in the open windows of one-bedroom homes.

The residents of Randfontein owed a lot to apartheid. They had menial jobs with parastatals like the railroads or the bus companies.

APRIL 1994: NOBODY TOLD ME THERE WERE WHITE TOWNSHIPS

The walls of their tiny duplicated houses were brick. Apartheid had provided them the modicum of dignity it had deliberately denied their black counterparts. And the people of Randfontein knew that the ANC's promises of houses and jobs for all would be kept at somebody's expense. If white people were to be sacrificed, surely it would be them. The weakest links are always easiest to sever. This made Randfontein the kind of place where extremists found followers, where people had everything and nothing to lose. So in the days leading up to the elections, officials were afraid that the people of Randfontein would sever the link with the new South Africa themselves before anyone else got the chance, blow it up before the ANC made it irrelevant. Once again this white township world possessed a peculiar danger that the black ones didn't.

Sarah and I had no idea how we would be received. The residents of Randfontein were, after all, hosting somebody else's party. The day before voting was due to begin, we arrived to prepare for it at the Randfontein Recreation Centre, site of the voting. We found a square room with a few lonely balls tossed into corners and two ropes hanging from the rafters; hardly a place where history would be made.

The only sign of the coming election were three tables lined up for handing out ballots and three or four partitioned booths for voting. Otherwise there was a peculiar sense of everyday abnormality about the place. A handful of local residents stood in the doorway to welcome us, smiling generously, even genuinely. No Afrikaner was going to let a little thing like politics get in the way of hospitality.

"*Goeie môre,*" they said in their sing-song fashion.

The women got to work in the center's small kitchen, crowded together as they cut slices of white bread, applied a thick layer of margarine and a thinner slice of pink luncheon meat. Large kettles of tea were being prepared and small bowls heaped with sugar. One woman was piling plate after plate high with small vanilla biscuits bought in bags of a hundred at the discount store, Checkers. The men, meanwhile, gathered outside, smoking cigarettes and relighting the butts of those not quite finished. They shared brief fragments of doomed thoughts – "Ag, time will tell, hey" and "Ag, who knows, really" – hints of the deeper hopelessness welling inside.

"They're really sad, aren't they?" Sarah kept repeating. As we checked each ballot for printing mistakes, we kept glancing up at the faces of the locals who had volunteered to carry in chairs and supplies. They looked like rural people trapped in an urban space, their faces plain, wide and open, their bodies sturdy, hands and feet big and worn. Some appeared handicapped, with distorted faces and hearty laughs that were too obvious and immediate.

Sarah was determined to understand the truth of this community, asking blunt questions, probing for clearer answers, lawyerlike in her approach. "How long have you lived here? Uh, huh. And how are you and Bakkies over there actually related?"

Late on that morning of preparing for the election, Sarah pulled me aside to a corner obscured by the hanging ropes. "Apparently, there's some inbreeding here, you know, kissing cousins, that kind of thing. So Theuns and Anneline, they're husband and wife and first cousins! Take a look, some of them have an extra finger or their hands are sort of webbed. It's like some sort of weird horror show!"

So completely cast off from the white South African world they ostensibly belonged to, the people of Randfontein had turned to each other to guarantee their future. I tried not to stare at their crooked faces. Once again, evil looked feebler up close, South Africa's reality as warped as the hands being thrust at me to shake. And once again I found myself preparing for the new South Africa with people who'd been imprisoned.

A smiley woman with a too-tight perm approached. "Hello, lady, would you like some tea and a sandwich?" I gently shook my head, no. I'd lost my appetite.

We continued unpacking boxes of ballots and creating orderly piles. Every so often Sarah and I would lock eyes and she would cross her eyes or stick out her tongue. I tried not to laugh, but a little light relief was welcome as bulletproof-jacketed police officers carrying AK47s paced back and forth outside the building and others trailed sniffer dogs searching out bombs. Some men nearby started whispering in halting English, as if for my benefit, "Yeah, they say some *okie* who's lost his job on the railways to some *dof* black has been threatening to walk in here and blow the whole place up with explosives strapped to him." They looked as if they were already assessing the damage.

APRIL 1994: NOBODY TOLD ME THERE WERE WHITE TOWNSHIPS

I glanced down at my ballots, pretending to focus on the written code of conduct I had been given. Rules, I wanted to memorize rules. More importantly, I wanted to believe they'd be followed. Or, if not, that the AK47s would work.

On the first morning of voting, 27th April 1994, Sarah and I started work in that surreal darkness that's neither morning nor night. People milled around the center with badges and clipboards, South African election officials, international monitors, police officers and reporters, creating a din of urgent whispers in those dark hours. The quirky locals were pushed to the kitchen and replaced by people whose faces were poker straight, whose lives revolved around symmetry, probity, making things right.

I kept repeating the rules and procedures in my head, occasionally giggling anxiously, wringing my hands and straightening my shirt to make sure I looked like an election professional. Wandering amidst this crowd, I half expected someone to demand to see my credentials, anything to prove I belonged here. Sure, the prisoners had accepted me; they didn't have a choice. Ajay was almost as desperate. But these officials looked so serious, so well trained; if they were interviewed on TV, someone would describe them as experts. Wouldn't one of them want to know why a young woman from Chesterfield belonged at such an important election? When would someone figure out I had nothing to offer and send me home? I took a deep breath and mentally recited my lines – *I have a conversational understanding of Zulu. I carried out voter education in prisons for three months* – and mostly held my breath, waiting for that tap on my shoulder telling me it was time to go home to my real life.

But it never came. Nobody outed me, nobody among the UN staff, the graduates of international studies at Georgetown and Harvard, the people who would be quoted by PhD students and those who would write their own magazine pieces. They let me stay and work among them. Maybe they, too, sensed some bravery in me. With each cup of Nescafé, I allowed myself to believe it might be true.

After a little while the official, important whispers became excited. "Look outside!" people said. Sarah and I rushed to the window to see what was happening, hoping it wasn't a phalanx of local protesters or that disaffected *okie* swaddled in explosives.

57

Although the sun had yet to rise, a line had begun to form outside the recreation center: a human chain, unlinked but not disconnected, curving around the building. As the sun made its way up into the sky, the line grew. Children riding past on bicycles stopped to stare. Randfontein had never seen such a thing.

"That's amazing," Sarah breathed. Even officials and cynics seemed to agree. I pushed my shoulders back and puffed my chest, proud of them for being here, proud of me for being here with them.

The color of the line in this so-called white township was black and white; nothing was ever black *or* white in South Africa. The blacks and whites didn't speak to each other, but they stood closely together. The whites exchanged a few whispers, but mostly people maintained a dignified silence. Maybe all the words exchanged for weeks before had exhausted them. A local, frumpy grandmother at the age of forty waddled around in an oversized jersey handing out biscuits and water.

"They're standing so nice and quiet, the blacks," she whispered when she came back inside. All of us kept waiting for some commotion to start outside, when patience would wear thin and simmering fears and anticipation would overflow. But it never came. The sun climbed higher, lunchtime came and went, and the sun sank again in the sky. The first day of voting was coming to an end while the line continued to grow. And still the people stood – reserved and resolved.

I stood too, all day long handing voters their ballots, which Sarah and other local staff would explain to them in an appropriate language. As I handed over each ballot, I looked each person in the eye, wanting to savor each moment, every connection I made with a stranger and their history. *Sawubona.*

"Where's Mandela?" a square old lady asked me in a voice loud enough for the room to hear. "Just show me his face. That's all I want to see." I'd been instructed not to talk to voters about their choices, which could be construed as coercion. But this old lady stood firm, unwilling to move until I showed her Mandela's face. She stooped her body over, used one hand to position the pen between the two fingers of her other hand and made a large, jagged X in the box next to it. "There. Done. Now where do I put this?" She shuffled away clutching her purse to her side, looking straight ahead.

APRIL 1994: NOBODY TOLD ME THERE WERE WHITE TOWNSHIPS

For months, election officials had repeatedly stressed that voting would be private, but by the time April came, most South Africans weren't concerned about retribution. They took their ballots and stood discussing them with each other. Some wanted to place their mark right in front of me, without the unnecessary formality of voting booths, others wanted to vote together.

"Oh for fuck's sake, why can't we vote together?" an old man said when I told him he couldn't vote with his wife. "Doesn't Mr Mandela approve?" Eventually he let his wife vote on her own, but he paced inches away. Then he clutched her elbow and they left the polling station together. A few minutes later a group of young black university students came in, almost dancing down the line, grabbing the ballot like it was a girl's telephone number. This was their party.

"How are you doing?" Jerry asked when I came home late on the first night. He sat with a cup of coffee in his living room, lit only by the television.

I flopped down on the couch next to him. "Totally exhausted. Totally buzzed. I feel like I could pass out and yet I want to stay up all night."

"Not surprising. Pretty amazing stuff you were doing today." *Did he just use that word?* I half nodded. Then, his tone gentler than ever before, he added, "Maria and I were talking tonight, and we agreed we should tell you we're proud of you."

"Oh, really?" I squirmed.

"Yeah, we've never really told you that, but we are. You've really thrown yourself into working here, and I admire that."

"It's a good feeling."

"You mean being here, being part of something so huge?" "Yeah, of course, that. But more than that." I paused, uncertain how to continue. "It feels good to be kind of ... important." I regretted the word immediately. "That sounds stupid, I mean obviously I'm not important. It's more just to be able to do important things, you know, to help people in a concrete way."

"To be powerful," Jerry offered with wry smile.

"Yeah, something like that, I guess. But in a good way, you know, powerful in a good way."

59

"That's why people come to Africa," Jerry said, "looking for power. Get some rest now," he said gently. I nodded and got up from the couch. "Jill ..."

"Yeah?" I turned to face him.

"You're doing good. Don't forget that, okay?"

***

On the last day of voting, when it was all over, after thousands of people had voted and no bombs had gone off, the people of Randfontein opened a bottle of sherry, pouring tiny tots into plastic cups. We raised our cups to toast each other and thanked them for being such gracious hosts. They said it was a pleasure, and I think they meant it. Leftover cookies were put back into a plastic bag, the powdered milk resealed. Tables and voting booths were quickly removed, because an under 16s dance was going to be held there the next night.

"Do you think brothers and sisters go with each other?" Sarah joked as we got in the car to drive away. Normalcy, Randfontein style, had resumed.

***

A public victory celebration was held on the streets of downtown Johannesburg on May 3rd after the election results were announced. Predictably, the ANC had won, gaining nearly sixty three per cent of the vote. Sarah and I drove through the empty streets of scared suburbs, blasting *Buffalo Soldier* through open windows. With victory official and power at least symbolically transferred, white South Africans waited for the banging on doors to begin, for televisions to be handed out through broken windows, for people who didn't even know how to swim to dive into someone else's pool with their dusty clothes on. I had thought about checking in on Elsie and Thys in the days before the elections, but I hadn't. Vereeniging felt too far away to reach with a simple phone call. Even many black South Africans kept their celebrations close to home, fearing the unknown. Angie had said she "couldn't be bothered" coming out, because all the *tsotsis* would take advantage of the night to "pinch purses". So in black and white

APRIL 1994: NOBODY TOLD ME THERE WERE WHITE TOWNSHIPS

neighborhoods across Johannesburg, lights were turned off, hatches were battened down and people kept vigil inside. As if quiet would beget quiet.

Sarah and I were two of very few whites in Johannesburg who decided to spend that night on the city's downtown streets. Teenagers ran around with an excited sense of purpose but no direction, like pin balls bouncing off kerbs. People danced in pairs and loosely formed groups, partners to everyone and no one. Others whooped and reeled through the streets in unorchestrated celebration. But it was just manic, not menacing; this party was all about revelry, not revenge.

We joined a group of people dancing the *toyi-toyi*, clapping and shaking our hips, ululating and shouting "Viva" every time the group did. It felt like a revival without a minister, and we were happy to be members of that headless congregation. I let my body follow the rhythm of the singing and music. I could have carried on dancing all night, completely lost and yet finally at home, as if I was up in those *koppies*, right in the center of my own circle.

I heard a voice so close to my ear say, "My name is Patience." An image of Thys and Elsie's maid flashed in my mind, but I opened my eyes to see a young woman with long, thin braids bouncing off her shoulders, so lithe, so alive, completely unlike the other Patience. She grabbed my hand and swung it back and forth in a girlish dance, much how my sisters used to dance with me when I was five.

"I'm Jill," I shouted.

"Jeel?" she shouted back.

"Yes, right, Jeel," I repeated, "*Ngingu* Jill!"

Patience barely missed a beat, "Ahhh, good, *kunjani* Jeel?" she shouted.

"*Ngikhona, unjani wena?*"

"*Ngikhona!*" she mouthed. Her smile brimmed so widely I wondered if she'd ever before felt this happy. I don't think I had. Then Patience started to lead, not with a hand on my back, but by forcefully tugging on each arm, as though I were a doll. She moved fluidly, with big, bold gestures of arms and legs. I tried to copy her, but while Patience looked like an acrobatic modern dancer, I looked like a disabled frog. Patience's smile bubbled into laughter, and only the excitement of the moment softened the knowledge that she was laughing at me. Didn't matter, I kept going, clumsy and ignorant, a hopeless copycat. That was the point: on that night, when the birth of the new South Africa had become official, brave Jeel was dancing on South Africa's most dangerous streets, with Patience taking the lead.

8

May 1994: Everything in South Africa is New Again

"Why aren't you going back to America, Jeel?" Angie asked.

"Because I want to stay; there are so many important things to do here." I shifted under her steady gaze.

"You want to keep going to those filthy prisons?"

"No, my work there is finished now the elections are over. I'm not sure what I'll do. I'm sure I can find a job. There's so much work to be done with the reconstruction, the RDP. I'm sure I can find some way to be a part of it."

"Is it a boy? Is that why you're staying? Because me, I'd rather be in America than stay here for the RDP!"

"No! God, no, I wouldn't stay just because of a guy. It's just that I can't walk away now. The elections were just the beginning, there's so much opportunity here to do good things, to change things!"

"Hmm," Angie surveyed her long purple fingernails, unimpressed. "Anyway," she looked up at me, "whatever you do, don't date the boys here. They'll tell you they love you one minute and walk away the next."

***

SHAME

I met Wayne Conradie at Nelson Mandela's inauguration and knew immediately. Not that he was "the one" – though I would convince myself of that within a matter of days – but that I *had* to get to know him better. What I didn't know was that Wayne would teach me the single most valuable lesson about life in Southern Africa. A lesson I had no idea I was learning: that public and private lives often bore little resemblance to each other, that people, including me, would mold and distort themselves into shoddy versions in the name of love or lust. That in the case of sex, dangerous and delightful were often one and the same. If only I'd been taking notes or at least paying attention. Maybe then I would have known, years later, to step out of the eye of the sexually transmitted storm flattening an already prostrate Zimbabwe. I would have respected that whisper-thin line between confident and foolhardy.

Al Gore was at Mandela's inauguration, along with Yasser Arafat and other less "infamous" heads of State. But despite the presence of officialdom, the event felt more like a carnival, complete with popcorn, cotton candy, Cokes and little kids running around barefoot. All that was missing was a rollercoaster. Which isn't to say there wasn't colorful entertainment. The biggest cheer of the day came when three fighter jets flew overhead, trailing the colors of the new South African flag behind them. Patriotism suddenly felt appropriate again, even cool.

The rowdy crowd fell silent when Mandela, angelic in a shiny African print shirt, his white hair apparently sprinkled with fairy dust, delivered a speech that was part therapy, part sermon, part political manifesto.

"Each time one of us touches the soil of this land, we feel a sense of personal renewal. The time for the healing of the wounds has come. The moment to bridge the chasms that divide us has come. The time to build is upon us" he said. How could I leave South Africa when its President was promising me personal renewal?

And then part of that promise walked towards me.

"That's Wayne Conradie," Sarah whispered. "He was this hotshot student activist at Wits." Student activist? My mind fluttered along with my eyelashes. "Just came back from exile. In London, getting his PhD in economics," she added.

MAY 1994: EVERYTHING IN SOUTH AFRICA IS NEW AGAIN

Exile? London? With every phrase Wayne became more intriguing: activist meets academic; Africa meets Europe; and perhaps most importantly, white meets black. Wayne was colored – a South African term for people of mixed race – with loopy hair and latte skin, the color of skin I aspire to in summer, and a thick Afrikaans accent that somehow managed to be sexy and smooth rather than prison-warden hard. Neither black nor white, neither them nor us, he seemed to embody Mandela's vision of a society without boundaries, free to express its desires. His very being seemed to suggest that crossing over and blending in might be possible, possible for me if I got to know him.

"Pretty horrid, he was in prison for a couple of years," said Sarah. "Think it left him kind of fucked up. Was tortured or something, I don't know. He doesn't talk about it much." Tortured! Wayne Conradie was literally a tortured South African soul, in need of healing. And now that tortured soul was smiling at me.

"We should meet up for a drink sometime," Wayne said, turning to me as the group began to disperse. "I'd like to hear more about your experiences in my country." He said "in my country" just the way Ntombenthle had. I glanced around, crossed my arms, giggled. Was he drunk? Was this Nelson Mandela-style racial goodwill? Hadn't Sarah told him I was just an intern, that I usually entered a room after her and mostly only to hand out stuff?

I tried desperately to channel the popular girl, cool and relaxed, used to this kind of attention from sought-after men. "Sure, sure," I said coolly. "Yeah, let's meet for a drink some time." Sarah watched me scheduling a meeting that didn't involve her, and I'd never seen her so confused.

"Terrence's, maybe, in Yeoville?" he offered.

"Hmm, yeah, great place, love it there," I lied. I'd never been to Terrence's before though I knew it was a big ANC hangout. Funny how quickly I took to lying to become a more attractive version of myself.

In all of my fantasies of my future life in South Africa, I was living and socializing in Yeoville, even though I had no idea at the time that's what it was called. But when I stepped foot there, I recognized it instantly as home of that groovy, jazzy popular-girl life I

65

was meant to have in South Africa. Yeoville was a hive of activists and ANC types, the whites trying to look rough, the blacks trying to look polished. Full of cheap flats, cheap beer and homeless people whose name everybody knew. Yeoville was Melville's sexy, skint cousin. Blacks and whites could live next door in Yeoville's anonymous blocks of flats and drink together in its bars, with nothing too groomed or grandiose outside to make them feel wicked. The whole place was sodden with grunge chic: tatty bookstores and street vendors who sold trinkets they'd fashioned out of wire, a grocery store where you had to pick through rotting fruit. A whole neighborhood that hid treasures underneath its rotting fruit.

Or at least that's what I imagined as I climbed off the bus and took my first steps on its dirty streets, aware that for the first time in four months I was walking in heels, the heels I'd thrown into my suitcase at the last minute. As I tottered along the pavement — yes, Yeoville actually had sidewalks — I was so glad I'd thrown those heels in because they forced my hips to move side to side, and the shifting hips made me aware of the soft rounds of my breasts beneath a layer of thin black cotton, my jeans tight around my legs. Finally, I grinned to myself, I'm really out in South Africa. If I could have run to Terrence's in my heels, I would have. Finally I understood what Keith Bernstein had meant about liberation being such a fabulous party.

I slowed as I walked through Terrence's front door. I'd said I'd been here before, so I had to pretend to be familiar with it. I thought I knew it, imagining it like the Green Mill, a moody, jazzy bar where you couldn't hear the conversations over the music, where the music and the quirky crowd, mostly fat black men and dissipated white ones, inspired me to order Irish Coffee or something involving Kahlua, a drink that was both grown up and sweetly childish.

But Terrence's wasn't like that at all: Terrence's was people talking over the music rather than finding space underneath it, it was sloppy kissing and spastic dancing, it was a party. It wasn't the kind of place where men invited women for dates; it was a staging ground for the simplest of seductions.

Wayne waved when he caught sight of me, then stood and offered me a kiss on each cheek, the sensation of his lips lingering like an imprint. We exchanged casual greetings, "hey, how are you", "fine,

fine, yeah fine" and I ordered a beer, Carling Black Label. I'd never had one before, but the name sounded authentic. It was difficult to get conversation started, because Wayne was constantly swinging his head around to see who was calling his name. Hey my *broe, howzit?* He'd get up and greet old friends with affectionate slaps and vigorous handshakes. His pager buzzed and he indulged it, the way important people did.

"It's Jakes at the Ministry of Labor," he whispered, and scurried away to the false quiet of a corner. It was okay, I mouthed, I didn't mind. I could have sat and watched him all night. I could have sat alone, surrounded by activists, no longer angry or afraid. It was like watching a victory parade whose floats just kept coming by.

You having fun? Absolutely! You said you've been here before? Yeah, uh, about a month ago I think, came here with some work people. Hmmm, you find your way into the right spots quickly. Doesn't take me long to get settled into a place. That's a good skill for a woman to have, particularly in South Africa. That's good, because I intend to stay in South Africa for a while.

This kind of fractured banter continued through the evening, any attempt at real conversation broken by the arrival of new "mates" and *boets*, Sonny, Marcus, Tito, I can't remember all their names. At around midnight a musician started playing a saxophone in a jazzy style that was more upbeat than melancholy, music to dance to rather than cry by. Wayne shouted a name – Abdullah Ibrahim. Turned out he was one of the greats of South African township jazz, though I'd never heard of him.

One o'clock in the morning, and Wayne and I were sitting at a table too small for the five mates who'd joined us to talk politics. Even against the din, these activists were still talking politics, their opinions becoming more definitive with each sip. *The RDP will only succeed with the involvement of the private sector! The private sector must be radically reformed because it's nothing more than an arm of the apartheid government! Education, not jobs, is the key to this country's transformation!* It felt like a conversation staged for the cameras by pundits paid to take a stance. But this was real and I was part of it. Better than any fantasy I could have had because I was on a date – well, sort of – with one of the people who was really going to change this country. I smiled my ever-ready smile, all pleased and privileged, the way voyeurs are, taking more and more sips of whatever I was drinking to hide the fact that I wasn't talking.

Wayne turned to a woman with long hair and short fingernails, who was ordering drinks for the table. Her name was Maureen, and from what I could tell she was a lawyer or an economist, possibly both, who'd had relationships with every man at the table. That wasn't surprising; it seemed that everyone at the table had either been in bed or prison together. Seemed that everything involved either bed or prison, sex or the struggle.

Eventually, as the rest of our tablemates broke away, attracted by the lure of political conversations elsewhere, Wayne and I did try to have one genuine get-to-know-you conversation. It mostly involved me getting to know Wayne, attempting to trace every year from his childhood to his work for the ANC. He boozily narrated a life story with so many fabulous chapter headings: first child to attend university, student activist, prison, exile, PhD. His words, his life, were more dizzying than the Carling.

Wayne's questions were coy and crafted, part of the game. How does a girl from the middle of America land in South Africa? He accepted my responses no matter brief or fatuous.

Three o'clock approached. We stopped trying to talk and started staring at each other, fueled to keep laughing by drink and lust. We casually entwined ourselves, my one leg curled inside his two, his fingers moving up and down my arm, resting over my hand. He leaned in and said he was going to tell me something I had to promise not to tell anyone else. We were already making promises!

"The ANC's offered me a job, in the Ministry of Labor, it's not official yet, but basically I'll be an advisor to the Minister, Tito Mboweni. Tito and I have known each other for ages." His eyes were full of intent and the flutter in my stomach turned into a heat in my thighs.

"That's, uh, that's great," I managed, "sounds like an *amazing* opportunity." And he kept edging closer. I didn't know anybody in Chesterfield who'd worked for government or as an advisor to a government. I allowed my legs to ease open.

Wayne ran his hand through my bangs. "You look stunning tonight," he whispered. The widening space between my legs grew moist. No guy had ever called me that before. Stunning – it sounded like a word reserved for models or pageant contestants. Wayne's face loitered close to mine, then he put his hand on the back of my head to pull me into his open mouth.

We'd spent the first part of the night stalking each other, seeing how much distance we could keep while still remaining together. The rest of the night – once he took me to his home in Houghton, unremarkable except for the red front door, which he said was "to let the whities know the communists had invaded" – was all about getting closer, closer and closer, as far inside each other as bodily mechanics would allow.

Desire came quickly, the kind that makes you look for things to hold on to: his shoulders, the headboard. I'd never seen a black man's naked body, but I didn't stare or search for differences. My eyes were closed as I reveled in joyous, juicy thoughts born in a pool of Carling and endorphins. I have a working class, Armani wearing, government-ministry-advising black man inside of me right now. And there's nowhere else he wants to be, except deeper inside of me.

I felt Wayne's body going in and out of mine while he murmured my name over and over, trance-like "Jull, oh Jull," the name hot on my ear, reeking of beer. He'd just introduced me to this sexually liberated, intelligent woman, Jull, and she would prove to Wayne that she could do amazing things.

9

Middle of 1994: Setting up Stakes

The conversation with my parents about my decision to stay in South Africa was surprisingly short, a reflection, I think, of their resignation.

"You're doing *what?*" my father shouted, then whispered to my mother, "Now she wants to move there!"

"People don't just *move to Africa!*" my mother yelped in the background.

"So what happened to being proud of me for being a part of history?"

"Yeah, we said that and we meant it," replied my father. "You've made history and now you can come home."

"The elections were just the beginning. Now it's about building a new South Africa, turning this into a place where everybody can grow and prosper."

"Grow and prosper? Jesus Christ, first you wanted to free them and now you want to grow them!"

"Whatever. You have no idea what important work I'm doing here. How I'm really helping people. I can't just walk away from that. I'm *somebody* here. I mean, I could actually be somebody here. You want me to walk away from that. To what? To come back to what? That total Chesterfield nothingness?"

MIDDLE OF 1994: SETTING UP STAKES

My father was silent, and I heard my mother ask in the background, "What, what is it? She's staying? She wants to stay there? It's not some boy, is it? She hasn't met somebody, has she?"

The rest of the conversation wasn't any more coherent. Few of my remaining conversations with my parents while I was in Africa would ever be coherent again.

***

In June, Jerry and Maria were scheduled to return to Chicago to spend the summer in Evanston, settling in and preparing for the new academic year. Jerry joked that they didn't want to "winter" in South Africa and were looking forward to long afternoons with the boys along the shores of Lake Michigan. I'd always known their departure would force a decision. Living in South Africa was easy when it involved living with someone else, but soon enough I'd have to find a job, a place of my own to live.

By June I was ready. Jerry and Maria encouraged my plans, helping me find a small cottage in Melville that sat at the back of a bigger property, again providing an illusion of family. They agreed it was a great time for a young person to be in South Africa, and, Maria confided on the side, they would enjoy continuing to live in South Africa vicariously through me.

The Van Rooyens threw a long, boozy barbecue or *braai* for Jerry and Maria the Saturday before they left, complete with *boerewors* and burgers, two kinds of salads, green and beetroot, one kind of beer, Castle, and one kind of white wine, Drostdy Hof, a fruity sweet variety that Elsie assured me, as she filled my glass to the rim, was just *puurfect* for a braai.

Although the occasion was somber, it was a celebration of sorts. The elections had passed without incident, the Van Rooyens still had their homes, and for now their jobs, the gun cupboards had remained locked, and the linen cupboards were still full of tinned food.

"We'll just be eating beans on toast for a while," Elsie chirped.

The old lady even managed a toast "to the future". "Yaah, maybe Seth Effrika will even have one!" she sniggered and the booze helped to stop everyone from cringing.

Late afternoon, Maria's eldest brother, Bakkies, started complaining about the *kak* music selection, and the real party started. Even Maria, whom I'd never seen touching alcohol, got tipsy enough to suggest a turn on the dance floor. All the sisters seemed more charmed by their husbands, their husbands more charmed by their life prospects. When night had truly fallen, everyone paired up for awkward dancing involving everything from disco to ballroom, attempts at break dancing, even something Anneline claimed she'd learned in her salsa class. Jerry found me sitting in a corner of the garden, admiring the stars. South Africa's stars captivated me every night, their numbers and brightness surprising me every time I tilted my face upwards.

"You excited about staying?" Jerry asked.

"Absolutely. I still can't quite believe it. I mean, it feels a little surreal to be staying here, in South Africa, trying to kind of make some sort of life for myself here."

"Any idea what you want to do now? It's not so straightforward now the elections are over, is it?"

I stared into my half empty glass of Drostdy Hof, watching a mosquito struggle to stay afloat, then looked up at Jerry and started to laugh. "Not really. I'm not really qualified to do anything! God, I've got a degree from a great university, and I'm not actually qualified to do anything, how pathetic."

Jerry gave me one of his avuncular, advisory looks. "You can write well, you have very good reasoning capacity – mostly."

I fished the mosquito out of my wine with one finger. "Yeah, but it's not like I'm a doctor or lawyer or an economist. I have no concrete skills to really help people here. Shit, I don't even have religion to offer them!"

Jerry glanced at his wife being twirled around and dipped by her younger brother, completely out of step with the popular music blaring from the radio. "Ah well, don't worry," he patted my shoulder. "You won't be the first unqualified white person to try to make something of themselves in Africa."

I laughed again. Just then, someone found *The Sign* by Ace of Base on the radio, and I hopped up. "Wanna dance?" I chirped, extending my hand to Jerry. He grabbed it and trailed behind me. It was nice to pretend to be in the lead for once.

***

A few weeks into my search for a job, Francine McCullough, head to toe in lavender and black, walked me to her sun-soaked office at BUILD, with its bold-colored cloths and woven baskets. She had a nest of white curly hair and large purple glasses rested on her cheeks. A two-liter bottle of mineral water sat on her desk. I learned later that she drank only mineral water, lots of it. "Can't really trust the pipes," she would tell people, then quickly add, "But you can't trust them back home either!" She loved to make comparisons between Washington DC and Africa: same potholes, same bad water, same corruption. Nobody seemed as thoroughly convinced as she was.

Cultural self-deprecation wasn't the only thing that made Francine the quintessential development worker. Single, in her forties, with no public relationship history, she had been living and working in Africa on and off for two decades. Devoted her life to it, she said. Starting in Nairobi, then Lusaka and Lesotho, she'd edged further south, collecting textiles and chunky jewelry as souvenirs. She'd done a brief stint in Bangladesh, but confessed she couldn't get Africa out of her blood.

As I settled into the chair across from her, she handed me a business card from the neat stack in the smallest of her woven baskets. I lied, telling her I'd run out of mine. Such a busy time with the elections, I said. Truth was, I hadn't even thought of getting business cards printed. What title would I have put under my name? Intern. African History Specialist. Lover of Wayne Conradie. Was that my best qualification at this stage?

The identity question had continued to hang over me for weeks after Jerry and Maria left, hardening with every week during which I didn't find a job or even a clear sense of what I should be looking for. Sarah suggested I look for a job with an American NGO, some place with big sturdy cars and air-conditioned offices. "They'll love you," she said. "Every international NGO in Joburg is filled with smart, skill-less people like you."

Sarah's pep talk worked. I edited my resumé to make it sound smarter, more skillful. Worked as a "paralegal" at the Legal Aid Support Unit in Johannesburg, had a "working knowledge" of Zulu, served as an election monitoring "official". By the time I was finished, it felt full and weighty, worthy of reflection. Still, when I saw the ad in the *Mail & Guardian* for a job at BUILD, I hesitated before pulling out my highlighter. BUILD's focus was on "capacity building" for South African NGOs. What the hell was capacity building? "Building" sounded nice – it's nice to build things in Africa – but what is "capacity" and how do you build it? They were recruiting for a "program assistant for training". Training sounded a lot like teaching and, hey, I'd taught people how to vote, I'm sure I could teach "capacity". Couldn't every smart but skill-less American be a teacher in Africa? Hadn't unqualified white people been teaching people in Africa for centuries?

"I assume you know a little about what we do," Francine started the conversation, putting the cap back on the water bottle.

"Capacity building," I beamed, like the straight-A student I'd always been. It's teaching, teaching people, right, to uh, have better – *stronger* – uh, capacity."

A crescent frown spread across Francine's face. "We don't really use the word 'teaching'," she said, using her fingers to form quotation marks. "We *train* NGO leaders to better manage their organizations."

"Right," I said, although still not certain how "teaching" was different from "training". Maybe I wasn't so smart, after all.

"We *facilitate* staff to be better project managers, financial managers, better people managers." Francine leaned into the desk to emphasize the word "facilitate". "And we *facilitate* organizations to develop long-term strategies, to create sound work plans, and to evaluate their programs. Among other things, of course. So our role is that of a facilitator, not a teacher, as such." I'd never heard the word "facilitate" used so many times in the same breath. Back then, I had no idea how many times I, myself, would breathlessly use that word during my work in Africa.

"So, it's kind of like management consulting?" I tried.

"I suppose that's one way to describe it, although I never have or would," she frowned and I smiled, trying to offer an antidote. "We create real relationships with our NGO partners. We don't tell organizations what to do – we help them find their own solutions."

I decided to start taking notes in order to keep all the words straight: facilitation (with multiple stars next to it), teaching (with a line through it) and partnerships = solutions (with a big smiley face next to it).

"Right," I said, still looking at my notebook. "So your work must be very much in line with the Reconstruction and Development Program."

"Absolutely! Our job over the next five years is to *empower* people as part of the RDP."

"So you sort of build the power of South African organizations to empower people, local people."

"Yes," Francine said, much as Elsie and Thys had when I finally pronounced *bobotie* correctly. And I was pleased, suddenly, with a whole new four-syllable word to describe my work in South Africa: empowerment! I'd empowered prisoners to vote, and now I was going to empower organizations to provide services to local people. Suddenly I wanted to leap across the desk and beg: please, I know I don't have a business card or any experience to require one, but please, please hire me to empower people!

"You went to Northwestern, right. English Major. So you have a pretty solid command of the English language."

"English and History. African History. So, yes, yes, I can write. And as you can see I speak Zulu too. Conversationally."

"Hmmm, I see that. Sweet. I remember when I said I had a 'working knowledge' of Swahili." She did the quote thing with her fingers again. "No, it's the English that interests me. You write well, you like to write?"

"Yeah, I guess so, I wrote so many papers at university, I wrote my honors thesis, I ..."

"That's great," she interrupted with a smile and wave of her hand. "When can you start?"

When I phoned Sarah to ask her to join me for a celebratory drink, her first words were, "Don't tell me: they run workshops."

75

"Something like that, yeah, I think they do lots of capacity building training. Why?"

"Cuz that's all the international NGOs do. You used to give out food and seeds and now you hand out breath mints and notebooks. Don't tell me; your offices are in Braamfontein."

"Yeah, how did you know?"

"Cuz all the international NGOs are there. It's like a township for smart but skill-less white people."

But even Sarah's cynicism couldn't dampen my spirits that night. I didn't mind inhabiting that kind of township because it was better than any air-conditioned office park I would ever have worked at in Chesterfield.

10

Mid to Late 1994: Part-time Lovers

Twenty-three-year-old women from Chesterfield didn't routinely have "affairs". We had dates, of course, in pursuit of steady relationships with cute and reliable boyfriends. We certainly didn't have "lovers". Lovers were for soap opera vixens or older, experienced women who wore silk nightgowns and fluffy kitten heels. I still wore a nightshirt with a pink kitten on it.

No, girls like me had boyfriends who watched Tom Hanks' movies with us, who ordered pizza with us and then ate the crusts. Familiarity and comfort were the key aims of our Chesterfield relationships, but I hadn't come to South Africa for that kind of Lazy Boy lifestyle. A certain amount of challenge was obviously on the agenda; I just had no idea how uncomfortable I was willing to be.

So for quite a long time, longer than perhaps made sense to anyone who wasn't a twenty-three-year-old woman from Chesterfield, I savored the novelty of an affair with Wayne. A form of relationship driven entirely by a base desire – desire, it seemed, for me. Me? Wayne wanted me? I'd find myself saying those words over and over in an almost irrational, all-consuming way. I couldn't imagine any boy-man in Chesterfield wanting me like that, so I added yet another point to my growing list of "things I never would have done at home": be the stunning, amazing lover of a hotshot activist.

"An affair!" Sarah gasped when I finally told her about the relationship, months later. Though I knew her reaction would probably annoy me, I couldn't keep the details to myself anymore. And she was the closest to a twenty-three-year-old Chesterfield woman I could find in South Africa.

"Well, yeah, I guess you could call it that." I'm sure I looked pleased with myself. "It's all pretty intense."

"Well, woo hoo, look at you," Sarah raised her glass. "Here for a less than a year and you're already screwing the big shots."

"God, you make it sound so crass."

"Have you met his family? Had a dinner party with his big shot friends? Hey, do you, like, have coffee with Tito Mboweni?"

"No, it's not like that. I mean, the whole having coffee, meeting family thing."

"So what's it like then? Shagging on the side? Do you rent a Braamfontein hotel room for the lunch hour?"

"No, I mean, God, it's not cheap and nasty."

"Look, just make sure you use condoms."

"Of course we do. Wayne insists." I paused. "Anyway, why do you say 'use condoms' like that, like it's a warning or something?" I added, doing the quotes thing with my fingers.

"It *is* a warning. These ANC types are all sluts. When they weren't *toyi-toying* or throwing bombs, they were bonking each other."

Slut? I'd never thought of that word in relation to Wayne, what with his wire-frame glasses and serious economic job. Maybe sluttiness had been part of the struggle, but this was the new South Africa, people were building things now.

"I'm pretty sure Wayne doesn't have time to be a slut," I said, looking down at my menu as a way of ending the conversation. Maybe there was at least one person I could end conversations with. And maybe it was better if, like my relationship with the Boat People, I kept this affair all to myself.

***

For months after that first night at Terrence's, Wayne and I maintained a once-a-week, during-the-week routine of meeting at fashionably relevant bars, places that combined rubbing shoulders with rubbing legs. Perched on a stool, heels still on, lips and cheeks rouged, boobs out just enough to feel like sexy Jull, I would watch Wayne work the crowd, occasionally invoking homeboy dialect like *sharp sharp* or *hey boet* as a shortcut to authenticity. He was among the first in South Africa with a cell phone – still thick and black and heavy in those days – weightier in status than any gold chain. Deep in pressing conversation with someone I imagined to be important, he'd glance at me and it didn't matter that he wasn't talking to me. Maybe it was better that way, because then I could be whatever Wayne imagined me to be.

The tight spaces of the bars allowed that initial thrill of desire to rage for months. The flowing beers meant the fractured flirtation still felt like full conversations. The loud music meant I never had to try to tell my brief life story. And the dim lights meant Wayne would never see any of my schoolgirl blemishes. In the shadows of Yeoville's bars I never felt exposed. I could be Jull, with a serious new career starting alongside a sexy relationship.

"An NGO?" Wayne repeated, when I told him the news of my new job. He tore open a bag of chutney-flavored crisps. "That's nice. What's the name of it?"

"BUILD," I replied, shaking my head when he offered me a crisp.

"Never heard of it. Anyway, that's nice, great that you got a job." I waited for him to ask for more details about the organization, about my new role, but he didn't.

"Yeah, they're doing lots of work with the RDP. I think they're like a major player in the RDP," I added.

"You talk to any NGO these days and they all reckon they're a major player in the RDP." Wayne dug his hand into the bag and stuffed a few crisps into his mouth. "Anyway, I'm sure it will be great. Let's have another drink to celebrate." He planted a wet kiss on my lips and disappeared to the bar. I wiped the crisp crumbs off my mouth, wishing I could learn to like chutney. As I watched Wayne get sidetracked in conversation with two people at the bar – one of them that short-fingernailed economist from the night in Terrence's – I knew I had to find something other than work to impress him. "Program Assistant for Training" was never going to hold its own next to "economist" or "government advisor". I had to make sure that even in rooms busy with important people, Wayne would want to find his way back to me.

Later that night Wayne was hungry and a little rough, and I followed suit. I let him bend my body over and push it up against a wall. I pushed back harder. Surprised a white girl from the middle of America likes it this way? I put every part of Wayne's body into my mouth, my tongue sucking, my lips kissing, my fingers caressing and probing.

"You're so passionate," he panted. It felt like the biggest compliment I'd ever been paid. He lingered after sex just long enough for our heartbeats to return to normal, then slipped quietly out of my arms. He always slipped away, and the reason was always the same: so much work to do.

"Why don't I go to your place with you?" I said one night, raising myself on my elbow. "I haven't been back to your place since I got mine. I can make dinner for you while you work."

Wayne gave a dirty giggle as he pulled his shirt over his head. "Don't you get it? I can't concentrate when you're around." He reached over and grabbed the back of my head for a kiss. "You're like a drug: intoxicating, maybe even addictive." I fell back onto the pillow, lightheaded. "Tonight was amazing," he said, keys in his hand. He kissed my naked shoulder and disappeared.

Wayne said I was like a drug, intoxicating and even addictive! I filled the empty space of my bed with fantasies of our future, when Wayne was truly hooked. We'd have a sprawling but sensible home in Melville, with lovely little latte children scampering around our yard. I would be the pretty, young mistress of the house and Wayne the powerful master, more powerful with every passing year. Over time the initial thrill of desire would, of course, mellow into a deeper, richer kind of emotion, but there would still be something hot, even fiery about our feeling for each other. The affair would grow deeper and richer, I believed, continuing to smolder rather than just burning out. But maybe that's what all twenty-three-year-olds from Chesterfield assume about affairs, that they would have to lead to something more permanent.

A couple of months later, I screwed up the courage to suggest to Wayne that we meet for a romantic dinner, the first time we would meet in a space without a band, a place where they kept the lights turned on all night. We would drink wine rather than beer, sit across from each other rather than on top of each other. And Wayne wouldn't know anyone else there; he'd be forced to talk only to me. I was ready to talk just to Wayne.

I chose Simpsons, a quiet, candlelit spot in Melville where people ate oysters and ordered more than one bottle of Sauvignon Blanc. Jerry had taken Maria there on their anniversary and they'd come home after midnight, bumping and giggling. Simpsons was a date venue, and both Wayne and I wore date clothes; he a collared shirt, me a skirt. There was a false air of formality around the night given the physical intimacy we'd already experienced. Wayne ordered wine while I surveyed the menu, sharing with him my little preferences – "I love pesto but sometimes it just overpowers everything" – enjoying the notion that he was noting them for future use. I could have mistaken the whole conversation for a genteel, even old-fashioned kind of courting.

"So I have to go see my ex-wife this weekend," Wayne said, tearing open his roll and shoving a pat of butter into the space in between.

"Oh, I, uh, I didn't know you'd been married," I replied, casually, almost as a reflex. "That, that you had a wife." The word "wife" came out dry and cakey, as all the moisture drained from my mouth.

"Yeah," he said with a flick of his hand, "it was a long time ago, back in Port Elizabeth, just after university." And then, in the time it took him to devour his roll, he summarized a chapter of his story that he hadn't shared in all those dark spaces we'd met in previously. She was a colored woman from his neighborhood, they'd met at university, she'd stood by him when he was in prison, getting pregnant and having his baby while he counted numbers of cinderblocks in his cell. "At least I've got my son to be grateful for, from this mad relationship."

"You have a son?!" I pictured a smaller version of Wayne, in clothes with animals on them and shoes without laces.

"Yeah, his name is Leon. You know, Leon Trotsky, great communist leader," he smiled at his own sentimentality and refilled my glass.

"How, how old is he?" Suddenly I longed to be back in Terrence's, music blaring, hands all over each other.

"He's five now, and he's the love of my life. I tell you, I just love that kid. My marriage didn't work out, but at least I've got my son. I'm going down to spend the day with him in East London tomorrow. I think we'll go to the beach; he loves the sea." Now I imagined a miniature version of Wayne in swim trunks, digging holes for moats around sand castles.

"You okay?" Wayne asked, taking my hand, "something wrong with your oysters? Sometimes Knysna oysters can be a bit too creamy."

"No, no, they're fine," I snapped. "It's just … I'm just surprised, I guess, that's all. Just a bit surprised."

"That I have a son?"

"Yeah, and an ex-wife. I mean it's pretty big stuff, and you haven't said a word about it."

"Well, we've been having such a nice time and it didn't really come up". He took my hand again, squeezing more tightly. "Look, I'm just not used to talking about things, personal things."

"I know," I relented, "It's just … we've been together for a while now. I mean, it's been like, you know, almost six months that we've been, uh, seeing each other. So I guess I thought you'd want to tell me. You can tell me anything." I grabbed his hand, "I want to know everything."

"I know that, Jull, and it's sweet of you to say. But the truth is," he lowered his voice to a throaty whisper, "every time I'm with you, I can hardly think straight. I don't want to talk. You're just so unbelievably sexy." I demurred, looking down, running my hand through my hair. "It's true," he repeated, "when I'm next to you, I just want to be inside of you."

It happened again, the fire running up my legs, the moistness rising inside them. Our fingers played with each other, our eyes locked. What only minutes earlier had felt like a betrayal, a denial of the truth that challenged the integrity of the relationship, now felt like nothing more than an invitation into another chamber of Wayne's inner prison that I would one day fully access.

As the waiter put down our main courses – I'd decided to try kudu because Wayne said I should try venison – I silently reasoned with myself: he's a father, not a slut! I'm having an affair with a South African man – a *man*, with a son and an ex-wife to prove it, not a boy from Chesterfield with no past at all. This kind of thing happened all the time with epic affairs on soap operas, secret lives were revealed, tortured paths to commitment followed. By the time I was scraping the last bits of gooseberry pie off my plate, I felt so committed to the relationship that all I wanted was to get Wayne home and prove to him that I was brave enough to accept his entire life, that I wanted him regardless of his past. And maybe he would accept my paltry past too.

Less than an hour later, Wayne held onto the short pieces of hair on the top of my head as my open mouth slid up and down, faster and tighter than usual. He used those hairs to push me down, so that he went as far back into my throat as possible. And I urged him on with hungry grunts, swallowing as much of him as I could, until I gagged and he came. Then I climbed on top of him and told him I wanted more. That was one way to make sure he didn't leave.

11

Still Mid to Late 1994: I Could See the Future

Francine sat me down about a week after I started working for BUILD to outline my first assignment: helping one of their leading consultants, Reuben Mandala, edit materials for a management course BUILD was running for senior NGO leaders. Francine explained that Reuben was amazing – I was pleased to know that somebody else used that word too – but his English language skills weren't very strong. Bantu Education, she explained, referring to the apartheid system of education that disadvantaged blacks. I would work closely with him, as an editor, a ghost writer of sorts, to make the materials stronger. I nodded eagerly, pleased to have more clarity about my role.

Francine's face darkened. "The thing is," she said, "nobody can know you're doing this. I mean if people knew I had a young white American woman basically writing Reuben's materials…" Her voice trailed off.

"Of course," I replied. What Francine didn't know, and what I hadn't yet acknowledged to myself, was that helping black South African men keep their real lives secret didn't feel all that strange or uncomfortable to me yet.

I slipped into the back of the Holiday Inn conference room, anxious for my first chance to watch the amazing Reuben Mandala in action, excited to see this facilitating–capacity building–empowering work in practice. Even before I sat down I could sense that Reuben had a presence; he was a presence. A giant man, the kind of giant that required him to buy tailored clothing and an extra airplane seat. His belt was like a lasso tied around him, catching his trousers.

Francine's pace always picked up as she approached Reuben, her arms outstretched for a hug. When they were in a room together, she never strayed far from his ample side, unabashedly besotted. Reuben was Francine's crown jewel, her black South African management guru who was living proof of empowerment. And, boy, was Reuben empowered.

As one of a handful of black South Africans with the combined education, experience, skills and charm to consult to international organizations and donors, he was an anti-apartheid millionaire. Reuben had four cars, each a German luxury brand, and four houses scattered around Johannesburg: one for himself, one for his mother, the others for choice. He'd been on management courses in Boston, co-written articles about South African NGOs for university publications, and claimed to savor a nice glass of Cabernet at the end of a long week.

The Americans, the Dutch, the Germans couldn't get enough of Reuben's work or his company. They invited him over for dinner after they signed their names to lucrative contracts – so many days, so many dollars. Reuben never apologized for profiting from the non-profit sector, and no one dared asked him to. Who were we to begrudge the success of a black man in South Africa?

Even among his friends, Reuben's private life was the subject of routine but intense speculation. "Where does Reuben live?" "So have you ever heard the final word on how many children he has?" "Is Reuben married?" His wife's name was never raised in public, only in brief whispered conversations among people who claimed not to be gossiping. The gossip was that Reuben had more than eleven children from several wives. That he had no wife at all. That he had women everywhere. Reuben kept the truth as elusive as his wives.

Back at the Holiday Inn, sitting upright with my notebook out and pen in hand, I assumed the familiar role of student, ready to learn about management from Professor Mandala. But I wasn't one of Professor Mandala's students, and I knew that. And this didn't look like any classroom I'd ever entered. It wasn't just the round tables rather than desks or the flipcharts instead of chalkboards. Or the lack of fresh white faces, just thirty black adult participants, women in somber-colored polyester pantsuits and patent leather shoes, men in mostly ill-fitting suits. What was most different – remarkable, even – about this room was its tone. Even in competitive Northwestern University classrooms, I'd never seen such a captive audience, not a single person slouched or slumped or drifting away. Even when someone poured water or unwrapped a mint, their eyes never strayed from Reuben as he lumbered across the room, riffing on the merits of planning. As he wrote one word on the flipchart paper, *vision*, then circled it with a flourish and put the pen down; as he rested on the edge of a table to catch his breath. Everything about Reuben was so weighty it seemed dangerous to ignore him.

Reuben shifted between English and Sotho and Zulu and Xhosa mid thought, mid sentence, sometimes in the middle of a word, his voice rising and falling to punctuate his points, his finger raised towards the heavens. And then he stopped in the middle of the room, hoiking up his pants as though he were preparing to demonstrate a dance move, his leather loafers bowing under the weight.

"Are we together?" he asked, followed by a dramatic pause. "Are we together?" he repeated, this time louder, more forcefully. And the participants, his followers, responded "yes" in hearty unison. I half expected someone to shout *Hallelujah*. Reuben gave a satisfied nod and started moving again.

His subject that day was an African approach to management called *ubuntu*, which was all about creating a sense of community and shared responsibility in the workplace. Reuben and other prominent South African business thinkers were excited about *ubuntu*, a distinctly African take on a subject that seemed so very un-African: management. Francine even had the word *ubuntu* carved into a piece of teak hanging behind her desk. "The West really has so much to learn from Africa," she frequently reminded me.

As they savored Reuben's words, the participants didn't just seem to want to understand the concept of *ubuntu*, they wanted to believe in it. To have proof that South Africa – which had just handed the world a lesson on democracy – had more to teach. They leaned in towards Reuben, nodding or involuntarily uttering "uh huh" or "yeeeesss".

There was Gladys from Bloemfontein who ran a women's education project and giggled when she introduced herself: "It's funny a woman like me without education running a women's education program." Until this course, she told the group, she'd never been given a chance to learn how to be a good leader – not just to call herself a leader, but to really *feel* like one.

And Patrick, a twenty-three-year-old director of a youth program in Nelspruit, his suit too big and his tie too thin, who stood up and cleared his throat every time he asked a question or made a point. Who argued the merits of periodic strategic planning over tea, "The communists liked five-year plans, but I think three years is more effective."

Gladys and Patrick and all the other participants were completely preoccupied with securing the future: theirs and their country's.

I spent the morning watching and listening to their discussion, and I fully believed the future was theirs. So driven by an ambitious desire to right apartheid's wrongs and help their people flourish, these participants would become the foremen of building the new South Africa. I could see it. Francine was right; this wasn't just some antiseptic form of management consulting. This capacity building – facilitation-empowerment thing was far more powerful and personal, something I would never have found at any Holiday Inn back home in the States.

"Are we together?" Reuben asked when he finished his session on *ubuntu*.

"Yes!" I shouted. Only a few hours had passed, but I was certainly together with Reuben. I sat on the edge of my seat, wanting to get closer to the group, even though nobody had noticed I'd joined it. My notebook fell from my lap but I didn't bother to pick it up. Who needed notes? This wasn't a lesson; it was a way of life. And who needed dusty streets and downtrodden people when you had business suits and bullet points, professional, powerful people who would build powerful organizations, who would then make powerful communities. Maybe I would emerge from this course professional and powerful too. Maybe one day soon I would feel as powerful during the day as I'd managed to make myself feel at night.

I milled around at lunchtime, my hand permanently extended. "Jill. Jill. Yes, Jeel, Jeel Reilly. Yes, yes, I'm the new training assistant. Jeel. Jeeeel. Yes, well, no, I guess it's kind of a common name in America." By this point I'd given up on saying *sawubona*. Professional, powerful NGO directors didn't want to hear me stumbling through Zulu, and besides I'd been hired for my English so I needed to show it off straight away. Everyone looked happy to see me; like the Van Rooyens, but better, because these people were black. And black people had never looked so happy to see me. How long had I been here? How did I find South Africa? "Beautiful, oh so beautiful, your country is just so beautiful." I think I even said their country was more beautiful than mine. Francine would have been proud.

In the back of my mind, I couldn't help hearing Francine's description of me as "a young white American woman". That's what I was, after all, and even though I'd worn glasses and a silky scarf that morning, nothing could disguise my youth. Still, as the lunch hour wore on, I felt more substantive, and it wasn't just the stodgy buffet food of roast beef and creamed cauliflower. Because even though I was young and white, everything about me – my pixie haircut, my accent, my funny one-syllable, neither male nor female name – had a glossy, imported quality to it. Like a Volvo. I'd imported myself into this little group, a necessary luxury among them, the English language expert with a shiny university degree. The longer I lingered with the participants' hands in mine, looking into their eager faces, the less I felt that "young" and "white" were such liabilities. Maybe they were the reason these older black South Africans had let me into the room in the first place.

"So you're the English *fundi*," Reuben chortled as I approached him over lunch to introduce myself. "The one who's going to dot my i's and cross my t's and all that?"

"Francine mentioned you might want some support in that regard," I replied, friendly but business-like.

"And you're happy to spend your days in the Holiday Inn rather than a township?"

"Sorry?"

"Most young people like you want to work with poor folks in the townships. Teaching people, healing them, all of that, in Soweto, Alex. Isn't that why people come here, to say they worked in Soweto?"

"I guess that's where I thought I would be working. But you can still make a difference in the Holiday Inn. Empowerment, right?"

"Yeah, but I bet you didn't think you'd be empowering a fat black millionaire with bad spelling!" Reuben laughing as he tucked his shirt back into his trousers.

I decided to go along with the playfulness. "Well, I guess the theory is that if I help you, you'll help them," I said, nodding towards the participants.

"And then they'll help the people in the townships," he continued.

"Exactly."

"You're right, that's the theory at least. We'll have to wait and see if it works out that way. Don't worry, we'll get you out to the townships eventually, you won't have to let down the folks back home."

"I think they'll be happy to know I'm in a Holiday Inn!" I giggled, now fully feeling the playful tone. And Reuben extended his hand to shake mine.

***

I started dialing Wayne's number moments after the glass door of the Holiday Inn swung shut behind me. I got his answering machine. "Wayne, it's Jill. I guess you're busy. Anyway, sorry to bother you, I just wanted to tell you about my day. I met the people I'm going to work with. Reuben, do you remember I mentioned Reuben? Anyway, it was just, uh, a great day, I mean really amazing, well, just like, really inspiring. And the people involved with this course, maybe you know some of them. There's this woman named Esther from PE ..." An inner voice told me to cut the message short, that I was starting to sound like a girlfriend in a pink nightgown. "Anyway, I'll tell you all about it when I talk to you. Call me soon. Okay, bye!" And then I started counting the hours until he returned my call.

12

1995-1997: African Renaissance

I had no idea at the time that the years 1995-97 were a golden period in my life in South Africa, or that they would one day come to an end. At twenty-five years old, I simply felt my life was blossoming according to plan and would continue to do so as long as I willed it. I could see nothing wrong with taking my place at a table among people thirty years older than me with twenty years more experience, or participating in conversations about issues I'd never experienced – poverty, HIV/Aids, early childhood development – and eventually trusting myself to lead those conversations. Why not? My white girl smarts would give me passage to all the interesting places that skill-less wouldn't let me go.

For two years I held tight to those feelings I'd first experienced on top of the monkey bars with a ten-dollar bill for the Boat People fresh in my school bag: the giddiness, the promise, the potential – theirs and mine, the power, oh yes, theirs and mine. The pure sense of rightness and goodness, the simple, succulent belief that I was saving lives. And even though it had happened once before, it didn't occur to me that this all-consuming belief would one day splinter into prickly shards.

For two years I committed myself fully to helping Reuben run more courses and better ones, reaching more activists, with even more empowering management training, so that South Africa would one day be full of power-filled, pleasure-filled activists reconstructing the country during the day, constructing relationships at night. I believed I would help Francine and Reuben build an empowerment empire. I had become an empowerment apostle, a capacity building convert, from that very first day in the Holiday Inn. Somehow, believing during the day helped me believe at night.

During those two years, the demand for Reuben's courses grew as the number of South African activists wanting his glossy brand of empowerment grew. I edited his materials so they were clearer and more compelling, put together flipchart presentations that were more colorful and engaging. All style, really, rather than substance.

But the substance soon followed: after enough days of sitting in the back of the dark conference room, listening to Reuben talk about participatory leadership, about visioning and adaptation, and with enough silent nights spent reading about the subject, my input became meatier. Month by month, suggestion by suggestion, at first whispered and then blurted, my role with Reuben grew and expanded. Our conversations began to focus on whether he should include scenario planning in his sessions, whether experiential games would help people test their leadership roles more effectively. I'd never run a management course before, but that didn't matter. Voting educator, training assistant, now management "fundi" – heck, Africa made me feel I could be a game ranger if I put my mind to it.

I could have sworn I was watching people's capacity being built right before my eyes. In the form of NGO staff huddled around tables setting ambitious targets for developing their communities; or financial managers setting up computerized accounting systems for the first time so they could handle more donor funding; directors who stuttered when they spoke English bravely picking up the phone to woo new overseas donors. I even swore that I met "empowerment" over the course of those two years, that I knew its many names: Jakes Madeira, Director of the Water Rights Trust in Uitenhage, Phyllis Tshabalala who headed up the Early Learning Action Center in George, and Griffiths Tsipang who was the Chair of the Board of the Small Farmers Association in Port Shepstone. Probably less than ten years education among the three of them, none of them knew how to drive and each typed using two fingers. They heaped their plates with food until pieces started to fall off on the way back from the buffet table and relished the privilege of ordering a Coke at lunch. It was the first time any of them had stayed in a hotel or taken an airplane. Every time Jakes wrote on a flipchart it slanted off to the bottom right so you had to cock your head to read it. Phyllis arrived early each morning, dressed in bold African print, to spend thirty minutes reviewing her notes from the day before. Her finger moved across each line of her notebook as she read. And Griffiths made rambling but relevant points, clearly more comfortable at a rally than in a classroom.

But it didn't matter that each of these people lacked all the social wherewithal and life experience that I associated with smarts, they were actually changing lives, their own and those of people in their communities. And there I was, helping to make it happen, not just watching it on TV. All of us were experiencing a golden period for the first time in our lives.

The entire country pulsed with that giddy sense of promise during those two years, when so many things about South Africa emerged new and genuinely improved: a national anthem with an unwieldy coupling of Afrikaans, English, Xhosa, Zulu and Sesotho verses that seemed to capture everything ambitious and unwieldy about the place. A new Constitution, one of only a few in the world to entrench equal rights regardless of "race, gender, sex, pregnancy, marital status, ethnic or social origin, color, sexual orientation, age, disability, religion, conscience, belief, culture, language and birth". As though the brains behind the new South Africa could see beyond the base politics of race to ensure even pregnant women got a fair shot. The launch of the Truth and Reconciliation Commission, with Desmond Tutu at its head, perhaps the only person more beatific than Nelson Mandela, was driven by a belief that the truth really did set people free, rather than just leaving them adrift.

Even the brutal sport of rugby, a sort of bastion of white Afrikanerdom, symbolic of so much old about South Africa, managed to reinvent itself in 1995. The Springboks, or *ama bokke bokke*, won the World Cup that year in Johannesburg, and in celebration the captain, Francois Pienaar, hoisted Nelson Mandela, wearing a Springbok jersey, on his shoulders. *Invictus*, indeed. Unconquered. It was so easy to feel unconquerable then.

"God, I wish you were still here, Jerry. I mean, I don't want to gloat, but I think you guys left at the wrong time." Jerry and I continued to talk from time to time, at first by phone and later by email.

"Yeah, I'm getting good reports from your side, along with some bad ones, of course. Can always count on the in-laws for the sort of Eugène Terre'Blanche take on things. But everyone seems to agree the government's certainly getting the window dressing right."

"I wouldn't exactly call a new constitution, a new constitutional court, window dressing."

"Yeah, but it's the bread and butter issues that are going to take some real time. Jobs, houses, health care, schools."

"It's going to take time, and it's only been a couple of years. A lot of the NGOs we're supporting are partnering with the government to work together on reconstruction."

"Yeah, but nobody in South Africa, nobody anywhere in the world for that matter, has experience fast-tracking development for this many people in such a short time."

"But there are loads of really strong people working in advisory roles in the government who've been in exile, well-trained at top universities. They're not just a bunch of bomb throwers in suits."

"No, they're bomb throwers in Mercs."

"Look, next time I'm just gonna call Elsie!" I laughed.

"Anyway, let's talk about you. You're happy with your job at BUILD, right, that's the name of the outfit?"

"Absolutely. I'm kind of right in the middle of things, building the capacity of some of South Africa's top NGOs. We're strengthening civil society so it can play a role in delivering just those services you're talking about."

"Well, listen to you," Jerry interrupted, "civil society." I knew if he were sitting across from me he would have been doing that quotation thing with his fingers. "Sounds like you're really hitting your stride."

"Yeah, well, I guess I sort of am."

"There's a student here doing her honors thesis on the elections.

I told her she should speak to you – you're the New South Africa expert, right?"

"Sure, sure I'd be happy to share my experiences with her," I replied. I barely heard anything Jerry said after that, my mind buzzing with the excitement of The Truth he'd just confirmed. In three years I'd gone from student to "expert". Who knew what the next three years could bring? As long as we kept believing, and didn't ask too many questions about what the bigger future would bring.

So I didn't – ask many questions, that is, of Francine or Reuben, and certainly not of Wayne. I'd been converted to him that very first day at Mandela's inauguration and was intent on making the affair as "pioneering", as "empowering" as possible, in line with the rest of my pioneering, empowering life. I looked for every opportunity to prove to Wayne that I was his brave and exciting Jull, believing he was becoming addicted to me. Addicted in the parking garage at the airport, the bathroom at Terrence's, in a corner at the Rosebank flea market, with a jazz band drowning out my grunts.

Once we both found ourselves at separate workshops in Cape Town, and Wayne phoned me at one o'clock in the morning, insisting he "had to have me", he couldn't sleep until he had. I became moist and light-headed, fumbled to put on mascara and lip gloss, rushed across town, naked under my coat, satisfied with the suitability of that tired cliché. Because I believed there was nothing tired or sordid about this affair: we were both unattached but busy activists, furiously rebuilding South Africa during the day and exploding in lust at night.

There were signs that Wayne and I weren't really building anything at night: the long periods he'd go without phoning me, the lack of introductions to anyone who meant anything to him, the number of times he didn't show up for a date we'd set. But there was always a good excuse.

"Ag, man, Jull, I'm really sorry. Tito called this meeting at the last minute, and I had to rush to the office. And the meeting just went on and on, and I couldn't get out of it and I couldn't turn my phone on. Before I knew it, it was already seven o'clock and then Tito wanted to have a whiskey. We've got a ridiculous timeframe to get this white paper to Parliament before they go into recess. It's just really intense right now. I know it's shit, and I really am sorry."

And within minutes I was just happy that someone working on white papers in Parliament was on the other end of the line with me. I'd remind myself that I never would have known a man like this in Chesterfield, and we'd arrange another meeting. I believed in Wayne, and in Jull. And being a believer requires you to ignore any hints or clues that might raise questions. Belief has no time for questions because once you start asking them, all that juicy faith and promise falls apart. I found that out when I was ten years old on the monkey bars, and I wasn't going to make that mistake again.

13

Early 1997: Crashing Off the Monkey Bars

Everyone agreed that an official celebration was long overdue. The New South Africa had empowered us all and the future was ours to celebrate.

Reuben and I had worked together for over two years, facilitated five management courses together, and capacity built close to two hundred of South Africa's finest future leaders. Reuben had long argued that the participants needed some sort of ceremony and certificates to mark their accomplishments, a privilege that Bantu Education had long denied them.

"Come on, Francine," he pleaded over lunch one day, placing his fleshy hand on her shoulder, "let's give these people some sort of diploma, haven't they earned it?" And with that, the graduation ceremony was pretty much official.

I glided among the participants on graduation night in the glittering ballroom of the Carlton Hotel, hugging, stopping to make a joke or take an order for the next round of drinks. Only two years earlier I'd watched these activists from the periphery of another hotel room during the day, my stomach churning with envy and curiosity. Now I was being twirled around and dipped by government officials, instructed by ANC committee members how to smoothly move my hips and shoulders to the sounds of township jazz. And I followed their lead, not worrying about whether my dress was too tight or my skin too white. This wasn't a night for worry.

"We never would have produced such professional materials without you," Francine said, putting her arms around me. She'd cornered me about half way through the night and held me in such a long embrace that I stopped holding her long before she stopped holding me. "You've done such amazing work over the past few years," she continued, her wine glass dancing in her hand, tippling onto her silky lavender dress. "If only I'd known how much that young woman who came through my door that day a few years ago would change my life ..."

I didn't try to deflect her praise. I knew I had improved the courses, and with each year the writing had become more of mine, the editing less. I'd earned a place at the front of the classroom next to Reuben, and he would even ask my opinion. Eventually he called me his co-facilitator though Francine never let him make that title official.

"Well, it's been a lot of fun, working with Reuben is really easy," I said. "I've learned so much, and he's been so generous teaching me things."

Francine lowered her voice, "Everybody knows this is really your work." She giggled like a little girl revealing a long-held secret. "They know Reuben wouldn't have done this, couldn't have. Silly me for even trying to hide you!"

"You think people know?" I pulled away from her, playing the ingénue. "Nah, Francine, everybody here just thinks I'm the young white girl editor." And I skipped away. You skip when you're in the middle of your golden period.

At around 11 o'clock the crowd started baying for Reuben and me to share a dance. He stood over me like an eclipse blocking out the disco ball shimmering above. Then he started to groove, smoothly jutting his hips to the left, then the right, further and further down. And I kept up with him, going down, down, down, the two of us jiving as if our bodies actually worked together. People formed a circle around us, cheering and ululating and shouting out phrases like: "Oooh, look at the little white girl go!"

When the song ended, Reuben and I shared a hug. "You're a great partner, Ms Reilly," he shouted.

"Thank you," I replied, "you're a pretty good leader." Reuben winked and mussed the top of my hair with his chunky hand, his gold rings gleaming under the spotlights.

At midnight, the room rocked as the dance floor filled. My head was spinning more than my body had and I needed some air. I saw Gladys Mabikwe, one of the course's matriarchs, standing by the doorway, sipping a cup of tea and surveying the antics. She looked like the only thing in the room that wasn't spinning so I approached, hoping she could make me feel as upright as she looked.

"Mama Mabikwe," I slurred, reaching for the wall. "Ma, I must tell you how much I respect you. Really, really respect you so much. I hope that by the time I'm your age, I can achieve what you have. You make me so ... so proud to be a woman. School principal, head of an NGO, grandmother – seriously, you're amazing. I just wanted you to know that."

Gladys sipped her tea and accepted my late-night love, but she had other things on her mind. "*Sisi*, why are you here by yourself?" I leaned heavier into the wall and took another sip of wine. "None of us has ever seen you with a man, and you've never mentioned anyone. Now here you are again tonight, alone. Such a lovely young lady, what are you doing so far away from home by yourself?"

I scratched my head. "A lot of people have to go far away from home to do what they want to do. And it's best sometimes to do that alone, when nobody else can hold you back. It's good to be alone, I actually like it that way. Look at Francine, she's by herself and ..."

"Nobody chooses to be alone, *sisi*," Gladys interrupted. "Why aren't you in America finding yourself a boyfriend? A husband! I know you're young, but you're not a child."

I put down my glass of wine and changed tack. Mama Mabikwe's company was having a sobering effect. "Who knows, maybe I'll find my husband here?" I offered a coy grin, half expecting some form of "girl talk" to ensue.

Instead Gladys looked at me, really took all of me in, then replied, every word deliberate. "If it's a white you're talking about, then fine, try one of them and see how you like it. But God save you if it's a black man you're looking for. I see too many of you young foreign girls chasing our black boys. They'll love you for a while, because you're pretty and smart and wear short skirts, and mostly because you ask so little of them. But it won't work, you'll never be accepted. Not by him, certainly not by his family. So take my advice. You have done wonderful work here. Now go home and find yourself a nice white man in whatever town you came from. Settle down there. You'll be much happier."

I put my hands on the wall to help me stand up.

***

I left the graduation party and headed for Houghton, parking my car just in front of Wayne's red front door, the first time I'd been back to his place since our very first night together. I wiped away the smudged mascara under my eyes, put on a fresh coat of lipstick, and sprayed myself with perfume. "God, I love the way you smell," Wayne had once murmured as he scraped his teeth along my neck. I walked up to the gate, back straight and shoulders bare despite the cool night, as invisible dogs barked all around. I rang the buzzer and waited, taking deep breaths and practicing a smile, until a voice answered. It was Sonny. I'd met him long ago at Terrence's, and he had a distinctive lisp.

"Hi there," I tried to sound perky, festive even. "I'm looking for Wayne. It's, uh, Jill. Jill Reilly. " A worrying silence followed, then a buzz as the gate opened. Sonny stood at the door in sweatpants and slippers, his arms crossed, as though I were about to try to sell him something.

"Hi there, I don't know if you remember me," I began.

"Sure, sure," Sonny replied with just the hint of a smile.

"I'm so sorry I disturbed you. Just, uh as I said, I'm looking for Wayne. I've been away, on holiday, so, uh, we haven't had a chance to speak." I fiddled with my small, beaded evening bag. "Is he here?"

"No, he isn't," Sonny said, his face slightly furrowed. "I assume you checked at his place?"

The words "his place" ignited heat on the soles of my feet and roared up my leg. "Uh, yeah, yeah, I did, of course." My throat constricted, "He, uh, wasn't there, so I just thought ..."

"I know he and Maureen were going away this weekend, down to the Cape to see Leon." I just nodded, slowly, blankly, my smile firm. "They probably already left. She wasn't there either?"

"Nobody was home," I managed.

"Yeah, well they go to his parents' place most weekends. You can probably reach him there if you've got the number."

"Yeah, sure, now that I think of it, I think he told me. Yeah, of course, I've got that number. Anyway, thanks, thanks so much. Sorry again for disturbing you."

As I turned away, Maureen's face confronted me: she was the short-fingernailed woman from Terrence's, the economist, the director of her own NGO, the whiskey drinker, the one who'd been in the struggle – in prison and in bed. Who'd commanded the table that night with drinks and conversation, who probably did ask a lot of Wayne, the one who had obviously been accepted by him and his family.

I closed the gate behind me, and in the same spot where Wayne and I had groped each other so happily two years earlier, I bent over and threw up. Alcohol, fatigue, confusion and despair splattered all over the ground in a desperate attempt to disgorge every sickening sensation I was experiencing. I sat down on the ground. I knew white women weren't meant to sit on pavements in Joburg at night, but I didn't care. My mind began ripping through images of so many blow jobs, of bending over cars and standing up in elevators, memories now rendering the relationship sordid. If I'd been a drug to Wayne then I'd been recreational, not addictive at all. I wiped my mouth. Wayne wasn't a slut; he had a stable relationship, a son he visited. But maybe I was a slut, the most pathetic kind – an unwitting slut.

14

Early to Mid 1997: Born Yet Again

The next morning I decided to follow the lure of those beating, tribal drums into Melville's *koppies*. They'd become commonplace to me by then, part of a background scene of loud domestics, snarling dogs, the tinny sound of a football match blaring from cheap radios, the occasional *haw haw haw*. Sounds I barely noticed anymore. But that morning I couldn't ignore those drums.

I'd barely slept, spells of dream-filled sleep soaked with wine and stained with relentless replays of every moment in front of Sonny's house. A few minutes that felt like hours. Minutes that made me shudder to recall. Still wearing my silky party dress, I'd alternately imagined Wayne and Maureen checking in at Jan Smuts Airport holding hands, and Wayne listening to my phone messages and chuckling before deleting them. Or did he let her listen to them as they laughed together? What would Wayne say when Sonny told him I'd shown up at his front door? Would there be a moment of concern, a fleeting "oh shit"? Or just a derisive laugh for the little American girl who sucked his dick every time he rang her?

I'd got up in the darkness of night and opened a bottle of Buitenverwachting Buiten Blanc, pouring it into a deep, wide plastic tumbler better suited for juice. I'd put on an Alanis Morissette CD, loud and insouciant, as though a party were taking place. Why had I ever left that graduation ceremony? How different I would have felt if I'd been left to believe that I'd graduated into a different class in life. I'd turned the volume from eight to nine, fuck the neighbors, I'd never met them anyway. I didn't know what was worse, memories of what had happened or visions of what might have happened afterwards. Why hadn't I just stayed at the Carlton Hotel, being twirled around by empowered activists, rather than getting dumped on the pavement by someone who had disempowered me without my knowing?

Two tumblers of wine later I'd turned the volume to level ten and started karaoking by candlelight. *I want you to know, that I'm happy for you. I wish nothing but the best for you both.* I'd stumbled around the room, tripping over my discarded handbag, flashing back to Wayne pressing me up against my cupboard door, a wire hanger digging into my back. *Did you forget about me, Mr Duplicity? I hate to bug you in the middle of dinner.* It was a slap in the face, how quickly I was replaced and *are you thinking of me when you fuck her.* Rewind. *Thinking of me when you FUCK her!* Rewind. *When you FUCK her!* Rewind. *FUCK her!*

I'd sat down on my bed, exhausted by memories of him fucking me, visions of him fucking her. Still I hadn't known which was worse, what actually happened or what might have happened after. I'd pressed fast forward. *Isn't it ironic, don't you think? It's like rain on your wedding day, it's a free ride when you've already paid.* Rewind. *Isn't it ironic, don't you think?* I'd eventually fallen asleep with my finger on the remote control, the tumbler of wine tilting from my hand, the candle burnt out. Music and wine had taken me away from reality for at least a little while.

Until seven o'clock in the morning, when the drums seemed to be offering me passage to another world. I pulled on sweatpants and hiking boots and headed for the hills, enjoying that first tingle of sun on my skin and the promise it made to bring a new day. Dogs were barking, but it was too early for the usual banter and bustle of domestic workers organizing lives other than their own. The clear sky allowed my hazy mind to focus on my left foot following the right up a narrow path, to note a beetle lying on its back, legs flailing, to admire the unlikely smoothness of an ancient rock. All the while, the people on the *koppies* kept singing. At least somewhere in South Africa people were still celebrating the dawn of a new beginning.

EARLY TO MID 1997: BORN YET AGAIN

I reached the top of the hill and saw them in the distance, a small circle of worldly angels clad in white gowns, lost in a celebratory dance with all the energy and exoticism of a *toyi-toyi*, but without its vigorous defiance. Far enough away to remain anonymous, I found a flat rock to sit on, feeling my bony knees against my chest. I felt safe there, even hopeful, like so many Sunday mornings in front of the TV as a child, watching exotic people from a comforting distance.

Except this time it was them who had the power save me. I lifted up my hand to reach out to them and quickly pulled it back again. My eyes steadied on the group's rhythmic movements; they would stay here all day going round and round and maybe I could stay too, not moving at all, just memories and imagination swirling round and round.

How long had Wayne been lying to me? Did he want to humiliate me or did he just like fucking around? The evangelicals couldn't answer my questions – I knew even these so-close-to-God people didn't have my answers – but maybe they could stop the questioning. Isn't that what believing is all about?

In the center of the circle danced a woman, apparently young though probably older than me, still light on her feet, with a body that looked as though it hadn't born children or the weight of raising them. She was smiling, almost laughing, her face turned up towards the heavens. I had to believe that what I saw was some version of pure exaltation, the kind I could only imitate. Then a smile made its way onto my face. I'd been so wrong about these drums when I heard them that first morning at Jerry's house. This ceremony wasn't a promise of violence, just promise itself.

A man who moved with the commanding presence of a leader spotted me, offering a broad, welcoming smile that I found difficult to reciprocate. For a moment I considered accepting the invitation, succumbing. Maybe these strangers would sweep me up and take me away with them to their world, make my body feel light and fluid again. The man waved for me, and I waved back "no", curling up tighter, my position as voyeur now untenable.

I walked in the *koppies* for hours that morning, noting the odd outcrop of green grass amidst the rocks, little white flowers flourishing without any apparent care. Tears gathered in the corners of my eyes and then dried again. I stumbled from fatigue and told myself I needed to get home for water, but I kept walking. I'd have to clean up the wine if I went home, look at my forlorn party dress and pry the wax from the candlesticks. Hours of one foot after the other, memory and imagination nipping at my ankles. How is it possible to have totally separate lives, to keep two realities so completely separate that they never have a hint of each other?

I carried on, haunted, hunted, slapping at my ankles to disperse bugs I couldn't see. Finally I slumped onto a rock and burst into tears. I just wanted to be alone, please just leave me alone. Nobody chooses to be alone, Gladys mocked me. I continued to sob, begging memory and imagination to just leave me alone.

Some part of my new life in South Africa had ended, but I had no idea how I was going to rebirth myself. Then, about a week later, the promise of birth came from the unlikeliest of places, it came from death.

***

"Aids? But I don't know anything about Aids," I said. "I mean, I remember all the stuff from the eighties, like Magic Johnson, the quilt, night sweats and all that. But Aids in Africa? I can't tell you the first thing about it. How can I run a project if I don't …"

"Oh that doesn't matter, you don't have to be some sort of Aids expert," Francine interrupted. "The Zimbabwean ASOs …"

"ASOs?"

"Aids Service Organizations. They've got the technical skills. We just have to strengthen their capacity to manage their programs better."

"I do feel I've developed a real understanding of capacity building over the past few years, how to help people be better managers," I mumbled, "but I've never even been to Zimbabwe. I mean, the Aids thing kind of freaks me out. Wouldn't a doctor be better for this kind of position?"

"Jill, I respect your reservations, but honestly your lack of Aids experience isn't a problem. You're very smart, a quick study, I have no doubt that you'll pick up the Aids stuff very quickly. It's just awareness raising, really, that's the main issue, people just need to be more aware of Aids and then they can deal with it themselves."

My mind flashed to images of me walking the aisles of hospital wards; marching through Harare's streets with singing activists; pacing Reuben-like at the front of a conference room; wearing a sensible linen dress with a red ribbon attached. Then I came back to reality, or what I thought was reality.

"Well, I guess Aids can't be any worse than apartheid, right? And I did sort of throw myself into the whole post-apartheid thing, didn't I, learning a lot quite quickly. I guess if I can deal with apartheid then I can deal with Aids, right?" I repeated, trying to convince myself.

"Absolutely, and this is a wonderful opportunity, a five-year project, so you can actually build something, really make a difference. You'd be the youngest project director BUILD has ever had."

***

To most people, Zimbabwe represented an idealized vision of Africa: without war or domestic weapons, without creeping, corroding poverty or the threat of random crimes. It had the highest literacy rate in Southern Africa, reflected in an exceptionally tidy middle class of men with neatly knotted ties and women with neatly knotted hair, working as accountants in neatly designed office parks with names I could have found in Chesterfield.

It was considered the region's breadbasket too, its bountiful lands raising cattle and growing corn, wheat and tobacco, all of which provided lucrative export cash. Its healthcare systems had succeeded in immunizing children and lowering birthrates, and its economy was home to multinationals and thriving local businesses alike. With game parks and lakes and even the World Heritage Site, Victoria Falls, this was a picture of Africa's natural and human potential fully realized, capacity built and ready to go.

I spent that first visit to Harare smiling; smiling at myself and my lovely exotic new home. I was an intrepid explorer again, this time with a title and 500 printed business cards: Jill Reilly, Director, BUILD, Zimbabwe. And what a delightful place to hand out business cards. Harare felt nothing like Johannesburg, so much more mannered, not nearly as confrontational, reassuringly organized, with well-timed traffic lights, mature gardens and wrought iron fences revealing comfortable ranch houses. Yes, the streets were lined with houses, not walls. Where the residents of Harare had walls, they weren't decorated with razor wire, just the property owner's name written on a plaque by the gate. It was nice to see houses from the street again, just like back home, where they also fought Aids and won, where people didn't have double lives.

I'd never been to Iowa City, but Harare was what I imagined it might look like: all swing sets, shopping arcades, fields of knee-high corn and flat, sensible shoes, even a homey quaintness. There were no highways, just two-lane roads without shoulders, busy with four-door sedans and aging busses with bad coughs. Minibus taxis didn't push other cars aside the way they did in Joburg, hungry for passengers and their fares. Zimbabweans weren't so hurried or ambitious. Yes, the city had its poor townships, rather clinically called "high density suburbs", and they were just as poor as South Africa's, but by all accounts these places were contained, their people possibly even contented. Rape statistics and recent crimes weren't recounted with awe, and no Afrikaners predicted our collective demise as they spat out cigarette butts. *Totsiens* Elsie and Thys, goodbye all you Terre'Blanche-type cynics, I'm moving to Zimbabwe, a land of hope, of promise, which reinvented itself long ago. Even Thys said I would have a nice life sipping cocktails under shady trees.

I sipped my cappuccino at the Italian Bakery, the coffee shop for prosperous black and white folk in Harare, and allowed myself to imagine my future life in this place. Instead of barking dogs and domestics, I'd hear children playing, people laughing as if good jokes were the country's currency, and perfectly enunciated English ringing like birdsong through the city's green spaces. Instead of fearing strangers, I'd admire them holding each other's hands, men and women, friends and lovers. Miniature golf courses and garden centers would provide weekend amusements. Maybe I would spend my Saturday at Borrowdale Race Track wearing a floppy hat and placing bets. At night I'd go to the ice cream parlor to eat freshly creamed yogurt while the teenagers flirted through eye contact. I'd walk the aisles of the supermarket, Bon Marché, buying feta cheese and penne pasta. It didn't have that same glacial, sanitized cold of Dierbergs supermarket in St Louis, but still people fiddled with torn-out coupons at the check-out, and some of the grocery carts had one wheel that didn't work. Maybe I'd attach my Bon Marché coupons to my fridge with a magnet, maybe that's what really grown up directors did.

I would be comfortable in Harare, even safe. Oh, this place felt safe, like crimes weren't committed here, either by violent strangers or even worse, by the people you thought you knew. I'm going to show you, Gladys, this is a place where people can live alone. Because alone is the only way to really be safe.

***

"I've left like a hundred messages for you. Why didn't you call me back?" Wayne finally reached me several days after I returned from Harare. Even though I thought of him virtually every day I'd vowed not to make contact with him. And days of ignoring his telephone calls felt satisfyingly karmic.

"All of the sudden you're desperate to talk to me?" I replied, my voice betraying no emotion.

"Of course I wanted to talk to you. I haven't heard from you in ages, I wanted to know how you are." I said nothing. "Sonny told me you stopped by, and so I just thought maybe we should talk."

"Talk? About what? You want to tell me about your girlfriend?"

"She's not my girlfriend," he sounded offended.

"You live with her, Wayne, please don't try to deny or explain anything, or how you've just been so busy you never had the chance to tell me about your girlfriend or wife or roommate or whatever the fuck she is."

"I wasn't going to try to explain anything," he tried to sound clinically calm. "There are just parts of my life you didn't know much about, so maybe now's a good time to tell you."

"A good time to tell me!" I scoffed. "Tell me what, Wayne, how you had a double life? Tell me about this whole relationship you kept totally secret, totally separate from me?"

"Well, you seemed happy enough."

"So you just thought I wanted to fuck you in parking garages for the rest of my life."

"I didn't know what you wanted for the rest of your life, Jull, you seemed to like what we had and never asked for more."

I momentarily heard Gladys' voice. "What*ever* Wayne, don't try to make this my fault. Like somehow I needed to say more, I needed to do more." I paused then played what I imagined was my trump card, "Anyway, I think I'm moving to Zimbabwe."

"That's a pretty extreme reaction." I think he was joking; I think I was supposed to laugh.

"Oh, spare me, it's not about you. Everything isn't about you, Wayne. It's a job, I've been offered a job, a big project, millions, millions of dollars. An Aids project."

"You're not an Aids expert."

"You don't have to be an expert in something to make a difference. Anyway, I'll make it work, just the way I did here. I managed to make a career for myself here, not that you would know much about that."

"Jull, seriously let's just meet, we can talk." But I wasn't listening anymore.

I didn't let go of the receiver for a while, staring off into the distance, picking over the previous years. Wayne was right; I'd never asked for anything more of him than our fleeting visits, never questioned his silences or demanded to meet his family or friends. I had calibrated my needs to meet what Wayne had to offer. That's what I believed an affair required, how I thought it would eventually deepen, by never challenging the requirements of the moment. The truth was, I had been content with whatever time Wayne gave me; Jull felt lucky to have any time with him at all.

Tears came to my eyes but I wiped them away. None of this mattered anymore. I was moving to Zimbabwe and life in Zimbabwe would be different, lovely. I would get to know these simple, smiley people without struggle or sluttiness, and perhaps they would know me too. Jill, perhaps they would know and accept Jill too.

EARLY TO MID 1997: BORN YET AGAIN

By my second visit to Harare, I was already setting up my new life there, anxious to cleanse myself by crossing the Limpopo. I fell for the first house I saw. Suburban houses in Zimbabwe were usually built for big families and lots of leisure, like trapped amusement parks, but this one was simpler. Snowhill Close, high atop a hill, too slanted for a swimming pool or tennis court, it had just two bedrooms, one bathroom and a wide verandah that I imagined sitting on every weekend, watching the old men on the road below struggling with the chains and tires of bikes older than them, domestic workers gathering to gossip at the kiosk on the corner. Without brick walls or razor wire, I could actually shout out *I see you* to the Harare life unfolding beneath me. *I see you* it would shout back.

Again, I used the Italian Bakery as my informal office during my visit, imagining I would spend a lot of time there in the coming years with fellow directors, new friends and officials. I'd sit surveying stacks of reports, immersing myself in Aids statistics and data whilst sipping cappuccino and munching on ciabatta smeared in pesto, enjoying the balance between discomfiting reading and comfort food.

For now, I found myself underlining and highlighting and placing stars next to numbers and letters that no matter how many times I read them seemed to be describing a very different place from the one I was in. I started writing questions and notes for myself next to the statistics: one out of every four Zimbabweans has HIV/Aids, and over five hundred thousand Zimbabweans have contracted the HIV virus.

I looked up from the pages and stared into a parking lot, where mothers unclipped their children from car seats, where young touts looked for money to wash cars. What a pleasant plague this is, I thought to myself. My waiter's hands weren't covered in scabs, the crowd hanging around the box office of the nearby cinema didn't look particularly thin or sweaty, funeral processions didn't clog the streets. The pall of death didn't hang over this city. So, were the statistics exaggerated, or did I simply have to look closer to see the truth? How did this great African success story possess such a fatal flaw? Why do such educated people need so much Aids education?

I closed my notebooks and gathered my things to return to my hotel, only vaguely troubled by the disconnect between the reports in my bag and the reality outside of it. I should have been troubled, having just been exposed to the realities of Wayne's charade, but I was new to Zimbabwe and a born-again believer: in my new life, in Zimbabwe's ability to "fight HIV/Aids", in the fact that I would take this important job and doing *amazing* things with it. And remember, being a believer requires you to ignore clues and will yourself to look away. How long would I be content not to ask more than the obvious questions?

"So, Gordon, what can you tell me about Aids here in Zimbabwe?" I asked the bartender at the Meikles Hotel, as I nursed a gin and tonic. Throughout the evening Gordon had refilled my bowl of macadamia nuts, given me miniature bottles of mineral water and wiped the bar in front of me, all the while maintaining the perfect balance of silence and chit chat about the weather, soccer, what living in Johannesburg was really like. By nine o'clock, three gin-and-tonics had encouraged me to delve into more testing subject matter.

"Come again, madam?" Gordon replied.

"Aids, HIV and Aids, apparently Zimbabwe has a big problem with Aids, one of the biggest in the world."

"Ahhh," he laughed. "I don't know about this Aids, I myself have never seen it, have you?" he continued wiping glasses as he spoke.

"Well, no, not really in person."

"Well then, if nobody has seen something, how can we know for certain it exists?" he laughed, though the strain in his voice hinted that he wasn't enjoying himself.

"I'm pretty certain it does," I said. "People just need to be more *aware* of it, to know how to keep it from spreading."

"I'm sure you're right," he said, polishing the bar. Then he put down his rag and looked at me, "But please, can you explain how you can educate people about something nobody can see?"

15

Early to Mid 1997: Becoming Mrs Reilly

"So it *is* about black people dying in Africa."

"What?"

"I told you, the only reason people go to Africa is to work with dying black people," my father bellowed into the phone.

"People don't have to die of HIV/Aids, Dad. It's totally manageable, totally preventable."

"Last I heard, Aids killed people, but I thought it was the gays. And Magic Johnson, don't know what's going to happen to that guy."

"It's not about gay men in Zimbabwe, Dad. Eighty per cent of HIV and Aids transmission in Africa is through heterosexual contact."

"Oh Jesus, Jill, give me a break. It's 11 o'clock in the morning, the last thing I need to hear is 'sex' and 'Africa' in the same sentence."

"Whatever. I'll be the youngest director in my organization." I'd spent weeks imagining uttering those words to my father. "Really, they thought I was good enough to make me a director."

"Weren't you an intern about five minutes ago?"

"I got a lot of experience and now they want to give me more responsibility. I'm in charge of a five-million-dollar budget." I was sure that line would finally see him crack.

"Isn't five million bucks like more than the budget for the whole of Africa?"

"Aids is a major problem; we need a lot of money to try to control it."

"So what happened to the whole elections-democracy-giving birth to South Africa thing?"

"I've done that, now this is another challenge, maybe even a bigger and better one."

"I gotta hand it to you, kid, you're the only person I know who could call Aids in Zimbawe a better challenge."

"It's Zimbabwe, Dad, with two Bs. Zim-bab-we."

"So, do I have to call you something else now that you're a big-shot director? Miss Reilly? Ma'am?"

"Jill will be just fine."

***

The only person in Zimbabwe who didn't call me Mrs Reilly at our first meeting was Mike Soderberg, project officer at our donor, USAID, the arm of the US government that provided funding to projects all across the developing world. He stuck with Jill, sometimes even "kiddo", the only one for whom white skin and the title of director didn't necessarily translate into me becoming somebody's "Mrs". To everyone else – the manager of Standard Chartered Bank who set up my personal account, Chipo, who sold me a teak table to sit outside my house under the frangipani tree, the Zimtel technician who offered feeble promises that I might get a telephone line within six months – I was simply Mrs Reilly.

I didn't know this Mrs Reilly and wasn't prepared for her to come forward when I crossed the Limpopo. I hadn't known about Jeel or Jull either, but meeting them had felt like the pleasant result of a blind date with a hitherto unknown side of myself, whereas meeting Mrs Reilly was like being forced to shake the hand of a version of myself I wasn't supposed to know yet, artificially aged and not at all exciting. Mrs Reilly frightened rather than intrigued me, but perhaps she was the only one who could pull off this job as director.

EARLY TO MID 1997: BECOMING MRS REILLY

Mike Soderberg was an old hand at USAID, with previous postings in Peru, Tanzania, Vietnam, Nepal, Cambodia and Gabon. He was at once world-wise and unabashedly American, wearing a New York Yankees cap on what he called his "bad hair days", driving a Chevy Bronco, and throwing around "you bet", "lots" and "folks" and other shorthand contractions that other expats avoided in an attempt to emulate the correct colonial English. Mike managed to balance a comforting mix of cynicism and enthusiasm, high ideals and realistic expectations. He wore the same kinds of checked shirts, cardigans and jeans as Jerry, and I could have called him a dork if I had still been in the habit of using that word, and if Mike didn't have a certain air of mischief about him, born out of a cheeky smile that often peeped out from under a moustache so thick as to look outdated.

He and his Italian wife Veronica held pool parties every weekend where the kids usually put themselves to bed and somebody ended up in the pool, usually with their clothes on. Mike carried his tennis gear to work with him most days for a quick game after he'd shut down his computer. And he could often be heard extolling the importance of balancing work and play, as though he'd been the first to arrive at such a profound conclusion. "Particularly in our business," he'd say, "you just gotta save time for a little rec-re-ation." He and Veronica could always be counted on to know when South African wine was on special at Bon Marché.

I arrived early for my first meeting with Mike, smiling – *masikati, masikati*, good afternoon – to every guard and secretary I encountered. And there were many guards and secretaries, checking purses and registration plates, slowly and carefully writing my name in a ledger, giving the whole process an official, almost militaristic feel, the way one might expect things to work in darkest Africa. I felt that tingle of excitement again. Because it all felt so much more African than Johannesburg, certainly more than Braamfontein, with all its medium-rise office buildings bursting with smart but skill-less do-gooders.

USAID was housed in a gracious Karen Blixen-like estate, a perfectly white, perfectly shaded vestige of Zimbabwe's colonial past, now housing people perfectly focused on the country's future, filled with helpers carrying computers rather than platters of tea, in ties and polyester rather than drapey cotton. And here I was walking among them, Karen Blixen-like in all my bullish inexperience. Not a *memsaab*, but something better, something modern and *Glamour*-magazine-like. "I'm a director!" I silently gloated as I was led along leafy paths, groomed by silent blue-jumpsuited men.

When I stepped into Mike's air-conditioned office, decorated with framed certificates, acknowledgements of USAID service and photographs of boys in baseball caps, he shook my hand vigorously, his broad smile making the corners of his moustache point upwards. I offered him my business card, self-conscious, the first time I'd handed it out, aware that Mike obviously already knew my name and position. Still, he accepted it and handed me his. Then we sat across his desk from each other making small talk, discussing Clinton (where had all the liberal promise gone?), how you could get copies of *The New Yorker* sent directly to you from the States, and how Luculus, the little Portuguese grocer in town, was now selling tortillas and salsa. Then it was time to get down to business.

"So Francine wasn't kidding. You are pretty young, aren't you?" he smiled.

"Youngest project director BUILD has ever had," I beamed, but something about the way Mike looked at me made me feel for the first time that this wasn't a badge of honor.

"Well, I hope it means you've got lots of energy, lots of ideas. Cuz there's lots of work to be done here."

"Absolutely, yes, I know that we're facing a major HIV/Aids challenge here. I mean, with one in four people HIV positive, five-hundred thousand HIV-positive people …"

"Yeah, of course, all that, I mean that's a given," Mike interrupted, taking a swig from his insulated Starbucks coffee cup, the kind made for sitting on your dashboard during long commutes. "But what I'm talking about is how you need to start spending some money, like tomorrow!" he laughed. "You're going to struggle to spend five million over the five years here with the Zim dollar dropping in value so quickly. And you've got to get some money into the pipeline quickly otherwise my bosses back in DC will start to wonder what the hell's going on out here." Another chuckle. "Even though we're in Africa, we can't spend on African time, ya know!"

"I know we've got a considerable mandate here with a corresponding budget. So we have to get a move on," I said, using what I considered the perfect blend of lofty director-ese and plain American speak. "Anyway, I think I'm pretty good at spending money," I tried on my own cheeky smile.

"Good, so get your office staffed up, get all your computers, cars, etc." He said each letter separately: e – t – c. "Run some getting-to-know-you workshops, whatever, just start spending money." I nodded, saying nothing. It seemed to have worked well with Francine.

"I assume you have a good sense of what your top priorities are?" he continued. "I mean, to my mind, there are three."

My heart raced, the way it always had when I knew the first answer of a test. "Uh, yes," I replied, "absolutely. It's imperative I establish BUILD's office here and get staffed up, meet all the project directors, I mean really establish a presence here."

"Yes, all those things need to get done – again, by tomorrow," he interrupted. "But from my perspective your top priorities are first deliverables: your five-year strategic plan, your first-year work plan, and your M&E plan. We've got to have those on file by the end of the month. It's in the cooperative agreement; I'm sure you've seen it."

My heart raced again, this time from terror rather than joy. I'd never even read the cooperative agreement. Francine had, and she'd signed it, just the way my father had signed all my admissions forms at Northwestern University, the application to open my first bank account.

"Of course," I stumbled, "all of those are in process, and I think we're on track to submit them to you on the date agreed." I felt quietly pleased that I'd somehow developed the director's art of bluffing only three days into my official role.

"Good, cuz if we don't get those docs on file, then the proverbial shit really does hit the fan. And leave plenty of time for me to see drafts of all those documents before they're officially submitted."

"Of course," I nodded.

"Oh yeah, you talked about the directors. Remember you gotta get out there and meet these guys. They need to see you, to know you as the face of BUILD. So let me rephrase this, you don't just need to meet them, you need to *impress* them." I nodded again, the only response I had available. It seemed to satisfy Mike.

SHAME

Ten minutes later we exchanged parting pleasantries by the door. Mike asked if I played tennis – no – and whether I ran – no. He couldn't hide a certain disappointment, as though these had been requirements for the job that Francine had failed to screen. I said I really liked to work out at the gym, but Mike didn't brighten.

"You got a husband, kids? They're going to join you here?"

"No, uh, no, I'm here alone."

"A singleton!" he whooped. "We haven't had one of you in a while! Ah well, it'll give you plenty of time to work!"

As I left, I tried to steady my spinning head, filled with required papers and plans I hadn't known existed, newly set deadlines and a whole new vocabulary to describe myself: "kiddo" and a "singleton", both of whom managed to co-exist with "Mrs Reilly". Who were these people? And when would I meet up with Jill again?

16

Mid to Late 1997: The Singleton who was Never Alone

A singleton, Mike had no idea how wrong he was to call me that. It implied I was freewheeling, unburdened by the care or maintenance of others. What Mike didn't know, or perhaps took for granted, was that although I had neither husband nor children to tie me down, I had eight people – four in my house and four in the office – who rather thoroughly relied on me for their livelihoods. Well, they relied on Mrs Reilly.

I'd never intended to establish this ersatz family, certainly not in my own home, but had no choice. When I signed the rental papers on my new house, the estate agent, Marlene, all gold rings and helmet hair, said, "I'll introduce you to the staff when you fetch the keys."

"Staff?"

"Yes, the property comes with a caretaker, a domestic – you can have her full or part time – and a contract with a security company." She cracked her chewing gum, still looking for the right papers.

"I don't need *staff*; I mean it's just me."

"Exactly! That's exactly why you need the staff. You didn't think you were going to live *alone* in a house in Harare, did you?"

I pictured Gladys grinning. "No, er, no of course not," I mumbled. Mrs Reilly wasn't supposed to look stupid.

For the next three years, I would have even more people around me than when my mother's hands wiped my mouth and my father's steadied my bike. Hired hands that would find rings I misplaced or glue together plates I broke, hands that would prepare my favorite meals and leave them waiting on the stove for dinner, hands that would ignite blazing fires with paraffin to warm my house before I came home at night. I would return home every day to the ghosts of the people who inhabited my home during the day; people I didn't live with, but who surely lived with me, off me.

For the next three years I would never be alone in Zimbabwe, but I would feel the profound loneliness that comes with being cosseted by strangers.

Rutendo, the caretaker, emerged from the far corner of the yard the day I moved in, his hair matted, feet bare, legs like sticks out of dusty, baggy shorts, eyes glassy, as if at three o'clock in the afternoon I'd woken him. He was about twenty-five years old, and although his pace quickened as he opened doors and gates, deftly selecting keys that looked old enough to hold the secrets to treasures, he was more laid back than subservient. He said his job as caretaker was to "make everything right" on the property. "I can fix things," he said, "wood, wires, garden. I can fix anything." He showed me how to jiggle keys in tricky locks, which doors swelled in the summer, and the clump of acacia trees at the bottom of the property that he worried would die before the rains came.

Rutendo knew the property, that was clear. I pictured him drilling holes and digging holes, maybe even helping me hang a picture, the way Mr Reilly was supposed to. Make everything right? Maybe Rutendo could.

"Where is your husband, madam? Is he coming?" he asked before he turned to walk home, a tiny concrete house at the farthest corner of the yard.

"In South Africa," I lied easily, "he will join me in some time." Rutendo nodded. "Soon," I added.

Sarah Chuma, the new domestic worker, dragged her legs up the hill to my house, panting and dabbing her forehead as she rested on the verandah. "I don't know why I'm so fat," she laughed, "I barely eat a thing." Sarah was a mother to two grown sons who she said were probably as old as I was. She shook her head, "No work. For two years now, no work. It is a problem." All this unsolicited narration of Sarah's life came with doleful stares down at her flat, vinyl handbag.

"Shame," I mumbled and made her another cup of tea.

Sarah kept talking, telling me how she lived alone with her sons in Kuwadzana, a dreary "high density suburb". Her husband had left her years ago and her sons had dreams but no obvious way of realizing them. Sarah struggled just to pay her rent, never mind paying for food and extras. All this made the accommodation on my property all the more appealing. By all accounts, that tiny concrete house – derelict to most, desirable to these few – should have been hers. Maids were usually first in line for such perks. So when I told Sarah the house belonged to Rutendo, her face curdled.

"Caretaker?" she scoffed. "You mean the gardener."

"Yes, yes, the gardener. But he does other things as well. Fixes things."

"Hmm, I'm sure he does" Sarah replied, her chin up, as though a bad smell hung in the air. When Sarah and Rutendo met a week later, it was one of the few times I saw Zimbabweans offer each other such cursory handshakes, reluctantly exchanging greetings without smiling. Power struggles can be the most vicious among those with the least amount of power.

I'd been fully prepared to negotiate a simple, lean arrangement with Sarah, as little time on as few as days as possible. But by the time she waddled down the road, with bus fare and a bit extra slipped into her handbag, she was on board for four full days a week, with a meal provided, far more time than was necessary. But who was Mrs Reilly to be the stingy madam?

I also had two security guards, Simon and Shadrack, who covered the day and nighttime shifts, eight till seven and seven till eight. Each would arrive on his bicycle, having traveled miles from his home in some high density suburb, and salute me, hand rising uninspired to his eyebrows. They wore standard oversized blue uniforms like those worn by Zimbabwe's police officers, but they had neither weapons nor any apparent physical prowess. In fact, it wasn't entirely clear how either Simon or Shadrack would protect me or defend my property in case of emergency, though the military affectations did give them a certain air of grit and stamina.

Although it appeared the easiest job in Africa, to me being a security guard seemed the lousiest: days maintaining the appearance of being observant in the heat and wet; nights pretending to fend off sleep at the time the body craved it most. And it was a job without any of the usual domestics' perks. Because guards came contracted through companies, rather than being hired directly, a distance existed between us and them, a lesser sense of responsibility for people who held such enormous responsibility for us. That didn't seem fair. I'd already agreed to give Rutendo and Sarah food during their working shifts, and I couldn't imagine leaving Simon and Shadrack out of the deal, not when half their lives would be spent sitting on my verandah, protecting me more from society's fear than from any real threat.

So on my first night in the house I walked out with a plate of white bread and tea, the staple diet of Zimbabwe's servant class. Shadrack bolted up and saluted, clearly surprised by my gesture.

"Evening, madam," he said, alert.

"Evening," I replied gently, but formally, aware of the inherent awkwardness of interacting with madam in the dark of night. "I just thought I'd bring you something to eat, a little something. I hope it's alright." I placed the food down next to his chair, but Shadrack kept staring forward, not a hint of eye contact.

"Thank you, madam," he said as I shut the door behind me. A clean plate and mug sat next to my front door in the morning, as it would every morning after that, the two of us maintaining this polite ritual of giving and receiving.

Inside, I turned the television on and flipped back and forth through the three channels that the Zimbabwe Broadcast Corporation offered. All I could find were cardboard sets, stiffer and more dour than the nighttime news presenters who spoke in a sort of soothing monotone about Comrade Robert Mugabe cutting the ribbon on a new clinic, addressing what appeared to be hundreds of supporters wearing T-shirts emblazoned with his face. Mugabe was giving a rousing speech, equal parts promises and threats about giving people land, speaking in a combination of Shona and English that was difficult to follow.

I switched channels to a rerun of *Santa Barbara* where Cruz and Eden were in the middle of a grave discussion about their ever-imperiled relationship. I fell asleep to *Beadles About*, a seventies British comedy where people played tricks on unsuspecting members of the public. How pathetic and mean-spirited the show was, I thought as I drifted off, safe in the belief that Mrs Reilly had done the right thing by feeding the man in charge of securing her singleton life.

My work staff – senior programs officer, accountant, secretary and driver – weren't difficult to find. Zimbabwe was filled with educated, qualified candidates, many of whom had spent entire careers with international NGOs. They had advanced degrees, typed resumés, fixed bank accounts and telephone lines. Mostly it was just about finding the right fit.

Susan Moyo, my senior programs officer, said she'd wear a scarf imprinted with the US flag to help me recognize her in the crowded Meikles Hotel lobby. And there it was, wrapped around her neck in a festive, flouncy bow, as if she was a gift to America. She turned heads, this shining vision in red, white, blue – and a lilac business suit. While most of the men in the room saw a future in Susan's shaking ass, I saw instead her past as a nurse, the mother of two children, a former director of her own family planning project. I looked down at my chest barely sloping underneath a pale linen dress, at a twenty-six-year-old body that had never had to feed anything other than itself, and I couldn't help feeling that although I had dressed the part of a director, it was Susan who looked it.

We took to each other immediately, chattering like long-time friends, enjoying an easy informality rare in Zimbabwe, and certainly among a white potential employer and black job candidate. Susan was well qualified, connected and likable, making the interview feel like a formality. The conversation flowed so easily that I felt comfortable enough to venture, "Do you, uh, have HIV/Aids?" The horrified look on Susan's face made me realize I'd stepped over some line I couldn't see. "Well, I, uh, don't mean do you have it necessarily," I bumbled, "I mean do you have some connection to HIV, something that makes you want this particular job?"

"No, no," Susan protested. "No, I don't. I mean I guess I'm quite lucky that I haven't been affected by HIV/Aids. This just seems like an interesting project, a good chance to help some of the local NGOs I know are struggling with the epidemic and need a lot of capacity building. And I think with my background in family planning, in health education, you know, I'm well suited for the job."

I tried to steer the conversation back to the safe territory of reviewing job descriptions and agreeing terms. And I chose to ignore her reaction to the question about HIV/Aids.

Candidates for the positions of accountant and secretary were plentiful. Zimbabwe seemed to produce competent accountants and secretaries the way it grew meaty, yellow corn. Edward Chirumbuke was phlegmatic and bespectacled, as so many accountants anywhere in the world were, as if the wire frames were issued with the diploma. His goal was one day to be the chief financial officer for an international company and he was pursuing an advanced degree through a British correspondence college, which would qualify him to work as an accountant in the UK. The only qualifications that count, Edward informed me, were from the UK.

Florence Sithole, our young secretary, managed to be pretty and matronly at the same time. She pouted and preached and scolded, she took notes in shorthand, wore her hair in a chignon, and would never, even on weekends, be seen in a pair of jeans. This old-fashioned sense of propriety proved useful when by her second week of work, Florence had already established office rules and the disapproving looks we'd receive if we didn't follow them. Although she and Susan would develop a fond relationship, the two represented different types of Zimbabwean women: Susan with her blushed cheeks and press-on fingernails; Florence with her short, unvarnished fingernails and lack of any makeup at all. Everything about Susan suggested a good time, while everything about Florence suggested women shouldn't even consider the notion of a good time.

And then there was our driver, supposedly the easiest position of all to fill. After all, unskilled drivers were more common than accountants in Zimbabwe, and you weren't supposed to care whether their English allowed for easy conversation. But I suspected that my choice might be more important, because I knew that this driver and I would spend hours alone together in remote places, experiencing an intimacy of sorts. He'd see my bare knees as I hoisted myself into the passenger seat. He'd watch the makeup melt off my face as the day's heat rose, and he'd try to pretend he didn't see my head fall back and my mouth open when the day's heat overcame me.

Lovelace Mandiveyi was a young man with a long history of driving, a history he could prove by means of two driving certificates kept in a tight plastic folder. The first thing he did when we started our interview was to set those certificates down on the table and flash me a proud smile. Every day Lovelace wore one of the two ties he owned. At that first interview it was the one covered with dancing Mickey Mouse characters, another playful homage to America. Whereas other drivers seemed happy to dress as casually and uniformly as possible – some even wore a gardener's blue jumpsuit – Lovelace always wore one of those ties and a jacket, even when he was changing a tire.

His hands neatly stacked in his lap, he elaborated on his sterling driving record, references to "no accidents" and "no citations" spilling out in somewhat fragmented English. But Lovelace's past didn't interest me – obviously he could drive competently – it was his plans for his future that caught my attention. His wife had just had a baby girl, Chenayi, and he had a plan for her future.

"I am not good, not now, I am not good at the typing. But one day it is my wish to be a secretary." There was the smile again. I couldn't resist it, the Mickey Mouse tie, the baby, the dreams of something better and, yes, the smile. Lovelace wasn't just a sweet name; he was a man with emotion, ambition, a real human being whose company I might enjoy. I offered the job to him immediately.

"I am a big fan, a great lover," he blurted as we shook hands goodbye, "of America. You have a very good democracy. You should be very proud."

"Thank you," I replied, as though I had something to do with it.

17

Late 1997: Meeting my Fellow Directors

In that imaginary world that gave me such great refuge in Africa, one of my first tasks was to meet the Zimbabwean versions of Ajay Naidoo: harried and dedicated, a bit mad but endearing. Or the local versions of Jakes Madeira or Phyllis Tshabalala: simple, dedicated people who'd given their lives to fighting HIV/Aids in their communities, just as Jakes and Phyllis had fought against apartheid. And in this misty world of my imagination I was some sort of cross between Reuben (wise and inspiring) and Francine (businesslike and world-wise). As a director cum capacity builder, I even had a speech ready for these Zimbabwean directors.

"Just think about what has been accomplished in other places – in America, Europe, in some parts of Asia," I would tell them. "We can do the same here in Zimbabwe! Your country has everything it needs to fight HIV/Aids: the people, the infrastructure, the literacy rates, the economy. And we would like to strengthen your capacity to take the lead in that fight. Imagine really powerful organizations like yourselves all over Zimbabwe teaching young people the facts about HIV/Aids, supporting people who have the virus, demanding equality for people with HIV/Aids. We would like to work with you to strengthen your capacity so that you can empower people in your communities to control this Aids epidemic. I believe this is possible.

LATE 1997: MEETING MY FELLOW DIRECTORS

After just a few weeks in Zimbabwe, I believe that anything is possible here." Maybe I would pause here, then add dramatically, "Are we together?" I would turn my back as the soothing sound of "yesss" washed over the room. I would have followers in Zimbabwe. Well, Mrs Reilly would.

The golden period in Zimbabwe was much shorter than it had been in South Africa. Months rather than years. But for those several months, before I'd had the chance to deliver that speech to any of the directors, before the doubts started creeping up Snowhill Close, I reveled yet again in those *feelings*: the giddiness, the promise, the potential – theirs and mine – the power – oh yes, theirs and mine – and the pure sense of rightness, or maybe goodness. The simple, succulent belief that one day soon I would be responsible for saving a life. And this time it would really happen.

I had no idea that it was the Zimbabwean directors who would be making speeches to me, that my meetings with them would offer little glimpses into my future life as a director in Zimbabwe.

The weekend before my first meeting, I lay on my bed reading reports and memorizing jargon (there seemed to be no end to either), repeating lines as though learning a director's script: ABC – Abstain, Be faithful, wear Condoms; Infected and Affected; Mother to Child Transmission. Imagining what the coming months would bring as my relationships with the NGOs and their staff developed. We'd quickly charge through the getting-to-know-you piece – millions of people are dying, no time for pleasantries! – and dive into group think sessions. I'd sit with the staff of our local partner Tendai – I liked that name, which means "be thankful" – across a long wooden table, brainstorming strategies for public education campaigns, for an advocacy drive to change discriminatory labor practices. I'd throw out questions and they'd snap them up nimbly, filling page after flipchart page with arrows, lines and asterisks, like little maps drawn to an empowered future.

I could hardly wait for Monday morning at seven, the sun already warm and the domestic workers already chatting across fences, when Lovelace picked me up in our brawny white Toyota Land Cruiser to head out to meet the directors of fifteen of Zimbabwe's ASOs considered to have the greatest potential to make

125

an impact on the country's HIV/Aids epidemic. I had concealed my pimples and combed my hair. Susan had made the appointments for me, Florence had booked my hotel rooms, and Sarah had ironed my loose linen dresses. As we headed out of Harare, my nose was pressed to the passenger window of the Land Cruiser, just as it had been pressed to a bus window so many years before in Johannesburg. For, once again, I believed I was being delivered to a land where my true potential as a savior would finally shine.

The further you got from Harare the more houses gave way to huts, bricks to sticks, and gardens to pastures. Still, the countryside was something of an African idyll. The sun shone brightly as we rolled over Zimbabwe's smooth tarmac roads, their two lanes easily handling the scant traffic. This was the kind of bold, brutish sun that grew things. Zimbabwe seemed to grow crops without even trying, every piece of arable land, big squares and little ones, cultivated by farms and gardens, by white farmers and black peasants.

A tall sprinkler watered a large, lush commercial farm with corn so high their leaves would tickle your shoulders. And cows or *mombes* stood still and dumb not far from the road until a little boy with a stick came to herd them. People in jackets and ties walked with more ragged companions along roads, everyone usually smiling and chatting, apparently unconcerned about the passing cars or the lack of shoulder to protect them. Kids ran miles to school in their uniforms, ties loose around their necks. Those kids didn't look feral; this society didn't look fragile. On the contrary, it appeared sturdy, thriving, as if it required so little in order to thrive.

I started counting again, just as I'd done in those early days in Joburg, when the sensation of plunging deep into a new society was so strong. One, two, three, that fourth person – the young woman walking with a basket of mangoes on her head – has HIV. One, two, three – another woman, this one older, holding out a line of fish for sale – she has HIV too. One, two, three ... one, two, three ... there were too many and soon I stopped counting.

There must have been hundreds of HIV positive people on the one hour drive to Chipinge: a young man selling *The Herald* newspaper at the roundabout ("Ministers Warn of Arrests of Key Opposition Leaders" said the headline, but I was too busy counting to pay much attention); the taxi driver in the lane next to us tapping his fingers to music I couldn't hear; all of them looked healthy and happy and unaware of their fates.

"So, Lovelace, tell me about Aids," I turned to look at him, thinking answers might be inside the car rather than outside. "Tell me more about this problem." He chuckled but didn't take his eyes off the road. "I've been here now for many weeks but I'm struggling to understand the Aids problem." In the few weeks I'd known him, Lovelace had enjoyed talking at length about "his country", teaching me its customs and traditions as though letting a *murungu* (white person) into his secret club. Now it was as if I'd asked him about a country he'd never visited. He giggled and stalled.

"It's a problem. They say it's a problem," he managed. Lovelace's pauses usually passed once he'd found the next English word, so I sat in expectant silence. Instead he looked at me and offered up another nervous giggle.

A few hours later we passed a billboard funded by the Department of Health, which shouted to passersby: "Aids kills!" Lovelace pointed to it, "Ah, you see," he said, "there is Aids." And he giggled again. I looked out the window and started counting again, counting the smiling faces of the supposedly HIV positive people living in the bountiful countryside.

For the next few weeks Lovelace drove me around Zimbabwe, from Bulawayo to Beit Bridge, Mutare to Marondera, most of which were sleepy, tidy towns comprising fewer than five major roads and ten shops selling bars of soap and bags of rice. To meet the directors: people like Mrs Muzenda and Mr Chiruma. It was like that in Zimbabwe – you'd only ever know the first names of the least powerful people and the last names of those who fancied themselves the most powerful.

All of the directors had a typically Zimbabwean combination of warmth and formality, the way I imagined my grandmother might have carried herself back in the day, careful never to misstep. Mrs Muzenda had been the matron of a hospital outside Bulawayo, and had a raspy voice and gray hair to show for it. Mr Chiruma was the wiry former head teacher of a school on the border with South Africa, who told me to take a seat the way he'd spoken to his students. Both of them so upright and mannered, their years spent heading public institutions hanging around them like invisible diplomas.

"Hello, Mrs Reilly," they enthused, drawing out the word "hello" and offering their cool, creased hands. I shook their hands too long, just to buy myself some more time.

"Please, please just call me Jill," I tried, encouraged by the warmth at every introduction. But then there was that look of confusion, even annoyance, as though I was changing the social rules, as though everything about me, from my skinny body to my short hair, was nothing like them at all. We all clung to cordiality to disguise our disappointment. Some of the directors responded to "call me Jill" more quickly than others. Despite my youth and informality I was the white American director of a project that could potentially help them, so it was in their interest to respect my wishes. Which meant they would all eventually manage "Okay, Jeel," through a show of chortles. Laughter provided Zimbabweans with such pleasant, even playful, masks.

In every office a young, quiet, female cleaner or secretary would pour me a cup of tea, cueing the director to push a plate of vanilla biscuits towards me. "Thank you," I'd whisper, selecting one and trying to seem upright and mannered. Then we'd settle back into our chairs, savoring our drinks to the sounds of birds twittering or *hawing* and Lovelace making fast friends with the local workers, taking a break with a pint of milk and half loaf of bread under the tree next to our parked car. It was an easy, quintessentially African kind of quiet, under baking sunshine with power lines hanging like jump ropes from poles, *msasa* trees that grew long and flat-topped like caps providing shade for afternoon naps. Only after a comfortable settling in period, did we set down our tea and allow our official conversations begin.

Mrs Muzenda recounted statistics with the calibrated certainty of an administrator, while I scribbled notes with the discipline of a first year student. One in four Zimbabweans had HIV/Aids, she reminded me, though she suspected the figure was even higher in some areas. In towns along the Zimbabwe/South Africa border, surveys suggested that more than fifty percent of pregnant women were HIV positive. *Fifty per cent pregnant with HIV* went into my notebook. The orphan population numbered in the hundreds of thousands, she said. Within ten to twenty years Zimbabwe would likely have an entire generation of feral youth, without values or family structures. *Feral youth*, I underlined.

"This is ravaging Zimbabwe's villages," said Mrs Muzenda without any ravaging emotion, while my mind flashed back to the quiet collections of huts we'd passed along the way from Harare. "Let me show you what we have been doing already," she continued, directing me to a plan neatly drawn with a pencil and ruler, with *November 1997* written in cursive at the top. "We submit all of our plans on time to our donors," she boasted. "In fact, USAID, they say our plans are some of the best, on time and the clearest, that's what our project officer says."

"That's excellent," I replied. I wiped biscuit crumbs from my lap and leaned closer to take in their work. Fifteen training workshops for peer educators held every quarter, with over a thousand peer educators trained over five years. "I've read so much about peer education," I said, excited to be using jargon in conversation. "It seems such a good way to raise awareness, particularly among youth!"

This spurred Mrs Muzenda on. They had organized over two hundred youth clubs, she said, in each of the villages in their catchment area.

"And they talk to each other about the ABCs?" I queried, showing off my new knowledge. Mrs Muzenda nodded "of course". She closed with the home-based care givers who traveled to different parts of their catchment area on the same day every week, looking after the infected and affected.

"We've trained over two hundred home care givers," she said brightly. "Each one of them has been given a T-shirt, so that everyone in the community knows who they are. These ladies, they are mostly ladies, maybe there is one gentleman, they are very proud of the work they do." And clearly she was too.

'It's all really impressive, Mrs Muzenda," I said, leaning back in my chair. "Obviously you and your staff have been working incredibly hard."

"Yes, we have worked hard, and for many years. We have been carrying out these programs for years, you see. The staff, they are very committed."

SHAME

"So then awareness of HIV/Aids must be very high in the communities where you work?"

"Yes," she said, "in some places it is as high as eighty per cent."

"That's amazing! Who has been funding your work all these years?"

"Ah, we have had many different donors. USAID, Dfid, the Dutch. They all love the peer education programs. They just gave us another million to expand our coverage area."

"That's incredible. They must have real confidence in you. What are your long term plans?"

Mrs Muzenda started shaking her head, "It's difficult to talk about the long term, you know. For now, we are going to just keep doing more of the same. We will continue with our peer education and care programs and, God willing, we will make a difference."

That night I sat in the largely empty restaurant of my Chipinge hotel choosing between chicken schnitzel and spaghetti bolognaise, sipping a glass of cloying local white wine. I looked at two bored waiters watching the soccer match on the TV hanging high in one corner, at flowery curtains and waxy flowers, at overhead lights made darker by the dirtiness of their shades. One other couple sat in the restaurant, he in jeans with a beer, she in a dress with a Coke, the two of them hardly conversing. I mentally toasted myself, having become so comfortable with eating alone in public places, the way Francine must have done in Tanzania or Nepal. I was comfortable in this shabby little hotel in this shabby little town. Nothing about Zimbabwe felt particularly threatening, even this "plague" producing masses of corpses and legions of "feral children". Because Zimbabweans were strong and educated, had been independent for almost twenty years, and didn't have apartheid holding them back from a glorious future. ABC … one, two, three … Zimbabwe was going to beat this epidemic on my watch.

***

His background as a school principal and small business owner gave Mr Chiruma the self-assurance that he was the most professional of all the directors. He would never be seen without a tie, carried his

LATE 1997: MEETING MY FELLOW DIRECTORS

personal planner to every meeting, and liked to throw around business lingo, calling his program's beneficiaries "clients" and his donors "investors". What had made him walk away from his apparently lucrative career to step into the middle of an epidemic?

"Oh, opportunity," he replied, "the opportunity to really help my country. I feel such a sense of dedication to this country."

Mr Chiruma had decided to focus on workplace-based peer education because he believed that business should be at the vanguard of fighting HIV/Aids – "vanguard" was his word. And, because workplace education was currently in vogue among international donors, his organization was thriving.

"The donors love the workplace peer education," he reassured me. "I just got another half million from the Swedes to expand our catchment area."

"Excellent," I said, noting another apparently thriving organization.

Mr Chiruma took me through another set of perfectly outlined plans, illustrating a set of what seemed to be perfectly executed activities: one-day and half-day workshops held at offices across Matabeleland, training people to be workplace-based peer educators. Hundreds of workshops training several hundred educators, all of whom left with a T-shirt. How could BUILD possibly strengthen what appeared to be the best-run HIV/Aids program in all of Zimbabwe? Mr Chiruma was hoping we'd act a consultant to his organization, the Matabeleland Aids Association, to help him to "strategically manage" the epidemic. Sometimes, Mr Chiruma admitted, he just didn't feel like he was coping with the demand for services. "Perhaps we could perform better, even better, by learning from other countries."

"Yes, sometimes that's necessary" I beamed, "and that's what BUILD is here for. To really help you strategically manage this epidemic. So that together we can end HIV/Aids, so that Zimbabweans themselves can end HIV/Aids!"

Mr Chiruma appeared unmoved. "The donors are always talking about learning from other countries. Lessons learned, south to south exchanges," he smiled. "That's all the jargon right now, isn't it?" I nodded, quietly adding *lessons learned* and *south to south* exchanges to the long list of phrases filling the pages in front of me. "Perhaps," he continued, "BUILD could help us be at the front end – again, you know, the vanguard of this trend."

That evening, the sun was setting and Lovelace was driving us back to Harare when a radio news report came on, talking about Comrade Mugabe and his support for the claims of the war veterans to farm land. Lovelace looked disgusted and pushed in a cassette tape. Soon Oliver Mtukudzi was singing in the background, his rhythmic, trilling guitar playing the same danceable, lighthearted rhythm over and over, like music for a carousel.

My eyes blurred as I reviewed pages and pages of notes, capturing hour after hour of meetings. I opened the window for some air and inhaled the now-familiar smell of wood burning fires, becoming aware of the click, click, click of hard-shelled bugs hitting the windscreen. These NGOs had probably collectively held over ten thousand Aids awareness meetings, trained thousands of peer educators, and just as many youth activists, home-based care givers, workplace support teams. By all accounts there were little Aids apostles scattered all over the country, spreading the word, converting people to a life of sexual caution.

I put my head back and closed my eyes. These ASOs had a done an extraordinary job empowering people to deal with the disease; I just had to help them do more of it, to expand coverage and increase catchment areas. I imagined the months ahead, maybe exchanging visits with Mr Chiruma, helping Mrs Muzenda and others to plan long term. Are we together? Are we together?! I opened my eyes and turned towards Lovelace.

"The directors," I said, "they seem like good people, doing very good jobs."

"Yes, yes, they have very good jobs," Lovelace replied.

"No, I said, they're *doing* very good jobs," I chuckled, but Lovelace was serious.

"When you have jobs like these in Zimbabwe, with so much money, you don't give them up. You do what you must to keep them, to keep the people happy."

"Hmmm," I uttered, not really understanding what Lovelace was talking about. I shut my eyes again and rested.

LATE 1997: MEETING MY FELLOW DIRECTORS

"Evening, madam," Shadrack stood and saluted when he heard me rustle up the verandah stairs.

"I'm sorry it's so late, Shadrack, really sorry. I'll get your bread and tea. Just let me put my things down and I'll get it for you."

I was fumbling with my keys when I noticed a note stuck to the door with a piece of putty: *Madam – You came late So I didn't have the chance to see you. Sorry madam but I need some monies. My uncle has died in the rurals and I need to visit his funeral. He has a headache and now he has died. Please if you give me 500 dollars I will pay it as a loan. I have to leave in the morning. Rutendo.*

I flopped onto the couch, holding the dirty piece of paper in my hands, eyes fixed on the sentence: *He has a headache and now he has died.* Malaria? I reached into my wallet and pulled out a 500 Zimbabwean dollar note. That's all it was, one note among many, as much as a glass of South African white wine. Deciding I'd wake up early to give it to Rutendo in the morning, I went to the kitchen to make Shadrack's dinner.

"Do you have something to read, madam?" Shadrack murmured, as I set down the tea and bread smudged with jam on the cold concrete.

"Something to read?" What the hell does a Zimbabwean security guard want to read?

"Yes, madam, I am sure you have many things to read," Shadrack sounded chastened. "I would just like something, anything to read."

"Sure, yes, of course, let me see." It took me a while to decide, but finally I struggled back out the door with a library-worker-like stack of *Newsweek* magazines and dumped them next to Shadrack's chair, thumping like bags of grain hitting the ground from a plane overhead.

"Thank you, madam," he said, straightening the pile. His smile at the stack looked so bright and full.

"I'll give you the latest edition as soon as I'm finished," I promised, but Shadrack didn't seem to hear me, he just kept staring at the stack, his tea still steaming in the night air.

"Ah thank you, madam," he repeated. Shadrack was one of a

133

SHAME

few Zimbabweans who never acknowledged seeing me, but it didn't matter because I knew he had.

Inside, I flopped on the couch again. What a day it had been. Shadrack and Rutendo and all the directors needed my help to be truly empowered, and I could help them, I knew I could. In some cases it was as easy as fishing a note out of my wallet or reaching for my bookcase. I curled my legs tightly into my chest and rocked back and forth. This was why I had come to Africa.

18

Early 1998: Turning Promise into Paper

A major part of being Mrs Reilly, director of BUILD in Zimbabwe, involved producing documents: reports, plans, budgets, all the things I suppose Francine had been doing while I was sitting at the back of the Holiday Inn.

Mike Soderberg had said I needed to submit a strategic plan, a work plan and an M&E plan, all due within the next month. And although I was filled with excitement about helping the ASOs to expand their work to reach more people, I couldn't yet see how it would translate into goals, targets or objectives, or even what the difference between these was.

Late one Saturday morning I was sitting at my desk at home. With so many words and numbers on the notebook pages in front of me, it was time to come up with my own on the computer screen. *Women's empowerment, peer education, prevention, education, harmful cultural practices, needs assessment, evaluation, training, strategic planning, work plans, scale up, condom social marketing, home-based care, psycho-social support, care givers, infected and affected, rapid testing, counseling and testing, vulnerable children, risky behavior, partner reduction, protected sex, trans-generational sex, sugar daddies. Over ten thousand Aids awareness meetings. Thousands of peer educators, just as many youth activists, home-based care givers, workplace support teams.*

SHAME

I heard Rutendo slashing in some distant corner of the garden, slash, slash, slash. He loved his slasher, a primitive, machete-like implement I'd never seen anyone in Chesterfield use on their garden. Simon walked by, pretending not to see me, hinting that it was lunchtime, an excuse to leave my empty computer screen. When I delivered the bread and tea to the verandah, I noticed the pile of *Newsweeks* he and Shadrack had read was growing taller than the ones they hadn't, the pages growing waffled and dusty from sitting outside so long.

I wiped the crumbs off the kitchen counter, made myself a cup of tea, and decided to call Mike Soderberg even though it was the weekend. We hadn't spoken since I'd met with the directors. Besides, I needed to prove that my singleton status was translating into high directorial productivity. He answered on the sixth ring, and I imagined him bolting off the tennis court to answer my call. After a few effusive apologies from me and a few "nah, nah, don't worries" from Mike, I got down to business.

"I've really enjoyed all my meetings with the directors," I told him. "There's some really impressive work going on out there."

"Yeah," he replied, "they're good people, most of them, they just need a little help managing the scale of programming we expect of them. You know finances, people, fundraising, moving a whole lot more money, making a whole lot more happen."

"Absolutely, they all seem to be in the process of expanding, increasing their coverage areas."

"There's a shitload of money coming in right now for Aids and we gotta move it. So these guys need to figure out how to ramp everything up, you know, do it all at scale."

"Exciting times," I quipped. "I have some pretty clear thoughts on how we can help them manage that transition. Everything's in order to deliver the plans to you on time."

"Good stuff, looking forward to reading them. Now remember, kiddo, this doesn't need to be a science. Just set some targets, put some things out there to shoot for."

"Absolutely," I paused. "Of course I want to make sure those targets are accurate, that we can actually do what we say we will."

"Yeah, sure, but there's always time to adjust the numbers down the line. Basically, we just need some decent numbers on file to cover the formalities with the folks back in DC. I mean, I don't want to say make it up, but, ya know, make it up!" he laughed.

"Yeah, yeah, I can do that. Anyway, the good news is we're spending money. Lots of money! Well, I don't mean lots, but enough, I think, on salaries, computers, all my travel."

"That's my girl! Good stuff, I'm looking forward to reading your docs when they're ready."

Make it up? Did he just say make it up? I stared at the computer screen. Is that what I was supposed to be doing here, using my imagination? Was "planning" meant to be a creative rather than analytical exercise?

The hours passed. Rutendo stopped slashing, and I started reasoning with myself. Maybe Francine "made it up" all the time, maybe that's what all directors did. Maybe these plans are just an estimate, intended to provide a general direction. The sun went from hard yellow to a softer orange and the smell of cooking fires started to crackle through the air. I poured myself a glass of wine and sipped, gaining courage to experiment.

- Over three hundred NGO staff trained in relevant management skills (What exactly will we train them in? Figure that out later.)
- Over one hundred strategic planning meetings held
- Over a thousand T-shirts distributed. ("Ask me about catchment area!" "Ramped up and ready to go!")

This was kind of fun! I looked at the words as though they were furniture I'd rearrange to fit real life. I stared at my make-believe targets, feeling a sense of excitement over the sheer scale of what I'd just made up. Maybe we could hold a hundred strategic planning meetings? Maybe somehow I'd managed to make up just what the NGOs needed. I was suddenly thrilled by the endless planning possibility afforded by my imagination.

That night, the television news was predictable in tone and message. Dorcas, the frumpy female presenter, made Florence's matronly look seem glamorous. "Comrade Robert Mugabe warned of the rising threat of farm invasions should commercial farmers not heed calls for greater distribution of land to the majority," she intoned.

There they were again, ugly words like "threat" and "invasion" being used to describe life in lovely Zimbabwe. Where were these threats? In two months I'd traveled all across the country without seeing any rotting plague or invaded land. I switched over to *Santa Barbara*, to Cruz and Eden once again staring at each other doe-eyed and dismayed. But I barely heard what they said, preoccupied with why there was so much bad news out there when the potential for growth was so great. I fell asleep that night to the sound of magazine pages flapping in the breeze.

I thought I would bounce out of bed the next morning to continue creatively designing the future, but instead I woke to a tangle of thoughts. Thousands of workshops? Hundreds of peer educators in a small catchment area? T-shirts scattered all over the country? If this great work was being done by ASOs all over the country, why were so many people still dying? Why, if these NGOs had such good news to report, were the donors' reports filled with such bad news?

I was starting to ask the difficult questions, the ones that imperiled belief. But surely it was Mrs Reilly's job to do so? Later in the day, when the questions refused to fade, I made another telephone call, this time to Mrs Muzenda, hoping this stolid Zimbabwean matriarch, so sure of herself, might make sense of these discrepancies for Mrs Reilly.

"Ah, hello, Jeel, it's so nice to hear from you. I have been meaning to phone you to say we are really looking forward to our work with BUILD because we know that you are going to make us able to grow bigger and stronger, able to do even more good works."

"Thank you, Mrs Muzenda, thank you. I'm looking forward to it as well. Sorry to call on a Sunday, but I wanted to ask you a little bit more about your growth, your expansion. You see, we have to submit some plans, and I want to make sure I understood everything from our meeting."

"Ah, that's okay, I know what this planning is like."

"What I wanted to know is, just what you are planning to do with these extra donor funds you are receiving? What exactly are your long-term plans for growth and expansion?"

"Well, we are planning to do the same awareness raising, education and home-based care work, just for more people in different areas."

"So if you're going to expand this work you must have clear proof that it's working well? I mean, you wouldn't do more of something if you didn't actually know it was working, right?"

"Of course. My staff has been with these communities for years to get to this place. Remember that I told you that now we have eighty per cent awareness rates in some places."

"Yes, I do remember and that's a wonderful statistic. I guess what I'm wondering is whether you've seen infection rates going down in those places with such high awareness rates. Or even if you've seen people doing things differently, you know, using condoms, having fewer partners, delaying sex?"

"You are talking about behavior change," she said, sounding tired.

"Yes, measuring whether all of your awareness raising and care work has made people change their behavior and so infection rates are going down."

"You know, in reality, it's very, very difficult to measure that kind of change in behavior. Because all of the behavior change is self reported, you don't know if people are telling you what you want to hear." She seemed to be scrambling. "And the actual changes in infection rates you can't really measure for years."

"But, of course, you've been in these communities for years," I reminded her.

"Yes, but it can take many, *many* years to measure this kind of change."

"I see," I said, although at that moment I really didn't. "So you don't really have any data to confirm the impact of your work. You don't really know what's changing or whether anything is changing at all."

"We have the eighty per cent awareness rates."

"I mean beyond that."

"No, we don't have that data that you're talking about. But

God willing, if we continue with our good works, we will one day bring about these needed changes."

I stared at my computer, seeing my creased reflection. Did she just say she didn't know what she was doing? No, don't be mean, rephrase that. Did she just say she didn't know if any of their work was making a difference on the actual bottom line of infection rate? I sat for a long while, long enough to watch Simon turn into Shadrack, the woman at the bottom of the hill fold up her cardboard kiosk. Then I stepped into the kitchen, flipping on the back porch light. Within minutes a mass of moths clouded the light.

Every year, with the coming of the rains, the moths make their appearance. For the rest of the year they live underground, breeding, hatching, growing, until the first heavy rains start to fill the ground with water, forcing them out into the world, thousands of them fluttering and flapping their wings. There's something dazed about their flight, hapless and misguided, as if they know their time on the earth will be brief and unpleasant, their only intention to find light: streetlights, car headlights, the light over your front door, anything bright, they want it, cling to it, vie for position on it.

The swarms make it difficult to walk out your front door at night, obscuring sight on roads, darting around your eyes. I couldn't wait for those first weeks of rain to stop, because I'd been told that by then the moths would be dead. The light would have killed them. After touching the light, the moths dropped dead to the ground, creating piles that Sarah swept up every day.

How pathetic, I thought, as I watched them hungrily flapping towards that single bulb. How sad that the very thing they craved, the light they clung to, was deadly.

Then I saw it. Another note, the paper ragged and grubby, was stuck with another piece of putty to the window next to my back door, like a secret. Shame, I smiled to myself, Rutendo wanted to thank me for the money I gave him, but he wanted his gesture to be private, shared just between him and me and not the guards. I cracked the door open just wide enough to snatch the note without letting the moths in. My face fell as I read. *Thank you madam for the monies this is very kind of you. Sarah is wytch, this is just something I was telling myself you should know.*

19

Early to Mid 1998: Searching for a Future

I spent the whole of the next week troubled by three separate realities: that my cleaner was a witch, that my donor gave me permission to lie, and that one of my star NGO directors was a fantasist – or a fatalist, I couldn't tell which.

I slept badly that week. As I turned on my pillow, left, right and back to the left, I realized that Shadrack stopped flipping magazine pages at about one in the morning, presumably to sleep, though I chose to believe it was to keep a closer vigil. I noticed that the dogs eventually stopped barking around the same time and that a childhood fear of witchcraft felt particularly potent around three o'clock in the morning, when images of an old, fat woman brewing broths and sticking pins in dolls felt like the only clear thought you could have. I noticed that wind can be either a comfort or a fright.

That week I left my house uncertain of the world I was entering, reality suddenly suspect. I walked past Rutendo with a tight-lipped "good morning" still uncertain whether one should discuss witchcraft accusations – get to the bottom of them – or just ignore them. I took my twenty-minute drive to work in Harare, past gracious homes with satellite dishes, a billboard for Cadbury's chocolate, Italian restaurants, little reminders that everything in Harare was still just like Iowa City. At a stoplight, its colors faded and the lines loose and bowed, I scanned the headlines of the country's one independent newspaper, the *Daily News*. "Thousands attend MDC Rally at Rufaro Stadium." At the next stoplight *The Herald* would be selling the government-controlled headlines: "Farm Liberations set to Begin". Liberation. How many times had I used the word in South Africa? Somehow this felt different. I didn't recognize this version of liberation as the thing I'd celebrated by dancing with Patience that night in 1994.

I shut my office door and sat back in the swivel leather chair Florence had bought for me, listening to it twist and squeak, playful director's distractions. I pulled my three make-believe targets back up on my computer screen and tried to admire them again or at least feel excited by them. They felt like more make believe. I swiveled away again.

Should I ask Lovelace or Susan about the witchcraft? They would take me for some silly, fright-filled *murungu*, not the composed director of the organization they'd signed up to work for. I picked up the phone to call Mike Soderberg and put it down again; he just wanted his plans, he didn't want kiddo to ask him how to make them up. Francine, professional, businesslike Francine, maybe she'd be the voice of reason. No, she'd just be reminded that I was a young, white American woman, after all. There wasn't anyone I could call. I was Mrs Reilly, the director, not an intern or assistant or ghostwriter to an amazing man who couldn't write. Mrs Reilly was supposed know better, even if Jill didn't. So I called Susan in for our first real debrief since my fact-finding travels around the country.

"From what I can tell we're supposed to be helping these NGOs grow, expand, reach more people with more programs, that kind of thing," I explained.

"Yes, more or less, I think that's right," she answered. "There's so much money flooding into the sector right now, we've got to help them use it."

"That's all fine, but my problem is that it seems some of these NGOs want to keep doing more of the same, without any proof that it's working."

"I'm not sure I'm getting you, Jill," said Susan, almost the only person in Zimbabwe to call me Jill instead of Jeel.

"I spoke to Mrs Muzenda yesterday and she basically said she has no data to back up the impact her work is having, but they're going to spend another million doing it for more people. And 'God willing' they might eventually make a change. Do you really need God if you've got a good evaluation?" I glanced at Susan to make sure I hadn't gone too far with the last line.

"So you're talking about measuring impact, measuring behavior change?" she asked. I nodded. "That can be very difficult," she added.

"You sound just like Mrs Muzenda." I was trying not to sound exasperated.

"Well, it's true, change like this, to very basic beliefs, cultural practices, can take a very long time, and it can be difficult to confirm that it's changing because of your intervention."

"So in the meantime we pour tons of money into expanded programming and cross our fingers that one day it's going to work? It's like there's no clear sense of direction, no obvious endgame for eradicating Aids here."

Susan pushed herself back from the desk and started shaking her head. "Ah, Jill, you know it's hard to think about the future in Zimbabwe these days, everybody is just clinging on to what they've got." I shot her a quizzical look and she added, "Let's just say there are a lot of things we'd like to get rid of in Zimbabwe. But we don't really know how."

***

What do you do when the two things that offer you the promise of a future – sex and liberation – turn out to herald an end, when a dictator and a disease threaten you at the same time? I had thought that if I just stared long enough into the looking-glass of the HIV/Aids world it would give me answers to those questions. What I didn't realize was that the only things resembling answers would come from that crumbling larger world that had no neatly drawn plans, no funds pouring in, and certainly no ambition for ramping up, a world that was contracting rather than expanding, the real world of Zimbabwe, not the donor-funded neverworld of HIV/Aids NGOs.

And it was ordinary Zimbabweans who would be my best

teachers. Not because they ran courses or used flipcharts, and certainly not because I asked the right questions, but because I had the privilege to listen to them speak to each other freely.

Within just a few days of working together, the staff and I had established some firm office routines – the way we said good morning to each other, the way Florence wrote smiles at the end of your name on a phone message, even how we parked our cars in the driveway – all of them mundane but somehow vital for creating a sense of belonging for these five very different characters.

One of the most vital – in the literal sense that it gave us all shared life – took place at lunchtime, at around one o'clock when the day's heat was uncomfortable, when the peacocks from the dilapidated house next door started screeching at each other. Everyone prepared his or her own food in the kitchen and then gathered in the conference room where Florence set down placemats and Susan dropped a copy of *The Herald* on the table. Everyone but me chewed on meat and bones, while I nibbled on a sandwich, dropping crusts like inedible rinds of expensive cheese. They sipped sugary tea at the end of the meal whereas I drank Diet Coke with it. For the most part they would talk and I would listen. Discussion flowed easily, greased with familiar informality, jokes and laughter. It was lovely to watch. That's mostly what I did, watch, realizing every day that there was so much I didn't know about Zimbabwe, so much I didn't understand about its smiling people.

The discussions started like any other lunch discussion anywhere else in the world, sharing life's little details, looking for commonalities. The complimentary, *Ah Mrs Moyo, I love that skirt you're wearing today*, to the commonplace, *Chenayi still isn't sleeping through the night*. I once complained about the nighttime news and everyone commiserated. There's something so reassuring about small talk, its ability to breed a sense of familiarity rather than contempt.

But it didn't take long, days rather than weeks, before Susan, Florence, Edward and Lovelace began to share something much graver than life's little inconveniences or annoyances, something that seemed to threaten life itself. Rising prices, fuel shortages, power outages, commonplace across the continent, but until now unthinkable in lovely Zimbabwe. Florence was especially vocal, lamenting the rising price of flour as she repinned her chignon and pursed her lips as though sucking on hard, bitter candy. Peeling an apple, I watched and listened. I'd never bought flour in Zimbabwe or anywhere else, nor did I buy corn meal to make *sadza* or paraffin to light cheap, fierce little fires. The prices of both had also increased by over fifty per cent in recent weeks.

"We're not like the rest of those African countries," Florence sputtered, "the Democratic Republics of wherever."

"Ah, you just wait, soon enough our Zimbabwean dollar is going to be worth nothing, we will have a Zimbabwean *kwacha*," Edward joked, referring to the currency of their neighbor, Zambia.

"You just wait!" I'd heard that line before, over lunches with another set of Africans, who'd also grown up believing they were different from all those black Africans who lived far enough away for their imaginations to create and distort images of them. The conference room was so humid with uncertainty, I could have been with Thys and Elsie, only the absence of an aging woman's stifled tears and her husband's drumming fingers reminding me this was a very different group of Africans. Africans who discussed their country's downfall with knee-slapping humor, roaring like a paid audience at a comedy club. And I couldn't decide if I was watching a comedy or tragedy, if this was how Zimbabweans survived or why their survival was threatened.

As the days passed and the fraternity strengthened, the staff began to discuss even bigger issues, ones that forced opinions and exposed allegiances. With each sitting, the group tested one other's faith, slowly piercing the waters of the most precarious topics of all, the political ones. Until their obsession, their fury, with Comrade Mugabe forced its way through the laughter.

"He's a fool," Susan proclaimed, putting aside *The Herald*. "Did you see him on the news last night, prattling on about building another statue for some fallen comrade? Please, why do we need it? You wait, they'll run out of money and that statue will end up with only the comrade's feet!"

"My *sekuru* is no fool," Florence said. She was of the same Shona tribe as Mugabe, the *Zezurus*, and liked to tease the others by referring to him as *sekuru*, or uncle, a common term of respect for an older man. She was the most forgiving of Mugabe's excesses, but even her patience was being tested by the downward spiral of her dignified land. "You just wait. He'll get the last laugh on all of us!" Her eyes darted around to see if anyone would play with her.

"Your *sekuru*!" Edward took her bait. "Every time that senile old man wants support he starts talking about the liberation struggle again. Ah, liberation this and liberation that, and about taking the farms back from the whites. It's never going to happen."

"I don't understand," I jumped in, "why the farms?"

"Politicians make promises, you know, it's their business," said Edward. "Your Clinton has done the same thing, though probably with young ladies instead!" The group enjoyed a laugh before he continued, "So when Mugabe came to power at independence he promised he'd give huge allowances to the men who fought in the liberation war."

"Which he only just did," Lovelace chipped in, "only when the war vets threatened him did he give them any money."

"And," Edward nodded, "he promised to give land back to the blacks, to distribute it to everyone, which he never did. Basically, most Zimbabweans wish to have our own land for a farm, a *kumusha*, rural home, so it's a very big promise to make to us. But when Mugabe came to power he did nothing about it. For twenty years he left the farming to the whites, while he and his *Zezuru* friends," he winked at Florence, "made millions. Now people are thinking it's time for Mugabe to go, and he's back to talking about liberation and land again. That old man needs a new script, you know. It's almost 2000 and he's back in 1980."

"You'll see, he'll follow through this time," Florence smiled as she checked a chicken leg for any more pickings.

"Twenty years is too long," grumbled Lovelace, "nobody should be in power for so long. Don't you think, Jeel? This would not happen in America."

"Zimbabwe's a democracy," I said, twirling the stem of my apple. "Vote somebody else in." I hadn't realized I was making a joke, but the suggestion of a vote made the room erupt, forcing them to put down their legs and wings to enjoy it fully.

"Ah, Jeel, democracy doesn't work that way here," said Edward, wiping grease from his mouth.

"This is African democracy," Susan added, her laughter jiggling her stomach. "Everybody votes for the same party on the same day and they call it an election."

"Anyway," Edward chimed in, "Mugabe, he thinks he's the father of Zimbabwe, you know, because he got us independence. And, of course, you can't get rid of your father."

"No matter how terrible he might be," Susan added.

"But it is coming," Lovelace said, chewing on a bone, "he won't be around for much longer."

"Ah, Lovelace, you better be careful," said Florence, raising her finger. "You're all MDC, MDC these days. It's dangerous, my friend."

"Yes, Lovelace, watch who you align yourself with," Susan added. "There's going to be a fight. And we need you here. Besides, if they cut the brakes in the Land Cruiser, I might be in it. And maybe you want to die, but I don't!" The room broke into laughter again.

"You mean people actually get killed?" I gasped, eyes wide.

"Oh yes, you don't try to take power away from my *sekuru*, not unless you don't value your life anymore," Florence chuckled.

"Anybody who's ever come up against Mugabe before has had sooo many car problems," grinned Susan.

"Or health problems," Edward added, "very, very healthy people who one day drop dead from heart attacks."

"Oh, and they get visits, men in suits come looking for them, the CIO is suddenly sooo interested in making friends with them."

"CIO?"

"It's like your CIA, they do all of the government's dirty work, very quietly, always with a smile, so Mugabe can go to see his priest on Sunday with a clear conscience."

"It's so strange," I said, throwing away the plastic Sarah had used to wrap my sandwich. "I mean, it wasn't so long ago that everyone was saying how Mugabe was a model African leader."

"Ah, Jill, to be a leader you have to think about the future," said

SHAME

Susan, selecting a toothpick, "you need some sort of vision, some plan of where you want to take your people. Our leaders in Zimbabwe aren't interested in our future. All they can do is think about the past."

Lovelace looked at me. "Or how to keep their jobs," he said.

20

Mid 1998: I Can See Again!

That night I hurried home, delivered Shadrack's tea and bread, poured myself a glass a full-bodied red wine, closed the curtains, pried open my computer and typed out the details of my plans in a rush of words that for the first time felt right. Not because I suddenly had the right answers, but because I now had the courage to make what I hoped were good guesses.

This new confidence had come suddenly that afternoon after lunch as I stared out my office window at a non-descript brown bird flitting through a jacaranda tree. I watched it nibble and peck, and kept hearing Susan's words, "You need some sort of vision, some plan of where you want to take people." And then I heard Reuben proclaiming that same word *Vision* in front of a room of rapt participants. The little brown bird flew out of the jacaranda branches, and with it my mind travelled back to that Johannesburg conference room and Reuben's lecture on leadership more than three years earlier. There in the past, in that Holiday Inn conference room where Reuben's ideas felt like solutions, I thought I saw Zimbabwe's future clearly.

"Vision," Reuben Mandala had proclaimed, writing the word out in capital letters and scrawling a line underneath it, "literally means the ability to see. We all know that." Reuben loved these moments, when he had a definition to quote and people reached for their pens to capture the exact words of it. He allowed for the drama of a pause before continuing. "In business terms – in organizational terms – vision is the ability to see into the future and manage it, to have a clear long-term sense of direction for your organization that allows you to take decisions accordingly." Pens were working furiously. "I would argue," he continued, "that a clear sense of vision is the most critical thing an organizational leader needs to be an effective manager, particularly in difficult or rapidly changing times." The group went silent, absorbing, processing, translating.

"What good does this vision do for you?" shouted Sipho, the fiery wheelchair-bound director of a "disability rights" organization, who insisted that his paralysis wasn't a disability at all. "It's some pie-in-the-sky dream that just raises hopes without really contributing to your work."

"Oh but it does help, my friend," replied Reuben smoothly. "That vision serves to clarify everything; your strategies, your expansion plans, all of it will be defined by that clear vision. Without it, you're spinning wheels. What is it they say, if you don't know where you're going ..."

"You have no idea when you get there!" Sipho was quick to answer.

"Exactly!"

Now, years later, I was having another "Exactly!" moment. Vision, that's what these directors needed, the ability to see a clear future for their organizations with a clear impact on HIV/Aids. I started typing:

- At least fifty NGO leaders with the ability to lead their organizations to make concrete impact on HIV/Aids infection levels.
- At least two hundred strategic planning and visioning workshops held to enable organizations to develop clear visions and accompanying strategic plans.

My fingers started moving faster. This planning enterprise was beginning to feel genuinely exciting, as if I was plotting social revolution from a quiet corner of Snowhill Close.

MID 1998: I CAN SEE AGAIN!

- At least fifty NGO staff with the ability to measure the impact of their programming on HIV infection levels.

"I see you," I could finally say to my future in Zimbabwe; with my help, the NGO directors would say the same. I downed my last gulp of wine and sat back to admire my numbers, which were gaining the handsome air of officialdom, as though simply by positing them on paper I was proclaiming them a reality. I pictured someone at a clean desk in an open-plan office in DC looking at them and believing I knew what I was doing. I scrunched my legs up to my chest and rocked back and forth in my chair. But I was no longer a little girl in front of a TV. Now I was a director in front of a computer, and I'd done my directorly job: I'd made up a reasonable set of targets and possessed the singular belief that they were probably the right ones. I might not be able to do anything about Zimbabwe's supreme leader whose eyes rested solely on the past, but that night I was certain I would transform some of the country's other leaders.

I was back to being a believer again.

***

Now it was Susan who paced the Bulawayo Holiday Inn conference room, taking deep breaths, repeating lines underneath her breath, turning to greet someone. "Ah, hello, Mr Chiruma," she practically sang when she saw him come through the door. "It's so nice to see you again."

"Good morning, everyone!" Mr Chiruma's sonorous voice rose above all the others, and the crowd practically stood to attention. The room was packed with peer educators, community officials and church leaders who had all come together for their first joint meeting with BUILD, in order to create a long-term vision and strategy for the Matabeleland Aids Alliance, or MAA.

The Bulawayo Holiday Inn wasn't all that different from the one in Braamfontein where Reuben had preached of vision all those years before; it just felt like the poor relation. The biscuits were drier and the sweets harder, the coffee made from chicory. The air conditioner rattled and dripped, the artificial flowers didn't even try to look real. Still it felt like a treat for the people entering that room, who were themselves the poorer cousins to their South African counterparts, the men's suit sleeves shorter, the women's pantsuit materials even scratchier. Most were "community members", which was NGO-speak for the real poor people we were trying to "reach". And they weren't there to become better managers or future leaders; I'm not sure many of them knew why they were there at all.

Susan surveyed the room, a tough, unpredictable crowd. Mr Chiruma's staff, all suits and ties and black patent leather shoes, had led the way in, followed by old men who had lost their teeth and carried their hats, who had shared a ride in the village's one available pick-up truck. Then came the district administrators, well-fed bureaucrats in donated Toyotas and inherited polyester suits, followed by nurses in white ruffled blouses, custom-made for a choir. The young people, or Youth, as the NGOs liked to describe them, were last to arrive. Fashionably late in sideways caps and low slung trousers, the poorest among them in donated T-shirts bearing slogans like "Spring Break 1998 Daytona Beach".

If you listened closely you could hear the peer educators complaining that the room was too warm, while the community officials were busy speculating as to whether we'd provide tea before we got started. There was a certain suspicion where one might naively have expected gratitude, a suspicion that would never completely disappear even when gratitude appeared.

"Hello, Mrs Reilly," the MAA staff sang out, the only ones with the confidence to address me; community members just nodded. I smiled and nodded back and eagerly shook hands, having decided before I arrived that Mrs Reilly would be the one to kick off this process. Those men with ties but no teeth, the women in the frilly white blouses, they didn't want to "just call me Jill", they wanted to meet Mrs Reilly, the international white lady in charge of international money. If I was going to push this crowd to think more ambitiously and creatively, I would have to channel Mrs Reilly in all her linen-clad purpose.

I took my place at the back of the room, with Susan in the front. Even amidst the expectant din, I savored the fact that in five years I'd gone from parading cards in front of a roomful of prisoners, to pulling strings from the back of a room full of people I was certain I would soon set free. Look at me now, Dad! As the director, leader among leaders, I'd pulled these people away from huts and fields and schools to participate in a process I deemed essential to their future. I was suggesting they needed a clearer picture of a better future, but would they agree?

The meeting started with people's arms and legs crossed, bodies and minds closed, a welcome from the most senior district administrator in the room, then a prayer, quick and mumbled, followed by a song, led by the nurses and sung at full voice. Only then could we begin in earnest.

Meetings in Zimbabwe were microcosms of the country's social dynamics. Certain people always spoke first, while others weren't supposed to speak at all. Old men and people with white skin got the best seats. And most of the really important discussions took place in small groups, over biscuits and tea, or a lunch of chicken legs and beetroot salad, in places where you could whisper and still be heard.

Susan, her face glowing and violet lips fresh, looked like an African queen gliding back and forth, raising her voice without shouting, clapping her hands to get people's attention without looking like an elementary school teacher.

"So, how do you say 'vision' in Ndebele?" Susan asked. The group giggled and chattered until the word *umbono* began to rise above the din.

"Madam Chairwoman," the senior district administrator, rising and clasping his hands, took it upon himself to speak on behalf of the group. "We do not have a word for vision, but *umbono* means a dream. That is what a vision is, isn't it, it is like a dream." Heads nodded in unison across the room.

"Yes, but it's a dream you have during the day, while your eyes are open." Susan's eyes widened to illustrate her point.

"And a vision is something that must be realized, right?" asked another man, a schoolteacher, half standing so as not to eclipse the administrator. "It's not like a dream, which might not be real."

"Yes!" Susan exclaimed, raising her finger and walking closer to the participants. "It's like a dream that you intend to realize one day. A beautiful picture of the future your organization will work towards."

Everyone nodded their heads, a green light for Susan to move on. "That's why we're here today, so that together we can create our vision, our *umbono*, for the Matebeleland Aids Alliance, for its work on HIV/Aids in your community."

"It's all well and good to dream of these things, Madam Chairperson!" Mr Chiruma shot up. "But how will it help us? We need practical ways of dealing with HIV/Aids, like financial support and training, not wild dreams that we cannot achieve right now." He looked at the administrator and then at Susan. Everyone in the room was looking at Susan.

"But I'm not talking about today or right now," Susan soothed, "I'm talking about five years from now." Chiruma remained standing, arms crossed. "Do you know how much you can accomplish in five years?" she asked.

"With all due respect, Madam Chairperson, we are already accomplishing a lot every day," Mr Chiruma sounded exasperated, "creating a network of workplace educators across the country. We don't have the luxury of thinking about five years from now when there is so much work today."

"You don't have the luxury not to think about it," I blurted, unable to stop myself. The entire room turned to look at Mrs Reilly at the back of the room. I had no choice, I had to stand up.

"I'm sorry, Susan, I don't mean to interrupt you." She nodded and gestured for me to come forward, though I couldn't determine whether she felt saved or sabotaged. As she moved toward the side of the room, I took a place at the front and faced the room, smiling. Very few faces smiled back. "What we're suggesting is that we take the time to assess, perhaps to reassess, if you're doing the most strategic thing, that which would have the greatest impact on fighting the HIV/Aids epidemic in this country."

Some of those blank faces got bunched up, perhaps sensing that I was questioning their methods, even criticizing them. My words were getting me nowhere, so I decided to use somebody else's. "I believe that possessing this kind of vision, having this type of clear strategic direction, is the single most important thing for an organization to have. Particularly in very difficult, changing circumstances, because it helps to clarify all the rest of your work, all your other choices are made for you." A few people reached for pen and paper, and I took a deep breath. "What is it they say, if you don't know exactly where you're going ..."

"You won't know if you're getting there!" one of the Youth sang out, and everyone shared a gentle laugh. The young man beamed.

"Exactly!" I said, channeling Reuben's habit of dishing out praise. I almost asked, "Are we together?" but instead gave Susan a nod to carry on as I returned to the back of the room.

"So you see," Susan resumed, "as Mrs Reilly has pointed out, we don't have the luxury *not* to have a clear five-year vision, with clear targets for impacting HIV/Aids, because that vision helps to shape our planning today."

"Okay," Mr Chiruma was on his feet again, "but five years, it is not much time." Heads were shaking all across the room. "As we have all experienced, it is not very easy to bring about real changes, dramatic social changes, in five years."

"Really?" Susan said. "Do you all believe that's true, that nothing much can change in five years?" The heads that had been shaking now started nodding. "Well, think about how much has changed in Zimbabwe over the past five years." She paused, taking her time. "Have many things changed?" Silence as people looked around the room, seeking permission with their glances; they knew exactly what had happened to Zimbabwe in five years.

"Ah so much," the words finally came from a white-haired nurse. "Sometimes we cannot believe that this is Zimbabwe, so much has changed."

"So," Susan said, her arms rising, "imagine then how much could you change in five years! Imagine all the *good* changes you could make to HIV/Aids in five years, so that we have something to be proud of, so that we can say no matter what was wrong with Zimbabwe we managed to get it right with HIV/Aids." She was walking back and forth, faster now, preacher-like, but without the sweat. A few people turned to each other and began conferring under their breath.

"Ah Madam Chairwoman, I'm afraid there's a problem with your logic." It was the district administrator's turn to stand and talk, clearing his throat and flattening his tie with one hand. "Everybody knows it takes longer to build things than to destroy them." Heads nodded.

"Okay, then," Susan said, uncrossing her arms. "Ten years? Can we start to rebuild things, at least some things, in ten years?" Everyone looked at her blankly. "Look, I know that things are bad here now, but there are some things in this country that we can get rid of."

"Yes!" came a few voices from the back, the Youth again.

"So let us focus on the things we can do something about. HIV/Aids is one thing we can do something about." A chorus of "uh huhs" spread across the room and brought Mr Chiruma to his feet again.

"Fine, then, Madam Chairperson, ten years," he said, and Susan smiled. "Let us develop our *umbono* for ten years from now." And with that he sat down and the entire room stopped holding its breath. We really were together.

***

I returned home from the workshop at the end of that week to find Shadrack sitting on his chair next to the tired pile *Newsweeks*, the stack of "not read" now fully absorbed by the "have read". The night was clear and quiet.

"Evening, madam," Shadrack took to his feet and did his little salute.

"Evening," I replied, wearily. "I'm sorry, Shadrack, as soon as I finish the latest magazine I will bring it."

"Ah madam, I enjoy these pages," he mumbled, then searched for his next words, "but do you have books? I would like the books if you have them."

Shadrack wants books? Oh my god he's wanted books all this time, and I've been giving him magazines. I raced inside and found myself lost in front of my bookcase again. Male or female lead characters? Modern? American writers? Small print? Then my eyes landed on *Things Fall Apart* by Chinua Achebe, an African writer.

Surely he would prefer an African writer? Maybe I'd been boring him with an American magazine when what he really wanted was an African novelist. When I took him his tea and bread, the book slid easily from my hand into his, and I was certain my security guard had everything he needed.

A few days later I asked, "The book, are you enjoying it?"

"Yes madam, thank you madam."

"He's an African writer."

"Yes, " he said. I had turned to go inside when Shadrack spoke up. "I was studying, madam, to be an accountant. I was studying to be an accountant when I had no more money and had to stop my studies."

"Really?" We didn't make eye contact.

"Our Zimbabwe dollar, it has lost so much of what it is worth. The cost of everything is getting much more. So I am not able to continue."

"I see," I said and we shared a respectful silence. "Hopefully things will get better soon."

A smile broke across my face. My security guard is an aspiring accountant; he won't spend his life weathering boredom to protect me and other white people from our imaginary enemies. He has an *umbono*, a vision, and maybe I would be the one to help him achieve it.

21

Mid 1998: The Salad Kid

Susan and I staged a minor celebration a few days after the workshop with Mr Chiruma was over. Maybe it was premature, but when that last peer educator shuffled out of the Holiday Inn, leaving behind pages of flipchart paper with lofty visionary words on them for Florence to transcribe, it really did feel like we had accomplished something. Like something transformational was about to begin in communities across Matabeleland; like we had already started to transform people in our first meeting. We had given people a chance to dream again, to experience a sense of power and control. Before things really started to fall apart.

The Bulldog was one of a handful of bars in Harare where blacks and whites mixed comfortably, almost unconsciously. Almost everyone there was under the age of thirty-five, professionals with directly deposited salaries, deliberately selected music collections and dreams of beach holidays. Modeled on an English pub cum sports bar, it had green bucket-seat booths and beers on tap, a few cheap wines – you never saw the bottles – and a cocktail list comprising few drinks that didn't involve either gin or tonic. I didn't particularly like the Bulldog, but locals found it effortlessly cool because it felt imported, and, like Edward, many Zimbabweans still believed the best of everything was imported from England.

MID 1998: THE SALAD KID

Susan and I chose the Bulldog because it seemed the perfect place for celebrating Zimbabwe's future, even though my linen dress and her pendulous breasts put us far outside its obvious demographic. We didn't care, high that night on the belief that we belonged anywhere and everywhere in Zimbabwe.

By nine o'clock, Susan was on her third Zambezi and I was on my third glass of wine, and we were toasting after every second sip.

"To *umbonos*!"

"To Youth! Thank God they were there!"

"To Madam Chairperson, thank God she was there!" I laughed.

"You know, Jill, I wasn't sure about this visioning thing of yours."

"What do you mean, you were the one talking about vision," I reminded her.

"Yes, but I meant Mugabe, you were the one who could see it applied to these guys as well."

Throughout the week, as the MAA's vision started to emerge, Susan had kept saying things like "this is unbelievable" and "when do you think he's going to wake up from dreaming?" But once he'd felt the tide of the crowd turning, Mr Chiruma had thrown himself into the visioning process, grabbing the marker from Susan's hand to draw pictures, typing notes into his handheld organizer.

"Women make up the majority of the population, don't they?" he had said half way through the week. "So they are our future! They have the power to bring about change in this country, and when they change the entire community can change."

Everyone had applauded, a palpable sense of expectancy rippling through the room like the air conditioner. As we said our goodbyes, the senior district administrator had approached with his hand outstretched to shake mine.

"Ah, Mrs Reilly, we can see the future very clearly now," he'd said, and widened his eyes just as Susan had. "And we are very clear that we will achieve that beautiful future vision, with your help."

It was ten o'clock at the Bulldog and by now the conversation comprised little more than laughter. "I never thought I'd hear Mr Chiruma talk about women," Susan slurred. "To the future!" She raised her glass again.

"To ten years from now," I managed, "when I come back and find Mr Chiruma leading marches of women through the streets."

"Maybe you'll be here in ten years," Susan giggled. "You never know, maybe you'll find a reason to stay." I shrugged her off, but was quietly thrilled at the notion of finding my own Zimbabwean *umbono*. "Speaking of future," she continued, "there's our future, right over there." She pointed her beer towards a group of stylish young black people in the corner, "The salad kids."

"The what?" I shouted.

"The salad kids! That's what we call these young black kids. They watch music videos, wear jeans, eat all this lettuce and vegetable and other rabbit food you white people eat. These kids are so modern. They take what they want from the west, and still manage to stay Zimbabwean."

"We need a salad kid running one of these NGOs."

"They wouldn't do it," she said, "not sexy enough. They're all business people. Salad kids steer clear of politics and charities."

Just then I saw him, nestled in the patch of salad kids. He held my gaze that crucial second long enough to distinguish it from pure chance. He was the only one not staring at his mobile phone. I was enjoying the sight of him, this sexy salad kid, this buff *umbono*. Susan had to get home to her children, so after one final toast I told her I'd stay to settle the bill. And then I settled my eyes on him.

This wasn't Terrence's, and it wasn't South Africa. Zimbabwe was lovely, and I would be in control this time.

He was dressed much like my father, like any man in Chesterfield: Polo shirt, Dockers and loafers. With some crucial differences: the closely cropped hair, shaved, almost Seal-like, and the way his chest muscles pressed against the Polo shirt, providing a sloping definition where most men just drooped. No man at any country club in Chesterfield filled out his Polo shirt like that. Appearing neither Zimbabwean nor American, neither them nor us, he seemed to embody the *umbono* of a society without boundaries, free

MID 1998: THE SALAD KID

to express its desires. His very being seemed to suggest that crossing over and blending in might be possible, possible for me if I got to know him.

I let him come to me, stumble through the introductions, all the heavy lifting of a routine pick-up. His name was Matthew, and he was an Audi-driving project manager who worked in the Standard Chartered Bank building across the street. All the talk of banks and management brought me further and further back to Chesterfield, or at least to a Zimbabwean version of it, a comfortable, safe place of families and friends who met for holidays in appropriately themed sweaters and played ball games in back yards. Even my mother might love him.

Three years in South Africa, seriously? Yes, why? You look too gentle to survive that place. All a façade. So you're tough? When I have to be. Why so far from home? I like a little adventure. And what better place to come for adventure than Africa. Something like that. So have you found it? What? Adventure. I'll let you know later.

After two more glasses of wine, Matthew pretended to pick something out of my hair and then let his hand stay there in the soft spot behind my ear.

So you like Zimbabwe? It's lovely and the people are the loveliest of all – and you can get feta cheese. Did you think after South Africa you'd come here and be eating *pap* and *vleis* the whole time? No, I was just surprised how much was on offer. Oh, you have no idea all the delicious flavors on offer here.

I moistened my lips and fluttered my eyes as our conversation rolled, no mention of peer education or visions or shortages or white papers, just jokes that wouldn't have been funny on any other night, slurred attempts at wordplay, opportunities snatched to brush each other's skin. Around midnight, when the staff of the Bulldog started collecting glasses and the telltale smell of bleach wafted out from behind the bar, Matthew leaned in close.

"Can I tell you a secret?" he whispered.

"Sure," I replied, used to this kind of thing.

"I'm in the MDC, the Movement for Democratic Change. But nobody knows, not even my mother. You know, Zimbabweans are kind of weird about that stuff." I tried to stop a grin spreading across my face. My project manager was an activist! My Audi-driving Dockers-wearing project manager-activist has told me something that he wouldn't even tell his mother. "What's so funny?" he asked. "Why are you laughing?"

I pulled him towards me, planting a huge kiss on his face, moving my tongue into his mouth. As we pulled away, we were both smiling.

That night I didn't let my mind wander too far into the future – I'd learned the dangers of those kinds of dreams – just far enough to picture moonlight nights at my teak table with my closet activist. Until we were told the Bulldog wasn't "closing" but "closed", we spent a few minutes stumbling over the MDC's slogan *"chinja maitiro"*, fight for change. Our last kiss at the Bulldog was the longest.

And then there we were, Matthew and I, tripping up the stairs onto my verandah. Shadrack saluted me. Oh shit, I'm with a man. In my sloppy, sexed-up logic I considered introducing Matthew to Shadrack, then just tried to get my key into the door as quickly as possible, while Matthew waited, hands in Dockers, patient and polite, just as my mother would have wanted him to be. When the key finally found its way in, I blurted, "Thank you, Shadrack, thanks," for no reason at all, and Matthew followed me inside.

Although he didn't know where my bedroom was, Matthew seemed to guide us there, his hands and mouth exploring my body. We walked awkwardly, entangled, towards my bed and I glanced at my sheets, ironed by Sarah into skating rink perfection, a perfection that my single, celibate life preserved. Would Sarah see any stains on Monday? Forget about Sarah and Shadrack and Rutendo and anybody else, just be here, now.

Matthew kept repeating my name – Jill, Oh God, Jill – only the second person in Zimbabwe to say it as my mother intended. Mrs Reilly had fled, the linen dress pulled off in one neat movement, now lying crumpled on the floor next to the Dockers and Polo shirt, a whole world discarded. It was Jill in bed, young and hot and hungry, making love to this familiar stranger, some version of sweet sex so universal that two people with no prior knowledge and only the flimsiest of introductions could come together and do it seamlessly.

MID 1998: THE SALAD KID

Then we hit a seam.

"Condoms," I said, when I knew we could go no further without one. Even hushed and languid, that word sounded so clumsy, as if I'd whispered "dinosaur" or "ombudsman" into Matthew's ear. I thought he would reach for his Dockers, but he just showed a sudden and deep interest in my nipples. I tugged on his chin, pulling his face closer to mine, kissed him gently on the lips. "Do you have a condom?" I whispered.

"Come on," he whispered back, "we don't need those." He kissed my lips, "I trust you." I looked into his face, thinking he would laugh or offer up his stellar smile. Neither. Just more kisses, more words. "Everything about you is so delicious," he murmured. "Would you want to eat a sweet with the plastic on?"

I laughed, a Lovelace giggle, earnest and uncomfortable, the bones in my neck sharpening, trying hard to maintain that lilting whisper, "If the sweet was potentially poisonous I would." Now Matthew laughed too, uncomfortable. You weren't supposed to say this many words in bed with a virtual stranger. But then I said another word, one that haunted every night like this.

"It's just, you know ... Aids."

Matthew pulled away ever so slightly. "Oh come on, baby, do we really have to talk about that?"

I found myself retreating. "It's just I don't even know you, I mean I..."

"Okay, okay, whatever, we can try," Matthew kissed my neck. "Do you have any, do you have a condom?"

I reached for my drawer without pulling too far away from him, trying to forget that this future-focused salad kid had gone to the Bulldog without condoms. How could a salad kid not know his ABCs?

Matthew lifted himself up to put on the condom. "Anyway, maybe these things aren't so bad. I like it a little bit dry anyway."

"Dry?" I asked, still stroking his back.

"With a little bit of friction," he explained with the expectant smile of a man ready for action.

My neck bones sharpened again. "That might be hard, because

I'm a little, uh, wet." And then, trying desperately to conjure up sexy again, "Can't you tell how wet you've made me?"

"We can do something about that, some resistance is good."

"Resistance doesn't sound good to me." My writhing underneath him became more like wrestling away from him.

"Hasn't anybody in Zimbabwe taught you about dry sex yet? Without a lot of the woman's, well, what's the polite way to say it, lubrication." This wasn't charming or sexy at all. I wanted to go back to the Bulldog, back to *chinja maitiro*. "It's cleaner that way," he added, still running his lips along my neck, doing everything a man in a Polo and Dockers should.

"I think you should go," I said, my whisper now more urgent, "I'm not really into this anymore." Matthew pretended not to hear, positioning himself. "Please just go," I pleaded in full voice, pulling out from underneath him.

"What's wrong? What's happened to you?"

"I just don't want it. I just, whatever, I'm not in the mood. Look, please just go." I tried not to look at him, pathetic with the condom blousy and wrinkled over his shriveling dick.

"Look, I'm wearing the condom like you wanted."

"It's better if you just leave." He didn't budge. "Please, please just go. I don't want bloody dry sex!" I shouted, loud enough that Shadrack might hear. Matthew got up, shaking and muttering, putting on his Dockers and Polo shirt, the collar now bent. I wrapped a robe tight around me and could feel my chest heaving under the robe. Though I was standing still, my mind was spinning and lurching, back to another man leaving me alone in my bedroom, and all of the profound sense of stupidity and sluttiness came flooding back. I feared I might throw up again, but I just threw out words.

"What's wrong with you people?" I said, trembling with confusion and fury.

"Huh?" Matthew looked up at me.

"What the fuck is wrong with you people?"

"You people?" A disgusted look spread across his face.

"You like to pretend you're all progressive, all sort of hip and forward thinking, with your fucking mobiles and political bullshit, thinking you're some sort of Big Man who's going to save his country. But you're just like bloody cavemen wanting as many women as you can get, wanting to screw women on your terms. It's all about you, isn't it?"

"What about *you people*, you white people. You pretend like you're all progressive and just like the locals, but you're all the same, all you want is to tell us what to do, how to think. Jesus, you even think you can tell us how we should fuck."

"Just get out of here! Just get the fuck out of my life!" I flung open the door.

"With pleasure, madam!" he shouted and stormed out. I went after him, to make sure he left.

"Evening, madam," Shadrack said quietly. I couldn't return the greeting or look at him, certain that the quick departure of my salad kid lover was a sign that I was a slut or a failure or both. The cold air was seeping though the thin crack in my robe, up my legs to where it had just been so hot with life. I shut the door and held on to the curtain, unable to move.

I couldn't go back to sheets that were creased but not stained, couldn't lie in my bed alone again, so I curled up on the couch, replaying every moment of the night. Wondering why hadn't I read about dry sex, why this intelligent young man didn't think we needed a condom when his country was in the middle of an epidemic. How could he care so much about the dictator and not the disease? There was nobody to answer my questions, to teach me about this country I thought I was getting to know. So I just made myself smaller and smaller, hoping I might disappear into the dark shadows, sobbing and shaking.

Then I remembered I hadn't given Shadrack his food. Snot poured from my nose as I stood over the tin of apricot jam, smearing it on extra thick. And an extra spoon of sugar for his tea, everything thicker and sweeter that night. I opened the door and silently set the plate and mug down, tears plunking onto the cold stone of the verandah.

"Thank you, madam."

22

Mid 1998: Mrs Reilly Tries to Return

Nobody in Zimbabwe would ever know I'd taken a chance that night and let Jill out, because Mrs Reilly returned first thing on Monday morning, wearing her courteous smile and another long, loose linen dress, the kind they sold in sections of Dillards department stores that I had once vowed I would never shop in. Looking at myself in the mirror that morning there was a vague unfamiliarity, like catching a distorted image of yourself. I never would have worn a dress like this at home, I thought. And for the first time "never would have" didn't bring a smile to my lips.

Still, to everyone who asked in the weeks that followed, I was "fine" even though dry sex and witchcraft now tainted my lovely life on Snowhill Close, enough that I checked the locks on my doors at night and got up in the middle of the night to check them again. Forget about seeing Harare from my verandah, I was worried about what happened when I let it inside.

Like everyone else in Zimbabwe, I seemed "fine" regardless of any trouble brewing under the surface. Florence's chignon remained perfectly pinned. Susan wore a new weave every week, favoring some version of an African bob, then venturing into Sandra Dee-style ponytails. Edward's wife was pregnant with their first child, and Lovelace would soon be trying for their second. A new restaurant opened on the Mutare Road that served a decent Chilean Merlot and had plans to open a martini bar later in the year. Zimbabwe Broadcasting Corporation started showing episodes of *Friends* – okay, it was the first season, but it was better than *Santa Barbara* – and a new jewelry shop was opening at the Meikles Hotel, selling exquisite little silver trinkets that I could afford with my fat director's salary.

After Matthew left that night I looked through the notebooks I'd filled since arriving in Zimbabwe, scanning every page of starred and highlighted notes for some reference to "dry sex" or "witchcraft". But amidst descriptions of women's empowerment, peer education, prevention, education, harmful cultural practices, needs assessment, evaluation, training, strategic planning, work plans, scale up, condom social marketing, home-based care, psycho-social support, care givers, infected and affected, rapid testing, counseling and testing, vulnerable children, risky behavior, partner reduction, protected sex, trans-generational sex and sugar daddies, the words "witchcraft" and "dry sex" never appeared. Not once.

Didn't matter, I told myself. Dry sex and witchcraft belonged to Jill's life at home, and all I had to do was focus on Mrs Reilly's life at the office.

To Mike Soderberg, I was more than fine, I was great! Mike liked people who were great. I phoned him early the following week, as if to reassert my belief in progress, maybe to squelch any sense of the singleton getting screwed. We'd started our workshops and they too had been great, I told him, everything coming out of my mouth with an exclamation point. Mike chuckled at *umbonos* – he hadn't heard the word before – and kept repeating it with all of the broad "o's" of Coke. I told him Mr Chiruma's vision had focused on women, which wasn't just great, but "great stuff". "We like women" he reminded me, and I agreed. When I told him we'd be running workshops almost every week for the next three months, Mike enthused how that sounded great for money spending and report writing, "Lots of good stuff to fill up those pages!" For a moment I allowed myself to believe that filling pages might just be enough. His last words were, "You just keep focusing on those *umbonos!*" And I assured him that I would.

Mike had no idea that I had no other choice.

SHAME

For the next few months Susan and I traveled across Zimbabwe trying to pluck imagination and hope out of tired, frightened minds. Every week we traveled deeper and deeper into the heart of *zvaka pressa* Zimbabwe, a land where survival itself seemed a type of *umbono*.

Things are tough, that's what *zvaka pressa* means, things are tough, and it was a phrase as often on Zimbabweans' lips as that everyday greeting *masikati*. *Zvaka pressa*, I heard it so many times: from Lovelace as we rattled over potholes that seemed to increase by the week, from the green grocer who couldn't get cherry tomatoes because they'd become too expensive to sell, from Susan whose sons' boarding school could no longer afford to serve meals. Things are tough. *Zvaka pressa*.

Week after week Susan offered her opening gambit, "How do you say vision in Ndebele?" And week after week she looked out at blank stares and heads nodding. They were nodding politely, even obediently. Not a single person slouched or slumped or drifted away. Even when someone poured water or unwrapped a mint, their eyes never strayed from Susan as she shifted around the room. It was just that they couldn't understand what she was talking about, their captive gazes a result of confusion rather than inspiration. As though if they just stared at Susan a little longer she would explain what the hell a vision was and why it mattered so much. To these peer educators, head teachers, matrons and midwives, chiefs and councilors, *umbonos* had all the currency of *kwachas*.

"In order to see this vision, I want you to close your eyes," Susan would instruct. That usually brought giggles, a welcome show of emotion. "I want you to imagine that I've been away from Zimbabwe for ten years, but I've been hearing about all your good HIV/Aids work, and I've come back to see it." Susan continued moving around the room, her voice taking on a soothing, dream-inducing hush. "So you're taking me on a tour of your activities, telling me what you've accomplished. Have you managed to lower infection rates in your communities? By how much?" She got close to people as she walked, prodding them with her words. "Are community members willing to talk about HIV/Aids now?" Susan would continue elaborating possibilities, hoping she could script their imaginations. "And what's happening among the youth? Are parents talking to their children about HIV/Aids? I want you to see how different the HIV/Aids situation could be in this country in ten years. How *different* you could make it." More silence. "We can make things different here, you know."

Sometimes I half expected Susan to say, "Are we together?" But you only ask that question when you are sure of the answer.

I'd get up and walk around these still rooms, searching people's faces while they searched for a future, hoping to find a flicker behind closed eyes. Instead, I saw clenched eyes and contorted faces. No flights of fancy were taking place behind those closed faces, but something difficult and uncomfortable, an attempt to extract something buried alive – that sense of possibility, the illusion of power.

Finally, in week four, a young woman with fine cascading braids and a T-shirt reading *Batisirai Home Based Carer* told us the truth hiding behind those closed eyes.

"Mrs Moyo," she raised her hand and stood, "I am having a problem with this exercise." Susan smiled, encouraging her to continue. "You see, my problem is that I don't understand. Why would you come back to Zimbabwe?" She paused for a moment. "I mean, if I had the chance to get away from Zimbabwe for ten years, I would never come back to see what was going on here. I think in ten years everything will be broken completely." The room broke into laughter, while the young woman shyly sat down when she realized she'd made a joke. I watched the group enjoy that morose humor that served as their *sadza*-like staple. Even I couldn't help laughing. The Youth had once again told the truth: it was impossible to talk about the Disease in Zimbabwe, without the Dictator getting in the way.

How could they dream of building when their President was intent upon destruction? How could they focus on the future, when even the present was in peril? There was only one vision they could clearly see and share, not a dream of a new life, but a dream of death, the demise of their father, the Liberator.

"A single bullet, meant just for him, as he's walking into Parliament," Edward said at one of our regular lunch sessions. With every passing month the staff's discussion of Zimbabwe's political situation grew angrier. "Right between those tiny eyes, that's where I would aim." Edward used his thumb and forefinger to fashion a gun and then mouthed a sort of "pah" as his imaginary shot was fired.

"I'd aim for the moustache," Lovelace added, dropping a bone on his plate and licking his fingers one by one, starting with his thumb. "The MDC will get him; you just wait. You will see."

"Ah, easy, Lovelace, I don't know why we're talking about killing him," Susan said, staring into her bowl of *sadza*. "I think he must suffer, the way he makes us suffer. Dying is too easy for him."

"Torture would be good," Edward concurred. "We could all have a go at it."

Even Florence was unhappy: "He is like our chief, you know, he is our leader. But chiefs are supposed to consult people and listen to them. Bob's not doing that anymore." When Florence was calling her *sekuru* "Bob", things were getting bad.

For weeks I'd sat at the back of stuffy rooms – in local hotels, community centers and office conference rooms – allowing Susan the space to lead. But in Bindura, I felt that rush of blood once more and strode forward to help these blinded people see again.

The Bindura Aids Consortium had sat for hours – the old ladies fanned themselves, the middle-aged men emptied bowls of sweets, the Youth breathlessly raised hands, while the no-longer-so-youthful glanced down at newspaper headlines – debating what it would take to significantly halt the spread of HIV/Aids in their coverage area within five to ten years. Some participants were unwavering in the belief that more of the same peer education and condom demonstrations would eventually pay dividends: "Ah but the community likes the peer education, they are comfortable with it. And we are starting to build, what is it called, a critical mass." Others wanted to take the opportunity to experiment with new approaches that might see more returns: "Start younger, we need to start the condom demonstrations in the primary schools."

Then someone said, "We need to target people better; not just offer everything to everyone, but really try to reach the infected and their families, they are most at risk." I shot from my seat, my heart racing. I had a great idea! I strode to the front feeling a rush of smartness. Mrs Reilly had a great idea, the kind that others would consider a solution.

"I don't want to interrupt the, uh, flow of the conversation," I said, as Susan moved aside to make way for me. "I was just thinking that maybe if we want to know how to reach the infected and affected, how to have the best impact, then perhaps we should ask the people with HIV/Aids themselves. The PLWHA, People Living with HIV and AIDS, right?"

Silence. The desire not to answer, as though people were holding their breath, looking away rather than at me.

"Are there people here who have, who are HIV positive? Living with Aids?" I asked. It was as if I'd asked whether there were convicted rapists in the room.

"I don't think they came, the people with HIV/Aids," Susan stuttered, trying to ease the tension.

"No, no," Mrs Shambura, the director said, straightening her skirt. "The PLWHAs couldn't come today. Transport, you know it's a problem for everyone."

"So nobody here has HIV/Aids?" I paused, as much for dramatic effect as to allow the smoke in my head to clear. "Is that right?"

"No, no, they couldn't make it," Mrs Shambura repeated. "They couldn't get fuel for their transport so they couldn't make it."

"In this room of forty people working on Aids, there's, uh, nobody with HIV/Aids?" I squeaked, hoping some Youth might say something to salvage the situation, "even though one in four people in Zimbabwe is HIV positive?"

"Yes, that is right," Mrs Shambura continued as though she was giving testimony. "They are not here."

I drifted to the sidelines again, all the blood just drifting away, abandoning my heart and anything else that gave me life.

It had been a long week when I dragged my feet up the stairs to my verandah. It was a Friday night and somewhere in Harare Americans were playing doubles tennis, while Zimbabweans were at the Bulldog ordering another round. Shadrack offered his salute, and I managed my nod. Then Shadrack found the words to ask for another book; he'd finished *Things Fall Apart*. I brought him Nelson Mandela's biography, *A Long Walk to Freedom*.

"Thank you, madam." But it was me who felt like thanking Shadrack, because his *umbono* felt like an easy one.

SHAME

I poured my usual glass of wine and entered my home office, the perfect spot for a singleton on a Friday night. One of the quarterly reports Mike wanted was due the following week. The computer screen didn't stay empty for long, because I had numbers – real numbers, not make-believe – to fill it.

Eight workshops run with NGOs to develop strategic visions for long-term HIV/Aids impact

Over three hundred people participating in visioning exercises, increasing their awareness of impact.

As I looked at my words, I began to reason with myself. Maybe the mere fact that we'd gathered people for difficult conversations, caused them to think about difficult issues, was a sort of accomplishment. *Zvaka pressa*, yes, but maybe it was enough just to be talking about *umbonos*, even though I couldn't say if they would have any impact on HIV/Aids. Staring at the screen I started to believe everything was fine, or at least that it would one day soon be fine.

***

Marondera-based Thulani were very proud of their Aids awareness activities. They had reached fifty per cent of community members, though they couldn't confidently say how any of this had affected infection rates. Their *umbono* was to reach a hundred per cent.

"I can see it now, everyone in Marondera will have seen the condom demonstration," proclaimed Mr Sibanda the director, six foot tall and worryingly thin. Yes, they were keen to spread their well-documented condom demonstration and peer education methodologies, which they considered so cutting edge. They had plastic cocks and wooden cocks and supersized African cocks and pictures of vaginas accompanying both short and long lectures on HIV transmission. They boasted about their interventions with "sex workers", making prostitutes sound like factory workers who gave head, and all of it was perfectly appropriate, as if ordered from an international catalogue selling components of an Aids project.

But I started rocking in my seat, rubbing the furrowed space between my eyebrows. I couldn't help feeling something was missing – any real talk of love, lust, desire, fear, insecurity, ego, pride, obedience, anything about the fraught, emotional drivers of sex. All the reasons that HIV/Aids was so difficult to address seemed too embarrassing or complex – or maybe just too real – for Mr Sibanda and his crew to discuss.

As the discussion wore on, I started to picture trying to combat a massive flu epidemic if you were too embarrassed to talk about sneezing. You would draw neat pictures of their red noses, use models of wide-open mouths to demonstrate them sneezing without ever talking about snot or dirty tissues or how some women leak when they sneeze. Knowing I had to say something, I decided to ask a question rather than make a suggestion. This time Mrs Reilly would raise her hand and be the ever-obedient student of Zimbabwe.

"Susan, sorry, do you mind if I ask a question?"

"No, please, come forward," Susan invited though her faltering voice revealed some hesitation.

"As I'm listening to you speak, I'm wondering how much you actually talk with people about sex," I ventured.

"Very much, Mrs Reilly!" Mr Sibanda piped up. "As we've already said, we give the demonstration of the condom. We tell them how the virus can be passed in the semen, in the lady's bodily fluids."

"And that's really important, but what I'm asking is whether you talk to them about what they really do sexually."

"Talk to them? But we do, Mrs Reilly, we talk during the condom demonstrations."

"Yes, but I'm not talking about teaching people the facts about Aids or lecturing to them about condoms. I'm talking about having a dialogue, you know, to get to the heart of whether people actually wear the condoms, how hard it is to talk to their spouses or partners about HIV/Aids. Do you talk to them about the realities of what they do sexually, rather than just what the textbooks say they should or shouldn't do sexually?"

"The peer educators they do this, as part of the condom demonstration."

"So do they talk about dry sex?" The words just tumbled out, innocently enough, but I knew there was nothing innocent about them. The room fell silent, except for a tiny old lady wearing a ski cap in the middle of summer, who was silently laughing so hard that she curled over in her chair. My heart raced as I sought to fill the very silence I'd created.

"It's contributing to the spread of Aids here, isn't it? Among women, because of the cuts, the abrasions that it causes." I thought I saw a young woman, a nurse at the local clinic, flinch when I used the word "abrasion", but whatever conversations they were having with themselves, however much they might have been silently cursing me, nobody would say a word in the large group. So Susan stepped in. In the end she was going to be the one to save me from the difficult crowd.

"I think these are very good points Mrs Reilly is making, and things we need to discuss as we develop our vision for our prevention activities." People shifted in their seats. Then Susan started speaking in Shona, switching mid-sentence, midstream, taking the conversation back from me. And immediately the discussion gained momentum again, with people speaking passionately about what I didn't know. At first I nodded my head, pretending I understood, but with each passing moment I felt more and more marooned. I took my seat again, watching the remainder of the conversation take place in a language that most certainly was not in my blood.

Later that night, Susan and I shared drinks again, this time in the deserted bar of a second-rate Marondera hotel, the only place in town where internationals and professionals stayed. The bartender wore a soiled shirt, a few lonely men hung over their Hansa beers, and a few single women wearing bright lipstick and high ponytails, sex workers scouting customers, waited to see who ordered the next beer. This was *zvaka pressa* Zimbabwe, to be sure.

And this time Susan and I weren't raising our glasses, we were just staring into them, sipping, not slugging. We talked about the mechanics of the day – the food was terrible, let's talk to catering tomorrow – and how to make tomorrow run more smoothly, but we both knew it wasn't mechanics we needed to talk about.

"You can't do that, Jill," Susan finally said gently.

"Do what, talk about reality?"

"Talk in such a way that you offend people, talk about subjects that offend people."

MID 1998: MRS REILLY TRIES TO RETURN

"I'm sorry, I thought it was a workshop about an epidemic, not a tea party." I'd never snapped at Susan before, and I instantly regretted it. She remained calm, patient, the way she'd been for so many weeks before with the other people who simply couldn't see.

"If you offend these people then you can't work with them," she explained.

"Maybe somebody needs to offend them, maybe that's precisely what I should be doing!"

"Look, there's sex and then there's sex."

"You mean there's this sanitized NGO world of sex workers and condom demonstrations and then there's the real sex, the one that's killing this country. Dry sex is real, Susan," my voice trembled. "I read about it, in a paper, a USAID paper."

Susan stared over her drink at me. "Why are you so upset, Jill? I told you this visioning thing wasn't going to be easy, and you can't get frustrated just because they don't speak the way you want them to. Just because they can't always go there with …"

"It wasn't just through some paper," I interrupted, suddenly burning to speak the truth. "That's not how I found out about dry sex. I met this guy. A salad kid."

"What?" Susan's eyes widened with horror. "You got together with one of those …"

"Why do you look so shocked? You're the one talking about me staying here, about me finding a nice man."

"A nice *white* man!" Susan said, loud enough that the sex workers looked our way. "I wanted you to meet a white man, Jill. You can't try to date some Zimbabwean man and think it's going to work. And you can't bring your personal life into these workshops. It's not right."

"Can't I? Isn't that precisely the problem, that nobody talks about their real life in these workshops? That all of it seems packaged at some HIV/Aids factory, without any real grounding in their own experiences. I mean, what about you, have you ever been tested or, I mean, had anything to do with … "

I stopped as Susan's face, usually so bright and warm, went blank and cold.

"Jill," she said, as though addressing a patient or one of her children, "this is work, it's professional, it's *not* something that needs to be brought up in workshops or meetings." I could see from her face that this conversation, so many conversations that I could imagine, were now officially over.

"Whatever, Susan, you're right, I'm sorry. I'm really sorry I offended everybody. Now I know better than to try to talk about what's going on here." I scribbled my name on the bill. "I'm tired. Long day tomorrow."

I went to my room, tired, so tired of having to navigate real and make believe.

23

End of 1998: Bewitched and Bewildered

I had never been to a funeral before I went to Africa, though at the time I had no idea what a privilege it was never to have experienced that irrevocable loss of someone close to me, the burden of trying to fill their absence.

When one of my father's second cousins had died – she was tall and sturdy with a husky voice, and though the word "lesbian" was never used there was always speculation about whether she would ever be with a man – my parents decided I was too young to go to the funeral. The sight of an open casket would probably sully the sunny worldview of a twelve-year-old. They were trying to shield me from the realities of human mortality, but they didn't have to because growing up as a white middle-class person in middle America, I already felt largely invincible. My parents didn't really have to protect me; privilege had done it for them. My type of white people just didn't generally die young.

Years later I would reflect that this lack of familiarity with death was a something that separated me from most Africans, along with never squatting over a hole to go to the bathroom and always sleeping with a pillow under my head. All of these things made it clear that there wasn't any part of Africa in my blood, no matter how long I placed myself on its soil.

Maybe that's why I offered to hold a memorial service for Mavis Mthethwa, one of the directors of the NGOs, who "died suddenly from a short illness". I put those words in quotes because those were the exact words used, and they were used over and over again. There was a kind of novelty to hosting a memorial, another first, which seemed fitting to come in the middle of Africa, in the middle of an epidemic. There was a certain propriety and dignity inherent in hosting such a hushed affair, propriety and dignity that I'd perhaps lost by uttering the words "dry" and "sex" back to back in a crowded, rural room. Yes, that's what it was, the chance to reclaim some sense of belonging, or at least of sharing something in common, by participating in this universal ritual of mourning. At that stage, I was still pinning my hopes on universals.

From the outside it looked like any good Christian gathering, the kind a good Christian Zimbabwean would wish for, with lots of talk of that all-powerful Father and not their worldly "father" who just thought he was all-powerful. After the official service at the Catholic Church in town, we gathered in our boardroom to share a few further prayers and casual tributes to Mavis.

Florence clinched her eyes shut and mouthed her own prayers, as if she were speaking to her Father directly. She wouldn't let go of her rosary beads, her forefinger and thumb pushing, pushing against their smoothness. Edward's head hung heavy, while Lovelace kept glancing up to see when it was safe to raise his head, like a child fidgety with convention. Susan was frumpy in her black polyester suit and matted-down weave, all traces of lipstick wiped off. And I just stood with my hands loosely clasped, head down and little to say. Occasionally I'd make eye contact with Lovelace, then we'd both look down again.

"Let us all pray. Lord in Heaven, you are almighty and our lives are in your hands. We know that you have a plan for us, that you know what is best. We are at your mercy, and we ask that you guide and direct us in our work, and that you forgive us for we are only sinners. You are with us in our hearts each day. Amen."

When the prayers were over, we milled around, fingering plastic cups filled with soda, chewing on chicken wings or tiny English-inspired finger sandwiches filled with tuna rather than cucumber while

Linda, the hired cleaning lady for the day, cleared away used plates under Florence's close supervision. Misty regrets and remembrances were our small talk. *She was a lovely woman. Shame. Such a loss.* Nobody uttered *zvaka pressa* or railed against Bob or shortages at the Bon Marché. The men loosened tight ties, the women made sure enough food remained spread out on the table. And everyone stood close together in supportive pairs and circles, deep in conversation or happy to hang together in silence.

Only one woman wasn't a member of any group. Stella Chadzimura stood in a corner talking to her daughter, a conspicuous gap between her and the crowd. Stella knew everyone in the room, she'd worked with some of them for years, but none of them were talking to her and she was making no effort to leave her corner. I'd imagined memorial services were always uncomfortable, redolent with sadness and loss, reminders of what lay ahead for us all. But here the air here was thick with something almost sinister, despite the Catholic priest's efforts to remind us all of God's presence. A feeling one step beyond fear, just short of collective paranoia.

"Witchcraft?" I repeated Susan's words, uncertain whether to feel relief or revulsion; relief that what I was no longer keeping one of Zimbabwe's secrets to myself, revulsion that apparently it wasn't a secret at all. "What do you mean everybody thinks Stella's a witch?" Susan couldn't look me in the eye.

Mavis Mthethwa had died five days earlier at age thirty-five, leaving behind two teenage daughters who didn't cry once during the service as they stood encircled in their grandmother's arms. Mavis's husband had left her a few years earlier and word was he'd taken another wife. The daughters, surely salad kids in the making, were preparing to live with their grandmother in the rurals, returning to a life of boredom and labor, of long bus trips to the nearest store to buy the occasional Coke. They looked like sandy husks of their former selves.

Only eight months before her death, Mavis and her team had held their visioning workshop, and I remember feeling unexpectedly energized because Susan hadn't had to prod them to think big or to lift themselves out of their dutiful morass of home caring and peer educating.

"We can't, you know, just kind of manage this thing," Mavis had said. "We have to really get on top of it, really think creatively about how to stop the spread of this disease." She wore long gold chains, had a neatly tamed Afro and seemed always to be searching for a piece of paper to draw some idea forming in her head.

Mavis's brain really did seem to storm, and maybe that's what killed her.

I remembered wanting to get close, so close to one of Mavis' drawings of the future: the image of a chief – a big fat man, not at all a stick figure – hovering above his village, speaking out against what Mavis and others called "harmful cultural practices". Mavis was passionate about ending Zimbabwe's cultural practices that she believed put people, and particularly women, at risk of contracting HIV/Aids. She'd stood up amidst stony silences and fractious discussions to share examples of young widows who'd been "inherited" by their brothers-in-law after their husbands had died of Aids, or young boys who had died after dangerous circumcision ceremonies performed with unsanitary blades.

At first people had resisted, crossing their arms and looking anywhere but at Mavis, arguing that culture was all Zimbabweans had right now and it wasn't something you tinkered with to suit your preferences. But Mavis's passion eventually had almost everybody's heads nodding, and not just politely, not just because she was the director, but because they agreed with her. Some people had even stood up and clapped. I was one of them.

At the end of the week, Mavis, Susan and I had shared a drink in the bar of the Holiday Inn Monomotapa in Harare, filled with glossy sex workers, tourists who couldn't afford the Meikles and wilted former salad kids. Mavis was buzzing.

"Ah Jeel, for the first time my staff are really excited about what we're striving for, because we developed it. It's a Zimbabwean solution. Not just something we've lifted from some organization in Bangladesh or America."

"To the future!" Susan said and we all raised our glasses.

"To women taking control of the future!" Mavis added.

And now Mavis was dead. Was it an accident, I'd asked

Florence naively when I'd heard the shocking news, a heart attack? Both times, Florence shook her head no.

Now at the memorial, with a different kind of naïve disbelief, I said to Susan, "C'mon, you can't be serious. These people, these educated people," I looked around the room at people I thought I knew, "they work for NGOs, they can't actually believe in witches." I paced with a sudden urge to vomit up my chicken wings. It was enough to think that my cleaner and gardener were part of this shadowy voodoo underworld, but now all these smiley, just fine people, with their cell phones and shiny shoes and ties tied just like in any other part of the world, they also believed in it? I wasn't fine. I felt revolted.

"It's not that they necessarily believe it, it's that they accept it as a possibility. They believe it's a real possibility. Everyone was jealous of her."

Mavis was an avid golfer who liked to talk about what score she'd shot that weekend over lunch with her staff. "What kind of Zimbabwean woman plays golf?" people would whisper afterwards, when Mavis was back in her office. Some said Mavis was pretentious, even a little shady. "Where would a woman like her learn to play golf?" Mavis just thought they were jealous. She had gone to a Catholic boarding school, drove a 1980s Mercedes, and lived in the suburb of Glen Lorne, where most of her neighbors were whites, whites whose names she knew.

Then one day, Mavis "fell ill", as Zimbabweans always said, wording that characterized sickness as a kind of unintentional mishap, like a skinned knee. "The flu," Mavis explained and everybody agreed, lots of people were coming down with flu these days. But when she couldn't shake that flu, that's when the whispers started. *The husband always was a problem.* Mavis said she was under too much pressure – the HIV/Aids epidemic just kept growing and the donor money just kept flowing – and she couldn't take the time off to recover properly. But her staff knew what it meant in Zimbabwe when you couldn't shake an illness; it meant you probably never would.

Then came the telltale cough, Mavis's hand permanently over her mouth, like some sort of mask at a ball. But it didn't stop her working, playing golf, telling stories, searching for a future. Then came the brown spots clustering around her cheeks and later on her arms, and with them more whispers. *Her skin, have you seen her skin?* Still Mavis kept smiling, until even her lips became red and sickly, her smile only drawing attention to them. *You know they're really sick when they get those funny lips.*

"She died of Aids, Jill, everybody knows that," Susan said.

"What do you mean everybody knows? Nobody's said a word about Aids, I haven't heard the word mentioned once."

"Of course not, nobody's going to mention it now."

"So what are you saying? Did she know she was HIV positive? I mean, had she been tested?"

"I don't know. Nobody really knows the whole story."

"She was the head of one of the biggest Aids NGOs in Zimbabwe," I said, as though Susan didn't know that.

Then one day, Mavis' illness had threatened somebody else's life too. Mavis was sitting at her desk reviewing financial reports when suddenly she started crying, her body jerking over her desk, her head touching the papers scattered on top of it. The women in the office swarmed around her.

"Mavis, please, come now, what's wrong?"

"Get away from me," Mavis lashed out. "Don't touch me. Don't you dare touch me, you people!" The women stood back as Mavis hunched and reeled in different directions. "You're all so happy that I'm like this. You wanted this from the beginning. You never wanted me here." By now the rest of the staff stood on the perimeters of the room, paralyzed. Except for Stella Chadzimura, the financial controller, who stepped towards Mavis and held out a hand.

"Come, Mavis, why don't we get a cup of tea and rest a bit."

"It's you! You're the one, aren't you?" Mavis' face twisted as she shouted, her body rocking with each scream. "You're a witch, aren't you? You've cursed me!"

Stella stepped back. "Come now Mavis, stop this," she pleaded.

"No, I'm not stopping, I'm speaking the truth! You've cursed me because you've always hated me and wanted my job and now you've got what you always wanted, haven't you?" Stella stepped back even further and the other employees looked back and forth between the two women. Then Mavis collapsed under her own weight, the fearsome woman suddenly disarmed by her own fatigue.

For days an awkward silence blanketed the office. Paranoia and delusions often happened when people had these "short illnesses", and Mavis had been under so much stress for so many months. Still, it was true that Stella and Mavis never got along. They were two of the most senior women in the organization, so there was always an element of competition. Stella hated Mavis's boasting, and Mavis was Ndebele, Stella Shona, you could never tell with these things. To Stella's face her colleagues sympathized, but to each other over a cup of tea in the kitchen, they speculated otherwise. "You just never know, do you?" The office, always quiet with professionalism, fell to silence. One colleague was sick, the other accused, each a victim of fear, denial.

So now Stella found herself in a corner, her teenage daughter providing a kind of protection. Nobody had said anything to Stella at the service, that would have been impolite, but Stella knew the danger in such polite silences.

"So wait, it gets even better," I said. "You're telling me that the head of one of Zimbabwe's biggest HIV/Aids NGOs died of Aids, but she believed she was possessed?"

"Bewitched," Susan corrected. My mind flashed to that cutesy 1970s television show my mother sometimes watched during the day, with the blonde with the button nose and the handsome but hapless husband, Darren. God, witchcraft looked so cute in that show.

"But nobody here is saying a word about it, any of it," I whispered, "not the Aids, not the witchcraft." Susan didn't respond. "And nobody in any of the workshops over all the past months has mentioned anything about witchcraft. Not a single one of them has ever said a thing."

"No, I mean, it's not the kind of thing ..." Susan tried to maintain the quiet calm of the event, "not the kind of thing you talk about in a formal group setting like that." She was struggling, searching. "Not that some American NGO has paid for, anyway."

"It's just too impolite to mention," my voice dripped. I rubbed the scrunched space between my eyes, trying to be perplexed rather than disgusted. "My gardener, he left me some cruddy little note and I haven't known what the hell to do about it, saying that Sarah, my maid was a witch. But I kind of thought, well, I guess I hoped, that it was just something uneducated people believed, you know, more traditional people. But that's not the case, is it?"

"Look, a lot of people think witchcraft has a role to play in people's lives," Susan responded carefully.

"Do you think that's why Mavis died? If you do, it's fine. I just want to understand."

"No, I don't necessarily think Mavis died that way. I think she died of Aids. Look, let's not talk about this now."

"So when, then?" I found myself straining to whisper. "Can we talk about witchcraft tomorrow at lunch with the staff? When is it ever going to be an okay time to talk about all these ugly things?" Susan looked down and let out a deep breath, unwilling to look back at me.

I went outside, seeking solace in warm air and sunshine, Zimbabwe's obvious comforts. Stella came out soon afterwards, standing at the edge of the empty swimming pool and staring into it. For a moment I imagined her wishing there was water in it so she could jump. I barely knew her; the last time we'd spoken was at the workshop, when she was part of a group working on ideas for "empowerment groups for girls". "Girl guides with an attitude," Stella had joked to me then, and I'd given her a "go girl" thumbs up that felt like some sort of Oprah-inspired international code that let white girls into that black-girl world.

Stella smiled gratefully as I approached, and we spoke softly for a few minutes, agreeing that Mavis' death was a terrible loss and nobody could really replace her as director, she was one of a kind. Then Stella began sobbing, just as softly as she'd been speaking a few moments earlier, staring into leaves swirling in the wind tunnel of the empty pool, her hand clenched in a fist over her mouth, hiding behind it just as Mavis had hidden behind her hand.

"I just can't believe this is happening," Stella choked. "That woman had gone mad, completely mad. And I don't know how she picked me." She looked straight into my eyes, "I'm not a witch, you know." Her face appeared to be melting under the heat of sun and tears.

END OF 1998: BEWITCHED AND BEWILDERED

"I know you're not, Stella. You don't have to …"

"They'll never be able to forget what she said. They used to avoid drinking from her teacups and now they're avoiding mine." She shook her head and then looked off into the distance. "Maybe I should just go somewhere else, but I don't want to take my daughter out of school, uproot our lives here."

And then I did a very Zimbabwean thing, offering up a weary nostrum: everything will be fine, eventually it will "come right". I sopped up her tears with words even I didn't believe. The reality felt too overwhelming, so I just made something up while inside people were busy whispering out another prayer, eyes firmly shut.

"Lord, we ask you to accept this woman into your kingdom who died at such a young age after fighting so valiantly against a terrible illness. We know you have your reasons for taking her from us and we know that you will look after her in your kingdom where she will wait until we join her. Although our hearts are heavy with her loss, we know that she is basking in your glory, that she has come home to you. And we wait to do the same."

***

Later that evening I found something propped up against my front door. Not a finished book or a wiped down plate, but a brochure, fold out, colorful. I bent to pick it up and smiled when I read the front cover print: American International College, Adult Continuing Education.

"This is my school, madam," I heard from behind me. "The place where I was studying before I had to stop. It is from your country," Shadrack smiled, his teeth white and perfect.

"I see," I replied, enjoying his smile. I hadn't seen a smile that day, a rare occurrence in Zimbabwe.

"The next term, it starts in two months." He shifted on his feet, and I became aware of the dogs barking somewhere in the distance, always that incessant barking.

"I see," I repeated.

"So I was thinking maybe, madam, if you could give me some

185

money, a loan, for fees, then I could start again. I have only two terms before I get my certificate. I will pay you." The cover of the brochure blurred in front of me, two young black people, they could have been the Cosby daughters, clutching books and smiling. My head began to throb, a dull ring in my ears that finally drowned out the barking.

"Let me think about this, just think for a while, and then I'll let you know. I'm just tired right now, Shadrack. Soon, I will let you know soon."

"Yes, madam," I heard as I closed the door behind me and locked it tight, making sure there were no gaps in the curtains.

I went straight to bed, dropping my bag and clothes onto the floor, the brochure on the pillow next to me. I switched on the television and found a replay of a Champions League game played somewhere in Europe. It looked like Madrid or Italy, swarthy and sweaty. I needed a place to rest my eyes, and I found it there, far away in Europe with its white people and their white-people ways. So many of my friends had gone to Europe after we graduated, tallying up mosquito bites in Athens, a broken air conditioning unit in Seville, a one-night stand with an Aussie at a hostel in Rome. It all seemed frivolous at the time as I practiced my Zulu clicks in the mirror at night, but maybe I should have joined them.

My eyes glazed over as the game went into penalty kicks, slowly, silently filled with tears. Slowly enough that I could ignore them. I reached for the brochure: Looking for a Chance to Advance Your Career? Inside were details of "internationally recognized" courses, providing "the best that America could offer" though I doubted any American university was actually involved. The text was decorated with snapshots of Zimbabweans speaking to each other in grassy fields, conferring over textbooks, studying in a paneled library, its shelves stocked with books, everyone in the brochure with their collared shirts and Dockers, their eyeglasses and ceaseless smiles. None of them had splotchy skin, putrid lips or wasting frames. And none of them looked like they'd ever seen a witch. Life in Zimbabwe looked so lovely in that brochure. And that life was Shadrack's *umbono*.

I got up, wiped away the wettest of the tears, and took all the money I had out of my wallet. It was almost enough. Then I went into the kitchen and methodically prepared his supper, back and forth, back and forth with the butter and jam, heap, heap, heap with the sugar. There were no shortages in my world.

"Here you go, Shadrack, your food," I set my offerings down on the verandah. Then I took a big sniff and I looked at him, allowed him to see my face. "And here's some money for your university, your course thing. I'll get you the rest on Monday. So you can finish, finish what you started."

"Ah thank you, madam," I heard, as I closed the door behind me, locking myself into the only world in Zimbabwe that made any sense to me, the only one with any hope of remaining lovely.

24

Late 1998 into 1999: Looking for Truth on Tombstones

That night after the funeral, after I turned off the television – *Comrade Mugabe has once again warned that war veterans will be forced to take action against white commercial famers* – I downed a bottle of Simonsig Chardonnay and went looking for my notebooks, the ones filled with bullet points and stars and highlighted words to remind me how important they were. The ones I hardly let go of those first few months after I arrived in Harare. I had been avoiding those strident reminders for weeks.

I paged through the notebooks from front to back. Then I started to repeat the jargon over and over, not to memorize it, but to hear each word as though it were real and not just the practiced language of some pretend universe. I inserted the word "fucking" into key places, to make it feel even more real. *Fucking women's empowerment, peer education, prevention, fucking harmful cultural practices, needs assessments, evaluation, training, fucking strategic planning.*

Giggling, crying, muttering, alternatively entertaining and depressing myself, fully embracing the curative powers of morose humor. Escalating from talking to myself to singing to myself then shouting at the walls, figuring Shadrack was too busy counting his money and dreaming of his future to care if madam was ranting. With every sip of wine the number of "fuckings" grew, as though I were some rapper cleaning out my closet.

Fucking counseling and testing, fucking risky behavior, over ten thousand fucking Aids awareness meetings, thousands of fucking peer educators, just as many fucking home based-care givers and God knows how many motherfucking T-shirts handed out.

I started cackling. It was another Friday night in Harare and somewhere out there the expats, tipsy or sweaty or maybe both, were enjoying some much deserved re-cre-ation after a long week of trying to fix a country that was busy breaking down right in front of their eyes. Who knows what most Zimbabweans were doing; I no longer pretended to know what really went on in the country I was living in. And this sorry singleton was keeping the company of words and wine, breaking down right in front of her own eyes. *Zvaka fucking pressa.*

I thought of Ntombenthle: Hey girl, I've got good news and bad news. The good news is that you were right, it would have been safer to stay in Evanston, but it's not the Zulus who are killing me. The bad news is that you were wrong about me, I'm not brave at all. I thought of Reuben: Hey big guy, let's be honest here, are we ever *really* all together?

Eventually I drifted to sleep with the wine bottle on my belly and woke hours later to nipples soaked in chardonnay.

That weekend and for several that followed, I left the house only to buy fruit, vegetables and wine, enjoying the excitement of seeing broccoli and cherry tomatoes at the local market, as though they were harbingers of some coming normalcy, tiny testimonials to Zimbabweans' ability to overcome chaos. I told myself I would make a recipe from my River Café cookbook, *farfalle con broccoli* or *linguine pomodoro*, and eat it by candlelight at my big teak table, the one I'd never used. Maybe I'd go back to the Bulldog and find a nice, white man to join me at my table, a landless farmer, somebody who knew what it was like to have an *umbono* taken away from him.

But I never cooked anything on any of those weekends, not from a cookbook or the back of a box or even from memory. I went home to bed and plucked the tomatoes straight from their plastic punnet the way some women eat luxury chocolates. I never left my glass of wine empty for long and only left my bed to use the toilet or organize food: Simon's, Shadrack's or mine. I avoided looking in the mirror. Eventually, I picked up the phone, promising myself I wouldn't cry.

"How you doing, kid? We haven't heard from you in a while." It had been a long time since I'd heard my father's voice.

"I've just been busy, you know, really busy. This being a director thing is hard work."

"I'm sure it is. It's never easy to be the boss lady, even in Zimbawe. You still doing good stuff out there? Fewer people dying and all that?"

"I don't know. I don't think I've stopped anyone from dying since I've been here. I'm not really sure what I've made happen since I got here." Don't cry, don't cry.

"That doesn't sound like you." Was that compassion in his voice?

"I guess it's all just more complicated than I thought it was going to be. God, that sounds kind of stupid. Like there's ever going to be something simple about Aids in an African country."

He paused before replying, "Look, Sweetheart, you've always just kind of thrown yourself into these things, like it's totally normal, like you're starting work in Cleveland. But it can't be easy. For most people, just going to Africa would be something to be proud of. Don't be so hard on yourself. Maybe it's enough just to be there trying."

"Yeah, right, maybe it's just enough to be trying."

As days became nights and nights turned into days, Simon to Shadrack, *morning madam* to *evening madam*, I stared from my bed out the window at smoke gathering across the street. Every winter, Zimbabweans burned open fields of long, dried up grass along the sides of roads. On our last trip to Bulawayo, Lovelace told me the fields were burned to prevent accidental fires igniting during the dry winter months, fires started in anticipation of others. But Rutendo told me the fires helped to fertilize the land before the rains started again, the ash feeding the earth so it could give life again, destruction a necessary precursor to rebirth.

For weeks, one of those fires raged on and off across from my house, in a field home only to power lines. Nobody appeared to own

LATE 1998 INTO 1999: LOOKING FOR TRUTH ON TOMBSTONES

the land, so it wasn't clear who had a vested interested in burning it. One day the fire just started with a fierce crackling, forcing the woman selling gum on the corner to cover her mouth with a cloth and swaddle her baby more tightly. Now I lay enjoying those flames from my bed, so far away and yet so close. How could I ever explain to anyone back home that I enjoyed watching something so destructive? I lost myself in those flames, seeing parts of my life passing away like little suffocated moments in time: the ten dollar bill I'd guarded in my book bag, the ballots and booklets handed out, all those excited coffees at the Italian Bakery when this life in Harare was still an expectant plane ride away.

Occasionally I wondered what was to stop a spark from traveling across the street and leaving its hot breath on my window. I'd have to run, grabbing photos and jewelry. Would Shadrack gather his book and run too, or would he try to defend me from the threat? I would never know.

***

"I can't take this anymore, Susan, I can't," I slumped into a chair in Susan's office about a month after the funeral. "I don't understand, I don't even know how to begin to understand. I don't ask questions anymore because I don't want to offend anyone or I don't know what questions to ask. I'm working with people who are leading the charge on HIV/Aids, but even they don't really want to talk about it. Well, I mean, they don't want to say anything beyond this internationally sanctioned script they're all reading from." Susan listened, her finger still hovering over her computer mouse.

"I've lived here for over a year now," I continued, "almost a year and a half, and yet I haven't met more than five people who say they have HIV/Aids. How is it possible to live in the middle of an epidemic, but not know anyone with Aids, to work closely with the very organizations dealing with Aids and yet not know anybody who admits they have it? Lots of people are apparently dying but nobody looks sick. And everybody claims to be a good Christian, yet everybody's having lots of sex with lots of people. And these good middle-class, God-fearing Christians believe somebody's died because she's been possessed."

"Bewitched," Susan corrected.

"Right, bewitched. So everybody's sick, but nobody's sick. Everybody's aware of Aids, but for some reason we need to keep raising awareness. And nobody, *nobody*, seems to really want to talk about the reality of any this, like if they keep repeating 'peer education' and 'home-based care', HIV/Aids will just go away. Like they're content to implement their little programs in the midst of the world's biggest bloody Aids crisis, fiddling while Rome is bloody well in flames, without any imagination or real conviction. I mean, God forbid you show some passion, some urgency."

And then all the anger stoked over those solitary, singleton weekends spent staring into flames gave way to sadness. Tears threatened. "I'm supposed to be working on something I can't even see," I whimpered. "I'm supposed to be helping people who won't even talk to me. Nobody will talk to me, Susan. Nobody will tell me the truth about HIV/Aids. Or show it to me. All I want is to know the truth."

Susan didn't look away. I was her young director, trying to make a difference, *dying* to make one, but I looked like one more thing in Zimbabwe that was broken.

"Come," she said, without pity, "let's go, let's get out of here."

She called Lovelace to get the car so I knew we weren't going for coffee at the Italian Bakery. But I didn't know where we were actually going until I saw it in the distance, in a town outside of Harare called Norton.

Few towns in Zimbabwe still had such English names, most were Shona or Ndebele names like Marondera, Bindura or Chipinge. Norton was in the provincial center of thriving commercial farms growing wheat, corn, and the country's most lucrative crop, tobacco. The farms, the ones Comrade Mugabe wanted, tucked off the main roads, their entrances marked by clusters of flowers and fanciful farm names like *Shangri La* or *Norton's Nest*, were almost all owned by white Zimbabweans.

The town itself was named after the Norton family that began farming in the area in the 1890s and was killed during what Zimbabweans called the First *Chimurenga*, or struggle, against English colonial rule. Zimbabwe's history was thick with *chimurenga*, but it was difficult to see any hint of struggle in Norton, where the locals went to work at the town's paper mill, the farmers' wives bought their children's shoes at the Bata store, and the train chugged past on the railway line. Comrade's Mugabe's threats to uproot such communities still seemed dim and distant, or maybe like all the other threats here they were just difficult to glimpse from the main roads.

I'd never been to a cemetery in Zimbabwe; the closest I'd been to death's rituals was Mavis's memorial and I'd run from that. But here we were at a cemetery, a dense concentration of simple gravestones with about thirty fresh mounds of brown dirt piled high.

"Come," said Susan, "let's go take a look."

The Norton cemetery wasn't immediately impressive, not like a Second World War memorial with its symmetry of crosses, its elegiac sense of human history and folly. Nor did the cemetery feel hasty, furtive or disrespectful. Crosses marked every grave, a flower sitting next to one, a plastic bouquet by another. This wasn't Bosnia or Rwanda; people hadn't been slaughtered by their neighbors for some primitive need to survive.

So although the cemetery felt unsettling, as any cemetery would, no truth appeared buried in the ground beneath me.

"This cemetery has only been here for six months," Susan said and I caught my breath. "It's true," she continued. "They had to open it up when the town's main cemetery filled up." She kept walking; there was more she wanted to show me.

Susan took me past "loving mothers" and "dear friends" straight to the freshest graves, where she began reading the tombstones aloud: William Chimarangwa 1970-1999, Gloria Moyo 1964-1999, Canaan Gazi 1974-1999, Runako Gwelo 1971-1999. I wanted to make her stop, but she just kept reading the same story, over and over. Of the thirty newly buried souls, thirteen were under the age of forty. Only two, Martin Carambwa and Blessings Haukozi, had the good fortune to grow old. Most of the other loving mothers and dear friends were my age or even younger; they hadn't lived to see thirty.

All these young people who had no chance of ever being saved or even empowered, who had maybe been students at an American college or longed to learn how to type, who had dreamed of one day owning a house of their own, a *kumusha*. I could see a tractor tilling land in the distance, hear birds twittering. For once I didn't hear dogs barking. Maybe that was just a big city thing?

I turned to Susan: "So all of these people died of a headache?"

"Yes, something like that, a cold, a long illness," she smiled sadly, her arms crossed.

"None of them died of Aids, right?"

"No," she said, looking at the tombstones, "of course not."

"And where did they go to die? Why do you see so few of these people?"

"To the rurals, they usually go to their *kumusha* when they get really sick, so that nobody will see them, so they can die there."

"Because dying of Aids would make them bad people, immoral people."

"That's right, and to be a bad person in Zimbabwe is almost to no longer exist. In your family's eyes, in your church's eyes, it's like you just disappear, like they want you to just go away, because if one person in the family is bad it affects everyone."

"So you not only disgrace yourself, but your whole family?"

"Exactly!" Susan said, as though now I was the good student. "That's the worst thing a Zimbabwean can do, bring shame to their family."

We kept walking. At the end of that row of fresh graves were the empty ones, about twenty neat squares dug for use the following day. I looked into the deep holes and saw unearthed worms, blades of grass, all of which would be buried the next day along with a young man or woman who had tried so hard to be an obliging lover, an obedient spouse. And that desire to be accepted, a universal need not unique to Zimbabwe, had got them killed.

"Are you okay?" Susan asked.

"I'm fine," I replied, quickly enough to reveal it as a lie. "Why, Susan? I know nobody wants to look bad, that's true anywhere. But Aids is preventable, completely manageable! I mean, is it really about helping people know more about HIV/Aids, making people more aware of it so they can …?"

LATE 1998 INTO 1999: LOOKING FOR TRUTH ON TOMBSTONES

"People know," she interrupted, standing straight and tall. "Most people know what HIV/Aids is. Whether they believe is another issue."

"Believe?"

"Believe they'll get it. Believe they can stop it. Believe in themselves. I don't know." She paused, looking down at another Gloria, another William and Canaan. "People are just scared, Jill. They're so scared right now with the country falling apart the way it is. And when you're scared you're kind of, I don't know, frozen, paralyzed. You don't know what to do, so you do nothing. You just hold your breath and hope, hope it won't happen to you, hope it will stop. I'm sure it doesn't make any sense to you."

I remembered lying in my bed all those weekends before, lying so still, practically holding my breath. "Of course it makes sense; I know what it's like to feel scared."

"It's just one more thing you can't control."

"But that's the thing; this is one thing you can control. You've said it yourself, at the workshops."

"That was for the workshops, Jill. The truth is that if you confront HIV/Aids, you might destroy your life in the process, have your husband walk out of the house, your mother-in-law think you're a troublemaker. You might not be able to pay for school fees if you don't have sex with the man who's got the money."

"Damned if you do, damned if you don't," I muttered.

"It's about survival. We're not like you Americans, who believe you have complete control your lives, who think you can just change something when you wake up one morning. You can't be so selfish here, you need your family otherwise you're alone, you're nothing."

I sat down on the grass. "So what do we do? If everybody feels so helpless, what can we possibly do about it with our little capacity building program?"

Susan paused, a response not coming easily to her lips. "Carry on. Keep doing what we're doing," she said eventually. How many times had I heard that answer from the directors in the months before? "Try to get people to think about how they really can control Aids, try to shift their thinking from just surviving day-to-day to how to try to build futures for themselves. We just have to keep fighting," she sighed, looking off into the distance to places where she knew the fighting was taking place. "*Chinja maitiro*, fight for change."

"*Zvaka pressa*," I replied and we smiled ruefully at each other. "I feel like such an idiot."

"Why?"

"Because there's nothing ABC about this epidemic; it's much more complicated. Knowing about HIV/Aids doesn't protect you from it, it just makes your life more complicated. All this NGO awareness raising is such rubbish."

"It's not rubbish. It's just that it's only part of the picture."

"A picture so complex it's hard to see it in focus, especially from the outside or through the windows of a Land Cruiser." I stood, still absorbed by the lives captured on those tombstones. "Thank you," I finally said.

"Ah please, Jill, you can't thank me for taking you to a cemetery!" Susan managed to find laughter again. "Thank me when I give you a nice birthday present or buy you a drink, but this is too depressing."

"The truth is a kind of gift, I guess." I thought about asking her to take me to visit somebody living with HIV, somebody holding on to the slim hope of a future. But I didn't. I had no clue what I would say when I got there.

25

1999: Haunted by the Truth

I wish I could say the truth had set me free. Instead I just felt more trapped. I wish I could say information had made me wiser. Instead I felt dumb. I wish I could say the graveyard visit energized me, but it left me huddled, trembling. Did dry sex send another woman into a damp grave today? Whose children had become orphans, cared for by an aging granny too tired to braid their hair? Stop it, stop thinking about them.

Every day Gloria, Canaan and William broke into my head, mocking or just shrugging their terrible bony shoulders. *What difference are you making? Why did they send you to Zimbabwe anyway? You're not Mrs Reilly at all, just a scared little girl.* They wouldn't leave me alone, wanting to know what I was doing to fight for change.

Wait a second, I wanted to shout back at them, we've run over thirty workshops, reached over five hundred people! *So did those workshops actually save anybody, even help anybody?* Come on, what about the directors? We've empowered over thirty directors to lead their organizations strategically. *Why is she always talking about "strategy", all those white-people words like "vision" and "milestone"?* I could almost hear them laugh, a real Zimbabwean laugh, the kind that takes some time to end. I wanted to fight back: But I've spent over half a million dollars! I've got so much money in the pipeline, money spent on you

Zimbabweans. *I think this girl is confusing spending money in Zimbabwe with spending money on Zimbabweans, she thinks paying for hotel rooms and Land Cruisers is going to save us!* They were all snickering at me now. Jesus, isn't it enough just to be trying?

Imagination had become much more cruel than memory.

"Fight for change!" that's what I'd told myself – told everyone from Jerry to Ntombenthle and my father – I'd come to Africa to do, long before I heard the term *chinja maitiro*. The graveyard visit should have left me animated. I'd told myself that if only I knew the heavyweight truth about Zimbabwe's HIV/Aids epidemic, I would face it down.

But it didn't turn out that way because fighting for change meant fighting Zimbabweans, facing down these smiling, polite people with all the messy realities of human existence that drive the spread of Aids anywhere in the world: lust, ego and duty; hypocrisy, cowardice and ignorance. It would have meant admitting Aids wasn't like the other man-made tragedies that had befallen them, brought about by racist colonials or that fallen "father". Face down the Elders in hand-me-down suits, and the Youth in hand-me-down T-shirts? I couldn't even face down my own staff, the people I shared an office and a meal with every day. Only now did I begin to see that the staff couldn't talk about HIV/Aids at lunch because that would have meant moaning about their husbands or their wives, their fathers or their mothers. It would have implicated them as bad people. And it was so much easier to moan about all those other bad people out there threatening your lovely existence.

And so for the most part I just stuck to the hand-me-down rhetoric.

To drown out Gloria and William and Canaan's voices, I took Susan's advice and did what directors were supposed to do, what it seemed all the other directors in Zimbabwe – white and black, those who went to church on Sunday morning and those who spent the morning reading *The New York Times* on line – had already decided to do. I put my nose down and carried on, hoping some of our work might make things better eventually. Carry on: that's what you do when the world you're living in is breaking into pieces. No matter that we'd like to imagine ourselves fixing things, sticking a finger in the air to menacing authorities, most of us just cope. Cope, that's our westernized word for it, the one the Woody Allens and Oprah Winfreys of the world made sound so normal. For an NGO director – white, black, Scandinavian or South African – coping mainly involves writing reports and spending money. That's what my visits to the directors had taught me, though it wasn't the lesson I was seeking to learn.

And so each month I spent money and I wrote reports, I wrote reports and spent money, hoping that every report written and dollar spent might make Gloria, William and Canaan believe in me again. I wrote beautiful reports full of symmetry and logic. The orderly world portrayed on the page was a world I inhabited every time I sat at my computer:

- Six workshops carried out in February.
- Two hundred people engaged in goal setting for their organizations.

The world in those reports was a world of progress and change, of problems being solved and lessons being learned, a world where organizations like BUILD were slowly, slowly passing on knowledge and resources to help Zimbabweans. Fighting for change? Maybe not. Facilitating change, yes, that's what we were doing, it's even what all our reports said. Wasn't that enough?

Still, as the date for a major review meeting with Mike approached, my confidence wavered. Would amiable Mike be impressed? Would he even be convinced? Convinced by my numbers, convinced by me, convinced that facilitating change really was the best possible way to spend five million dollars in the middle of one the world's biggest Aids epidemics?

I imagined that Gloria, William and Canaan could sniff out my weakness. *He's going to send you home because you're not making any difference here. And then what will you tell everyone at home? At least in the past white people built things – roads and schools. They smile more now, but they build nothing, they're too busy talking and smiling to build anything.*

I suggested to Mike that we meet at the Italian Bakery but he said their coffee was getting more bitter and expensive by the week. Bitter and expensive, that describes Zimbabwe right now, ha! We shared a morbid laugh. Mike said to come to his office and he'd provide the coffee. By that time, trips to the USAID offices had lost their glamour. All that gracious officialdom now felt tedious. Anyway, Mike's coffee turned out to be cheap and bitter.

"We keep hearing good things about your work," he opened, upbeat. "Seems your visioning and strategy workshops were a hit, and the follow-up seems to be on schedule too."

"Great, I'm pleased, yeah, I think they're going, um, well."

"Everyone says all the BUILD workshops are real professional, really helpful in getting them to see their future plans more clearly. Apparently your Susan's a leader for the future, hold on to her."

"Absolutely, yeah, she's done a great job. I've been at most of the workshops, the follow-ups, and it hasn't been very easy to get them to, uh, think boldly, you know, to sort of think outside of the, uh ..." But Mike wasn't listening.

"How many workshops have you run so far?" he interrupted as he paged through my report.

"Thirty." I conjured up a big, wide Midwestern smile, even though the number sounded so small compared to all the other HIV/Aids numbers. "We've done all fifteen and follow-up sessions with each NGO. Our follow-up has been in specific skill areas, finance, evaluation, so they have some tangible skill development as well, to support the execution of their visions."

"Looks like you're right on track. And the budget looks good too, you've spent all the money in the pipeline," he smiled.

"Absolutely, in terms of numbers we're right on track with where we said we'd be at this stage in the project. And mostly I'm pretty pleased with our progress." I looked down at my hands, trying not to let even a hint of concern register on my face. "There's just a couple of things I wanted to flag now, in case they come up later, to make sure we're, uh, on the same page."

"Shoot."

"The thing is, when it comes time for our mid-term evaluation, I think we're going to have a hard time proving we're really impacting the Aids epidemic. I think the workshops are good and it's obviously beneficial for the NGOs just to be going through the strategizing and skills development processes. But the bottom line is that we're going to have a tough time showing our capacity building is actually having a concrete impact on infection rates." Mike chuckled and took a sip of coffee that left drops glistening on his moustache. I plowed on. "I guess what I'm saying is that I'm not entirely sure this is the absolute best investment that can be made on the Aids epidemic." Even as the words came out of my mouth I wanted to pull them back in, like a bubble of gum I could deflate with a sharp breath. "It's just a thought," I added lamely.

"Don't you just wish we could go back to the old days?" Mike mused. "When we built things, actual schools, houses, when we gave people something tangible and knew it would help them? Not all this friggin' empowerment and participation and facilitation, which I know has its place, I mean obviously it's necessary, but..." he broke off, shaking his head, bemused but not frustrated. "The simple fact is that we don't know if most of what we're doing is really making a difference."

I paused to make sure I'd heard his words correctly. "Really, you think that?" I said, not sure of the implications of agreeing with him.

"Absafuckinlutely, but you'll never hear me say that 'officially'." He did the quote thing with his fingers.

"Couldn't we do some research, find out what really does work?"

"Oh Jesus, then we'll play right into the hands of the conservatives when we find out our programs aren't cutting it. I mean look at the HIV/Aids statistics; ten, twenty years into this thing and we can hardly point to any really big wins."

"Yes, the groups we work with hardly seem to focus on large-scale impact," I added, suddenly at ease with the moaning. "I mean, reducing new infections, things like that."

"Ah, screw impact, it's all about inputs, isn't it?"

"And yet you're giving them money to expand? Even though you're not sure they're really making a difference, you're still giving them more money?" Again I almost regretted my words but couldn't pull them back.

"Well, who else are we gonna give it to? At least these guys have a chance of doing something worthwhile. Everybody wants to spend money on Aids in Africa, and you have a pretty tough time convincing the folks back in the beltway that there's nobody investable in the middle of the world's biggest epidemic." I felt stricken, any smudge of Midwestern hope erased. "What choice do we have?" Mike continued, arms spread wide. "Stop doing it? Shut it all down? I mean, the whole development industry, it's like, what's that thing they say about a speeding train?"

"Get out of the way of it?"

"No," he said with an exaggerated shake of his head. "I mean you can't stop it. This is one fucking train you cannot stop." We shared a uniquely Zimbabwean moment, laughing at our own futility, but it passed quickly. After all, we were the visiting Americans, who had chosen to be passengers, if not conductors, on that speeding train.

"Anyway, you should feel good about Mr Chiruma. Heard great things about his work with women. Some of that workplace stuff was getting a bit stale, but now the donors are lining up to support him. Danes love 'em. The Scandis, you know, they can't get enough of all that women stuff. So keep up all that good work!"

Not long afterwards Mike showed me out of his office as though the previous thirty minutes of conversation had never taken place. One of their friends from the Swedish embassy was running Pilates classes from her home on a Wednesday night, the wine selection at Bon Marché was getting worse all the time, Luba's Blues Band was playing at the Arts Café on Friday, oh and he'd try to get out to visit some of the NGOs over the next month or so, when he had the time.

I left the USAID compound, walked down well-tended paths, past crouched gardeners, clipping and pruning. My head was far away, replaying *You're So Vain* by Carly Simon over and over, till I became aware of hammering and drilling coming from a corner of the compound. They were busy building a new extension in a style sympathetic to the colonial feel of the whole place. Men in blue jumpsuits were laying the shingles of a new roof, while others slept on the grass. Diseases and dictators meant growth for some in Zimbabwe: corrupt bureaucrats and aid agencies, the only ones whose cash flow increased with the chaos.

"Goodbye, madam, have a nice day." Her words brought me back to the present, to the smiling young woman holding a pen and the roster for me to sign. She had straightened hair and a smart gold chain, her chipped pink fingernails the only hint of imperfection. She could have been one of the people on the cover of Shadrack's college brochure. Maybe that's how you were supposed to look in the version of Zimbabwe the Americans created. Not a hint of *zvaka pressa* there.

***

Ten days later I was climbing into Lovelace's car, hoping yet again to find that world of earthly *umbonos* where *zvaka pressa* didn't exist, the one where everyone was fighting for change and winning. The world Americans thought we could build. I took Susan with me, knowing I needed a translator, not just for what I could hear but what I could see, as though the entire world created for and by NGOs was a sort of *trompe d'oeil* and Susan was the curator of the collection, explaining what it meant.

This time I kept my notebook closed; the notes had nothing to teach me. I stared out the window at the world passing by, the smiling people endlessly walking, the flat roads and flat-topped trees, the collections of huts.

Susan was dozing, so I talked to Lovelace. "Everything looks so normal. I'm reading about farm evacuations and killings of activists, and Aids is supposedly killing off the villages, and yet it looks so pleasant, so perfectly pleasant."

"It is difficult to see what's really going on in Zimbabwe from high up in this Land Cruiser," he laughed his uncomfortable laugh, but to me it felt like a commentary on my position in the country. "Ah no," he continued, " I mean the people are trying very hard, very hard to hold on, to send their children to school, to eat their *sadza*."

"To keep their lives feeling normal."

"Yes, something like that. But change is coming, Jeel. You must be patient, it's coming." I knew that Lovelace wasn't talking about the change we were hoping to bring about with our workshops.

"You always sound so confident, Lovelace. Of everyone in the office you seem the most confident about things coming right here."

"Because I know…" he searched for words. "Just because you can't see blood does not mean a fight is not happening. Do you know who this is?" he asked, turning up the radio.

"Mtukudzi. Oliver Mtukudzi."

"Yes, and do you know what he is saying? He is saying *wasakara*, you are finished, you must go. Everybody here knows who Tuku is speaking to."

I nodded and tried to share some of his optimism, to believe that this movement for change was bubbling all around, even though I couldn't see it. And for the rest of the car journey I felt buoyed by the notion that if I could be patient like Lovelace, change would eventually come. I just had to wait.

A few hours later, Mr Chiruma's *umbono* of "women's empowerment" sat in front of me: fifteen women, all probably in their twenties or thirties, in a circle suited for unholy confessionals. They all wore long, full cotton skirts and T-shirts with "Aids is With Us" printed in colorful letters on their backs, their full breasts straining against the white cotton. Mr Chiruma, neatly dressed in jacket and tie, pulled me aside as we arrived.

"It's going so well," he whispered excitedly. "Some members of the Danish Embassy have come to see our work with the women, and they are thinking of giving us more funding! Can you believe this is our *umbono* in action?!" I gave him a quick high-five before finding my seat.

Susan and I slipped into the back of the room, wanting to avoid formalities or upsetting the natural flow of the women's conversation. As we eased onto our chairs, we made sure our skirts covered our knees, our faces remained smiling and expectant. The room was filled with that unique Zimbabwean combination of laughter and weighty silences, discomfort and amusement blending seamlessly. A breeze blew through an open window, the sounds of heavy trucks and strangers' voices filtering through. Fifteen women in the Matabeleland's Aids Association's "catchment area" had formed a support group of sorts, to help each other deal with the pressures of being wives and mothers in an HIV-positive world, to educate their communities about HIV/Aids, and to educate their husbands and partners about condoms.

1999: HAUNTED BY THE TRUTH

"Our goal," Mr Chiruma reminded me with a smile, "is to empower these women. We have taught them condom negotiation skills to use with their husbands, so that they are more in control of the sexual act."

One of Mr Chiruma's staff members, a standout in her button-down white blouse and black patent leather shoes, was the official facilitator of this conversation, a chance for the women to discuss their experiences in putting their condom negotiations skills to use. She was asking the women how their "relations" with their husbands had been affected by condom use. No response from the circle of condom training graduates, just tittering and bowed heads.

Susan and I chuckled too, sharing an Oprah-style sense of female solidarity. I imagined one of them getting up, hands on hips, saying, "Men!?" before riffing on all their obvious shortcomings. But there was none of that here, in this room of giggles and glances away, where wives and mothers appeared reduced to maidens. Still, the facilitator kept probing them to share their personal "strategies" for protecting themselves from HIV/Aids. Finally, one woman spoke.

"What am I meant to do when he comes home at three in the morning? Uh, what can I do?"

"It is true," another woman joined in, "if your husband comes home looking for sex then you cannot say no. It is just not possible." The sound of a jackhammer from the road repairs nearby resonated through the room.

The facilitator refocused the discussion on more specific matters of condom negotiation. I found myself looking away too, suddenly uncomfortable as I recalled my own attempt at condom negotiation with a Zimbabwean man. How it ended with me curled up on the couch alone. Crying. The facilitator's voice brought me back: "How have you practiced your new skills to introduce the subject of condom use?" But the women couldn't match her enthusiasm. They looked at each other, looked around, looked away.

"We all know that sex is not something you negotiate with your husband," the oldest and largest woman said at last. "It is something he tells you to do with him. If it is not sex tonight, then it is tomorrow night and there is no way that he will let me talk about condoms." A quiet chorus of "uh huhs" rose from the circle.

"They just don't like them, the condoms," added another woman, "and if you talk about them, then it hurts you in other ways." The room returned to quiet, everyone looking at their feet, the facilitator still propping up her smile, searching for a question that might lead somewhere. Sensing the facilitator's frustration, another woman consoled her.

"We really have appreciated your trainings," she offered. "The talking skills you have given us, they have helped us." The women nodded their heads in agreement. "It is just difficult, you know, sometimes it is just difficult to deal with these things."

At tea break, the facilitator slunk off to the bathroom while the women huddled and bubbled around the kettle. When the facilitator returned, looking deflated, I said, "Good job. It's not easy to get these things directly, it will take time." I consoled her, resisting the urge to use the word "difficult". She managed a smile.

After tea, there was more of the same. Some women argued that they had to keep trying to get their husbands to use condoms, others shook their heads, hinting that their men would never accept it.

Above the sound of the jackhammer, a gentle sobbing rose from a young woman who had sat still and curved like a comma, her thin legs crossed, her shoes without laces, the only one in the room whose T-shirt hung loosely from her slight frame.

"He said he was going to kill me, kill me, if I talked about condoms again," she sobbed, her words muffled in the hands that held her head. "And I knew he wasn't lying. I didn't know what to do." She lifted her head and spoke directly to her fellow support group members, "My daughter was asleep in the next room."

The jackhammer kept digging outside. The other women nodded and looked down at their hands. Someone got up to shut the window. Even the facilitator stopped smiling as the young woman sniffled. Someone put an arm around the young woman, and she managed a weak smile.

Before Susan and I could discuss what had just happened, Mr Chiruma came rushing in as though a fire had just started. "I'm so sorry," he whispered, "I heard what happened. You weren't supposed to see that, that kind of thing."

"What kind of thing?" Susan asked.

"That poor woman breaking down like that." One of the secretaries brought Mr Chiruma a chair, which he pulled in close and sat down on it.

"That's exactly what we're supposed to see," Susan continued calmly. "The realities these women are facing."

"I know," he spoke into his long, fine hands, "but my staff have been doing really good work, and they wanted you to see all the progress we're making."

"It seems you are making progress with these women," I said, "it's their husbands who aren't progressing. How often does this happen, Mr Chiruma? A woman in that kind of situation with her husband?"

"It's difficult to say." He fiddled with his gold wedding band. "Quite often, I think."

"Often? You mean a woman is often physically threatened as a result of discussing condoms?"

"We've had several cases like that, yes. Married women are at greatest risk, of course."

I felt the queasy irony of women who are trapped by the very marriage vows that are meant to protect them. "So what can you do about it?" I asked. "What are you doing about it?"

"We've added some extra modules to the training, with role plays on handling, uh, difficult situations. And, and we've, uh, added some sessions on self esteem issues. So that the women can feel good, you know, strong in themselves. We got the materials from a women's group in America. Portland, I think." Mr Chiruma kept looking back to check if the women could hear him. "We're really trying to empower these women to make choices about their sexuality, not to have those choices made by men." He said it with the certainty of someone who had rehearsed it, confident of the person in Portland who had scripted it.

"So the women make the choice to talk to their husbands about safe sex, and their husbands choose to threaten them. That's not really a choice, is it?"

Susan turned towards me and whispered: "The problem is the

women are told by their husbands how and when sex is going to happen. It is not something that is discussed."

"So then why don't we talk with the husbands?!" I asked, sensing opportunity again. "Seriously, why don't we work with their husbands too? We could have discussion groups like this, but among men. If men are the ones who control sex, then let's talk to them."

"It's too difficult to try to change African men," Susan said. "They don't want to talk. Trust me."

"So instead we're asking these women to try to change their men? That's what we're doing, isn't it?"

"Our best hope with Aids is through women," Susan repeated. "They're the only ones who are willing to change."

"We're dealing with a sexually transmitted disease here!" I said, trying not to shout. "It doesn't work if only one half of the equation is willing to change."

Mr Chiruma was turning the ring round and round his finger. "We're already making plans for scaling up this work," he said. "We've got funding for scale up!"

"Do you really think it's a good idea to focus on scale-up when you're having major problems like this?" I asked, trying to sound conciliatory. Mr Chiruma shook his head as if I wasn't a director at all, but a dolt.

"There's no money out there for that kind of work with men," he whispered, rubbing his forehead. "The donors don't like men, they like women."

"Mr Chiruma, if working with men is the right thing to do, if it is the most effective thing to do, then we'll find the money for it."

The turning of the wedding ring got faster and faster, until Mr Chiruma turned to me, not a hint of a smile left on his face: "At our visioning meeting, you were very gung ho about this women's empowerment idea!" The phrase "gung ho" came out as if he'd heard it on *Friends*. "You and Mrs Moyo here were going on and on about how we needed new approaches, how, how, we had to get people – women – to deal honestly with Aids."

"I know," I stuttered, heart racing, sick gathering at the back of my throat, "but now you've learned that maybe it isn't enough."

"So now you're saying this work with women isn't enough? Now you want us to work with men too? Now you are not pleased with what we are doing!"

"It's not about pleasing me, Mr Chiruma, it's about helping *them*," I pointed to the women who were looking at us with concerned faces.

"You people," he spat, "you donors, international organizations, you're always trying to get us to do one thing then the next. All your priorities, all your plans. First it's peer education, now that's not good enough, it's got to be women, then it's going to be men. What do you expect from us, chopping and changing all the time to suit your needs?"

I stared at this once overweening man, now crumpled and exposed, genuine anguish on his face. "I'm sorry," I said, stricken, "I'm really, really sorry." Right then I didn't know who looked more sorry, me, Mr Chiruma or the frightened women from the group. Weren't we all just doing what we were told?

"You're not going to tell them, are you?" Mr Chiruma asked.

"Tell who, tell them what?"

"Our donors, you're not going to tell them what you saw today? We need this new funding to come through."

"No, Mr Chiruma, I won't tell anybody, don't worry." I sat back in my chair and for the first time I recognized myself in Mr Chiruma. I had thought I was so different from him, but there it was, a feeling that seemed so very common for everyone in Zimbabwe: the fear of exposure.

***

When I got home that night, *Long Walk to Freedom* was lying next to my door, Shadrack's silent request for a new book.

"Thank you for the book, madam. He is a good man."

"Yes, he is."

"Zimbabwe needs a Mandela," Shadrack mumbled.

For the first time in a long time, I looked directly into his eyes. And I saw it, a cataract spreading milky over his right eye, like a curtain closing. I tried not to stare, wondering how long it had been there and why I hadn't noticed it before.

"Yes," I said, "you do need a man like Mandela. Maybe Tsvangirai will be the kind of man," I continued, referring to the head of the MDC.

"I don't think so," he shook his head. "Zimbabwe doesn't make these kinds of men. Not for a long time."

"I'll get you another book," I said and went inside. The first book my eyes fell on at my bookcase was *The Great Gatsby*, which I snapped up without much thought. Maybe the story of a shattered 20th century dream was just what Shadrack needed. Then he would know that in America we have tarnished *umbonos* too. As I handed the book to Shadrack, I looked straight into his eyes, into that eye. It *was* a cataract.

For a moment I just wanted to cry, to soak in the irony of this thirsty reader who soon enough wouldn't be able to see, this aspiring accountant longing to spend his days poring over pages of numbers. But not a single tear came. Maybe in Zimbabwe blindness was better than vision. Maybe Shadrack would be the lucky one after all.

26

Late 1999: Hunted Because of the Truth

It's only in the movies that the weather portends evil, that storm clouds gather as the drums beat and the base guitar strums, telling you that bad people are about to do bad things or bad things are about to happen to good people. This was another perfect day in Zimbabwe, indistinguishable from most others: hot and sunny, hardly a cloud in the sky, just that blue expanse that was about the only thing that Zimbabweans could count on every day. The only thing that was neither expensive nor bitter.

I remember what I was doing on that sparkling day, not because it was particularly interesting or unique, but because I was doing exactly what I did every day, the only thing I could do in those days. I was writing documents and spending money; spending money and writing documents, pumping out the lifeblood of any good non-profit. By spending money and writing documents, I was ensuring there was ample papered proof of our utility, evidence that we were doing things right, even if we weren't doing the right thing. Reports, plans, budgets, there was always some other form of paper required by headquarters or the US government, and it was Mrs Reilly's responsibility to make sure that we complied with those regulations.

Compliance. The word has a satisfyingly supple, geisha-like feel to it, all those painted ladies pleasing their men. In the weeks and months that followed my visit to Mr Chiruma's circle of condom graduates, I found solace in practicing the art of compliance. Who needed *chinja maitiro* when you could allow compliance to spread like a milky cataract across your eyes, blinding you to anything but the computer screen in front of you? Who needed to venture out of the office over those flat two-lane roads, the kind a child would draw, which lulled you into thinking it was the kind of country a child might conjure, only to sit on the outskirts of another circle of trainees or addicts or victims, or stalk another conference room wall-papered with flipchart paper, trying to stoke up American-style arrogance and ingenuity and bravado.

I'd let Susan do that, while I stayed in my comfortable office sipping imported Twinings tea, inhabiting an imported world where budget numbers added up in a perfect one-plus-one-equals-two sort of way. Where details of our project activities rang with a cheery ABC kind of logic that now seemed lost in the chaos beyond the computer screen. Where I could feel like I was writing a brochure for Shadrack's college, one where the Americans promised to make everyone look like a character from the *Cosby Show*, smart and sharp and wickedly self-possessed. Where, with my eyes focused solely on my computer screen, I could believe for a little while that that we were doing some sort of good. I could even allow myself to imagine – imagination had become quite useful again – that some prospective do-gooder might eat cashews and drink tomato juice while reading my reports on the flight to Harare and by the time she strode through the little airport she might actually think she understood what was going in Zimbabwe. Maybe she'd even think *I* knew what was going on here.

On that brilliantly sunny day, I spent the morning writing about the fifteen workshops we had carried out in the previous three months, and the seventeen more scheduled for the next three months as we helped NGOs implement their visions and become better managers of the Aids epidemic. *My staff are dedicated! So dedicated! We'll do this capacity building for years if we have to!* I wrote of US$455 000 spent in the past three months. *We're busy, very busy!* Of the $350 000 we expected to spend in the next three months. *All the money in the pipeline!* I was sitting back to admire the way our work, our world, appeared on paper, when Gloria, William and Canaan invaded my thoughts again.

This stuff you're writing, it's rubbish, they mocked. It's not rubbish, all of it is true. *Have you ever stopped to think that the truth can be rubbish? All these numbers, all these workshops and meetings, do any of them really matter? Have you stopped HIV/Aids from spreading today? Have you saved a life today?*

What exactly do you want me to do, quit this job? Tell everyone this whole capacity building thing is a sham? Tell the NGO leaders they're busy fiddling with awareness raising and ABCs while Rome fucking burns?

A knock on my door roused me from these imaginary challenges.

"Jeel, there are some men here to see you," said Florence. She was standing in the doorway, eyes widened and fixed. Something was wrong.

"Men? Who are they, where are they from?"

"I don't know," she squeaked – Florence, who made it her job to know every reason for every visit.

I slipped on my sandals and went downstairs to meet the two mysterious men. They stood next to the pegs for our jackets and the cubby holes for our mail, probably in their thirties, their suits a fraction too long, their ties too narrow, their smiles wide and full, hands clasped.

"Hello madam," one of them said, looking down at a notepad, "Mrs Reilly." We shook hands, keeping our practiced smiles in place. In any other country I would have guessed such men would be selling religion or encyclopedias, but I knew these two had nothing to sell. I felt my hands trembling because Florence the busybody had gone back to her office and shut the door behind her.

"Mrs Reilly, we don't want to trouble you, because we know you're a very busy woman, as the director of this organization," the fatter of the two men paused for a moment and looked down at his notebook again. "BUILD."

"It's not a problem," I said, still trying to be casual. "How can I help you?"

"Your driver is Mr Lovelace Mandiveyi?" the man said, holding his hands behind his back, still smiling.

"Yes, yes he is." Were they police officers, coroners, undertakers?

"Is he here? We'd like to speak to him." A sense of euphoria washed over me; at least Lovelace wasn't dead.

"No, no he's not here. Is there some kind of problem?"

"No, no problems," the one doing all the talking said. He didn't take his eyes off of me, while the other one kept looking around. "We would just like to speak to Mr Mandiveyi."

"Are you with the police?" I blurted and immediately regretted it.

"We're conducting an investigation," the spokesman replied, without missing a beat. "Do you know where Mr Mandiveyi is?"

"South Africa." The lie tumbled out of my mouth. Florence had told me that morning that Lovelace's mother was ill and he'd gone to his *kumusha* to see her. I let my arms fall to my sides, "Lovelace, uh, Mr Mandiveyi, he's in charge of looking after our vehicles." I couldn't stop talking, I didn't know what would happen when I did. "We have two Land Cruisers – Toyotas – and they need some new parts. So we sent him to South Africa to get them. It's getting so difficult now, getting Toyota parts here. And they're so expensive. Everything is so expensive these days, isn't it? It's difficult."

Their smiles faded. Commiseration wasn't going to work with these two. It was compliance they were after.

"When do you expect him back?"

"End of the week maybe. Depends on how long it, uh, takes in Pietersburg. And then at the border, Beit Bridge. You know things can sometimes get jammed there. So it's difficult to say, really." I crossed my arms again.

"Well, when Mr Mandiveyi returns just let him know that we've come looking for him."

"But, uh, who should I say came looking?"

"He'll know," the man said, with smooth certainty. They walked towards the door, then he turned back, "Thank you, madam. You foreigners can be so helpful. We know that's why you're here, to help Zimbabwe."

The next few minutes were very still, with everyday sounds amplified, the squawking peacocks next door, the huffing engines of secondhand Nissans and Suzukis that polluted Zimbabwe's roads. I could feel my lips drying.

Florence and Edward crept out of their offices and found me on still the stairs.

"Who were they? Some sort of police officers? Investigators?" I asked.

"The CIO, the Central Intelligence Office," Edward replied.

"How do you know, I mean they could have been…"

"You just know these things, Jeel," Edward interrupted.

"These are the ones responsible for all those sudden illnesses and brakes failures?"

Edward nodded, "And worse…"

"What do you mean, worse? I mean they're still with the government, there must be some limits, some…"

"Ah, there are bad stories come out of the rurals, beatings, torture. Who knows if it's true. Mugabe is scared, anything is possible."

"But what do they want with Lovelace?"

Florence and Edward glanced at each other, stalling. Finally, Edward said, "He's got more active … in the MDC. With the strikes and stay-aways, he's been a leader in Chitungwiza, organizing people."

"Lovelace's in the MDC!?" My thoughts reeled, the words "beating" and "torture" ringing, ringing in my ears. "So where is he? Is his mother really sick? Is he on the run or something?"

"We don't know, he's just gone away for a few days while things quiet down."

"To his *kumusha*? Won't they find him there, won't they go looking there?"

"He's not really there, that's just the story that he put out."

"Why didn't somebody tell me? Why didn't *he* tell me? Maybe I could have helped, done something."

Edward took his time with his answer. "We didn't think you needed to know. We thought it was safer if you didn't know."

SHAME

Florence finally found her voice: "There are just some things you don't talk too much about, Jeel." I nodded, as though finally accepting the message I'd been told since my first month in the country.

The drive home that night felt longer than usual, past the oversized Chinese restaurant with its empty parking lot, through the traffic lights so dim you could barely see the changing colors, past flower sellers who chased your car with their bunches of red roses if your eyes so much as strayed in their direction. I started counting again: one, two, three, four, that one has HIV, the one with the fancy blond weave, and the other one over there, with a matching patent leather handbag and shoes. And how many of them were in the MDC, hiding their political affiliations like the HIV-positive hid their status? Did some of these men in suits work for the government – beating, torturing, raping people because sometimes being a thug is safer than being a victim? The streets were filled with addicts and victims and activists I couldn't recognize because they weren't sitting in a circle in front of me, wearing donated T-shirts.

In the midst of this reflection, a slight flutter darted through my stomach, a desire to pick up the phone and call someone when I got home. Jerry? Sarah? My father? See, I really am in the middle of this fight for change! I'm not just complying, I'm harboring a freedom fighter! That's why I'd come to Africa, right? To be a part of a fight like this.

It's not your fight, you know, Gloria, William and Canaan mocked. But it didn't matter; it just felt good to finally know someone who *was* fighting.

I found Shadrack hunched over his book.

"Evening, madam."

"Are you in the MDC, Shadrack?" I asked as I turned the key in the lock.

"Madam?"

"Are you in the MDC? Do you support them, the MDC, Tsvangirai?"

"Ah madam, you know … politics …" He stared down at the tiles streaming with ants.

LATE 1999: HUNTED BECAUSE OF THE TRUTH

"Because you know, if you are, I'll support you. I mean if there's something I can do. I don't know if you need time off, if …" I trailed off, uncertain what else to offer.

"Yes, madam," Shadrack replied.

"Anyway, if you need something, I'm here." I pushed the door open and entered my silent house.

A few days later, Lovelace came into my office at eight, right on time. I wanted to stand up and hug him, shake his hand, pat him on the back, offer some sort of greeting appropriate for a returning warrior. But I did none of those things.

"I'm sorry," he said, looking down at his hands.

"You have nothing to be sorry for," I gushed. I had so many questions to ask: When did you start with the MDC? What exactly do you do for them? But now such questions felt prying. Maybe there were some things you simply didn't talk about.

"I never thought they would come," he said, shaking his head. "I never thought they would come to the office."

"You can't control them; you can't predict what they're going to do. Anyway, are you okay?"

"I'm fine," he said, dismissive. The smile returned to his face. "They just like to scare people, you know."

"It worked!" I laughed.

"Oh, you are scared?"

"I'm fine," I shrugged, "I'm not what matters." There was a pause. "I'm so proud of you, Lovelace, really, I'm so proud of you taking a stand like this."

"Ah, Jeel, I was running away when they came looking for me! Nothing has changed yet, there is no reason for pride yet."

"At least you're trying to bring about change."

"People are dying for this, they are being killed. It doesn't matter if I'm just trying." I didn't know what to say in reply. Then Lovelace turned to the door, "The car needs washing."

"Be careful," I said. "Remember your daughter, your wife."

"I know. They are why I am doing this."

27

End of 1999: Another Unwanted Visitor

Friday night a week later, there was a knock at my front door. It was around eight o'clock – I know that because a repeat of *The Bold and the Beautiful* had just ended, Brooke and Ridge had got remarried – and I was on my third glass of wine, savoring the hazy sense of giddiness. Mike had invited me to go out to some gallery opening. I'd lied and told him I was busy; expat conversations about home leave, game reserves and delayed deliveries of *The New Yorker* just didn't appeal.

When I heard the knocking, I turned the television volume down. Who could it be? At seven o'clock Rutendo had left for the night, wearing his shiny black it's-pay-day pants. I'd already given Shadrack his bread and tea. I caught my breath as I pictured those men, the two apparently upstanding men, crowding my doorframe while Shadrack cowered in the bushes.

Then came another knock, not hard and official, but soft, desperate. I crept towards the door as lightning washed out the sky, flashing not crackling, promising that rain would lull us to sleep rather than keep us awake. Through the gap in the curtain I saw Susan looking pale and shrunken, shrouded in tiny insects. In my nearly two years in Harare, Susan had never shown up at my house unexpectedly. She had been off most of the week with a cold, missing the Lovelace intrigue. My stomach and throat tightened. I held my

END OF 1999: ANOTHER UNWANTED VISITOR

breath anticipating the words that would come through the open door: Lovelace is dead; they've killed him. She's come to tell me the bad news because Florence and Edward couldn't face it, I thought. Please tell me he was shot, died a quick death, please tell me he wasn't tortured.

"What is it? Is it Lovelace? Is everything okay?"

Susan couldn't look at me. She scuffled over to the couch, heels clacking on my parquet floor, and dropped heavily onto the cushions. I waited, knowing I would soon hate the words I was now so desperate to hear.

"I'm dying. I think I'm going to die." Susan's throat was so dry the words could barely slip out.

"Wh, what?"

"I went to the doctor today. You know I haven't been feeling that well lately." Susan wiped her nose and looked at me, then started sobbing. "He took my temperature, looked at my throat and, and he said maybe it was HIV, that he'd seen it before and it looked like HIV."

"C'mon Susan, what can somebody tell just from looking at your…"

She shook her head, "He's an old white man, Jill. He knows these things. I'm going to die. He knows I'm going to die."

I sat down next to her, repeating *shhhh*, *shhhh* and rocking, as though these universal actions would ease the pain. I patted her back and felt dizzy, every sensation lunging towards me: the TV still chattering from my bedroom, the smell of the pasta sauce I'd made earlier, the pages of Shadrack's book flapping open as the rain started to pat steadily on my roof.

I held Susan, firm and strong, and I decided in an instant that I would do so for as long as she needed it. No matter how heavy she got, when my arm fell asleep, when the nubs of her hair extensions started to form dents in my neck, I wouldn't shift or slump. It was the first time a Zimbabwean had truly leaned on me, and I wasn't going to budge.

Our bodies started to rock together gently, back and forth like a tiny boat lost at sea. I was at once anchored to her body, that sofa, that moment, and off wildly chasing some future truth. Susan's beautiful face could soon be covered in telling splotches, she'd fake a smile through putrid lips. She'd keep telling jokes and moaning about Mugabe over Nando's chicken until she took to bed in her *kumusha*, forced to stop pretending. Would Florence stop rinsing her coffee cups? Or would Susan be the one accusing Florence, unveiling jealousies and tensions I'd never known existed?

Stop it! Susan has a sore throat, that's it. I don't know how long we sat there. Shadrack coughed a few times, the opening sequence of the news started. Which of Comrade Mugabe's lies was Dorcas selling us tonight, her monotone delivery either the ultimate act of compliance or defiance?

There are just some things you don't talk too much about. Would I hide in a polite silence now, even after all I'd seen and thought?

"Susan have you been tested for HIV, have you ever been tested?"

"No," she whimpered, mascara streaming, lipstick smudged.

"Have you had unprotected sex? Could you possibly have been exposed?" All that ABC, one, two, three Aids awareness jargon finally felt useful.

"Yes, with my husband, of course," Susan's replies were now equally quiet, rational, almost testimonial.

"Have you been unfaithful to him?"

"No."

"Is there a chance he's been unfaithful to you?"

"Yes, of course, there's always a chance with a man. I don't think so, but of course there's a chance." *Christ, Susan is just another vulnerable married woman. Underneath the expensive weaves, the chardonnay and wise words, she is just another Mrs Somebody who isn't in control of her own life.*

"We'll get you tested," I declared. "We'll go to a clinic tomorrow and get you tested." Susan nodded her head against my shoulder, like a sad little girl. "And then we'll know, we'll know for sure. Right now we don't know anything for certain. We can't be sad when we don't know anything for certain yet, you hear me?" Susan kept nodding and sniffling. "Do you want me to call your sisters?" I offered. Susan was the second oldest of six sisters, whom she often

END OF 1999: ANOTHER UNWANTED VISITOR

referred to as her best friends, so I thought she'd want them around her.

"No!" she barked and pulled away from me, eyebrows knitted over wild eyes. She stood and started pacing, her skirt bunched over her knees, the wind squalling and thunder gathering outside. "No, you can't call them! You can't call anybody! You can't tell anybody, nobody from the office, not my family. You mustn't tell anybody!"

"Okay, okay," I soothed, bringing her back to the couch. "It's alright, it's fine, I won't tell anybody." We started rocking again, returning to the familiarity of hushing and shushing, escaping in the silences.

"Can I stay with you tonight?" she asked.

"Of course, of course."

"They think I'm at a workshop," she said, before descending deeper into her tears.

"Shhhh, shhh, it's okay, it'll all be okay." Even as I was saying those gentle, generic words, my head started to throb with the reality. Susan had reached out to me because I was so irrelevant here, my disconnect from Zimbabwe's real world made me the perfect hiding place. This educated woman, who for the previous two years had traveled this country with me preaching to NGOs about "speaking the truth" and "voicing the unspeakable", now didn't want anyone she loved to know that some white doctor took one look at her throat and said she might have HIV/Aids. I felt sick gathering at the back of my throat. This was the face of Fear, which showed little regard for the logic of ABCs or the apparent sophistications of middle class, urban life. If Fear could fell Susan like this, how brutal must its power be to destroy the hundreds of thousands of Mrs Everybodys living in Zimbabwe's villages? And if she didn't feel safe from Aids, who in Zimbabwe ever would?

Susan fell asleep, overwhelmed and exhausted, her breath hot on my arm, her body growing heavier as she started to snore. Slowly, tentatively, I pulled out from under her and went to the kitchen for a glass of water. I started to pace, playing the tape in my head: *women's empowerment, peer education, prevention, education, harmful cultural practices, needs assessment, evaluation, training, strategic planning, work plans, scale up, condom social marketing, home-based care, psycho-social support, care givers,* infected and affected, rapid testing, counseling and testing, vulnerable children, risky behavior, partner reduction, protected sex, trans-generational sex, sugar daddies. Over ten thousand Aids awareness meetings, thousands of peer educators, just as many youth activists, home-based care givers, workplace support teams.

Susan Moyo 1961-1999. That's what it would say at the top of her tombstone, I could picture it perfectly, one of the bigger tombstones in the cemetery, always decorated with fresh flowers. Susan was so popular, a loving mother and wife. *She's a real star, you should hold on to her.* Popular Susan Moyo passed away recently from after a short illness – or would it be a headache she died from? Dorcas could read it on the news together with her bigger parade of lies. And what would I do when all this bullshit started to pile up at my feet? Readjust my mask and make a donation to the chorus of baleful lies? Or make some fiery speech at her funeral about honesty and stigma and truth and how it all might set us all free? I couldn't picture myself making that speech; my imagination no longer had the capacity to envision Mrs Reilly, or even Jill, doing something so brave. Neither one of us had made a single fiery speech since setting foot in the country, other than in front of the mirror, to an empty glass of wine.

The tape started playing again. *A five-year project, you can actually build something, really make a difference. Just think about what has been accomplished in other places. We can do the same here in Zimbabwe!* It was like seeing your life flashing before you as you drown. *In order to see this vision, I want you to close your eyes.* I began pacing again, caged and agitated. *I'm not a witch, you know. You're not going to tell them, are you? We thought it was safer if you didn't know the truth. Chinja maitiro. Zvaka pressa.*

Fuck, fuck, fuck it! What the fuck am I doing here? What did any of these lines mean now, when this shining example of women's empowerment lay on my couch certain she was dying? I went to the toilet, willing myself to throw all of the emotion, all of the experience, up and out of me. But no matter how far I stuck my finger down my throat, nothing came. I was empty.

I sat on the toilet and started sobbing quietly, repeating *sorry, I'm so sorry* to everyone, no one, mostly to Gloria and Canaan and William, who'd been right about me all along. Maybe I could fake it as a director, but I could no longer pretend to myself that I'd be the activist I had once imagined myself to be.

END OF 1999: ANOTHER UNWANTED VISITOR

You win, you win. I'm not useful here for anything but compliance. That's all I know how to do, really, comply.

Gloria and Canaan and William seemed to be nodding. *You can't solve Zimbabwe's Aids problem, we Zimbabweans must solve it ourselves. You must just go back to America, buy yourself a nice new car with all the money you have saved living in our broken down country, find a good white man who might cheat on you once but probably not many times, even have a baby if you feel you must have a project. Look after your own life and accept that we must do the same with ours.*

You won't tell anybody, will you? That I just gave up, walked away, lost the will to keep fighting ... even to keep waiting?

We are dead. The only person we can tell things to is you.

28

Early 2000: A Farewell to Mrs Reilly

It was my farewell party and the directors' hands were filled with tea cozies and aprons, serving platters and dishes, the perfect gifts for a young woman who said she was going back to America to start a family.

"Finally!" one of them said, "you'll have a real family. Maybe even a child!"

The word "finally" was whispered a lot that night. It seemed that although none of the directors had said it directly to my face – there are some things you don't talk too much about, after all – many of them had worried that I was too young for such a big job, that it wasn't healthy for a young woman to be in Zimbabwe all alone. They believed, as Gladys had so many years earlier, that nobody chooses to be alone. I no longer knew if they were right.

It seemed fitting to end my time in Zimbabwe with a gentle, white lie that would make my public departure more acceptable. A lie that would save me from having to use words like "burnout" or "despair" as I looked into Mike Soderberg's eyes, save me from having to tell people I was desperate to flee their lovely, lovely country. Save me from admitting to Mr Chiruma that I no longer saw victims or villains, just lots of people politely conspiring to suffer, or confessing that I lay in bed dreaming of my future back in America. The

EARLY 2000: A FAREWELL TO MRS REILLY

innocent, airy silences, the only squabbles between the birds. The absence of cries you cannot hear but know are out there, farther than the wind can carry. The absence of conversations in languages you still don't know even after three years. The absence of requests, demands, warnings, apologies. Laughter, I wouldn't even miss the sound of acrobatic laughter because I knew how often it was fleeting, false. I couldn't bear to tell anyone in Zimbabwe that I longed to feel once again what it was like to truly be alone.

***

We did get Susan tested at a clinic and a week later she'd returned to my house for her results. I'd given Sarah the day off and sent Rutendo to the shops for bread and milk, creating the thinnest veil of privacy up there on Snowhill Close.

"You call them," Susan pleaded.

"I can't do that, they won't give me the results," I replied, only too aware of the confidentiality of such private matters.

"Come on, Jill, this is Zimbabwe. Do you really think anyone will care?" she responded with an ironic chuckle that conveyed no humor.

Susan was right, nobody did care. They just put me on hold while they looked for her results. "This fucking country," I thought, "how is this possible after twenty years of Aids work?"

All the while Susan lay prostrate on my bed, looking defeated. Until she heard me say the word "negative".

"Negative?" I repeated, still not quite believing I was having this conversation on Susan's behalf. "Let me just be sure I heard you correctly, Mrs Moyo's results are negative?"

Now Susan was jumping up and down, dancing across the room, moving faster than I'd ever seen a woman her size move. "Oh my God, Jill, I can't believe it," she squealed, rocking me back and forth, back and forth with a "thank you, thank you, thank you" on each side.

I wanted to jump up and down with Susan, like little kids feeling our feet landing hard and flat on the parquet floor, but my body felt leaden. I couldn't help feeling I was still in mourning. Belief, if not life, had been lost, and maybe the loss of belief was worse.

"That's great news," I managed with sufficient enthusiasm as to not distract from her celebration. "Really, really great. Wow, what a relief."

Susan kept jiggling and bouncing in front of me, all the life returned to her face and her limbs. She smoothed her hair, applied a fresh layer of purple lipstick to chapped lips and smiled at her reflection. Mrs Moyo was back in business. She was going to drive to the clinic to see the results for herself; she wanted to hold the paper in her hands. Then she wanted to celebrate at the Bulldog that evening, did I want to join her there?

"Come on, Jill, I promise I'll steer you away from the salad kids!" But the mere notion of a celebration – the vague reference to sex – almost made me shudder. I wasn't sure there was anything to celebrate.

"No, no, you go with your friends, you have a good time," I said.

Susan picked up her purse to leave. "Thank you so much, Jill. You don't know how much you've helped me. I couldn't have done this alone. You're a true friend."

I said nothing; I'd lost the will to play counselor or confidante or cheerleader. As she bounced down the verandah steps, I wondered if she would tell her husband, talk to her sisters.

She left a deathly quiet behind. I busied myself, putting her tea cup into the sink, straightening the creases her body had left on the bed, all the while shaking my head and fulminating. How could she pretend she was some fucking Aids activist when she so obviously didn't have a clue? When the bed was completely flat and unlined, I slumped onto it, head in my hands, tears running down my wrists. Still, all I wanted was to throw up all the pain and confusion raging inside, as though I could expel a disease from my body. And still there was nothing coming out of me. I thought of that other night when I did throw up, when all the pain of my relationship with Wayne threw itself up onto a cold pavement in Houghton. I had so wanted his approval, desperately needed his desire to make me feel good about myself. So I had led a double life, the rational me during the day and

EARLY 2000: A FAREWELL TO MRS REILLY

the emotional me at night. Just as Susan and everyone else in Zimbabwe was doing right in front of me. "You fucking hypocrite," I chided myself, "what makes you think you're so different? You didn't have a clue then either." Nothing in Africa had ever been what it seemed. Including me.

Tugging myself back to the present, I turned my computer on and started to compose a letter. It was the first time in months I believed every word I was writing on my screen. Susan had been given her life back, but I couldn't help feeling that my life in Zimbabwe had been taken away.

When I told her my decision to quit, Susan cried quietly. I offered neither apologies nor satisfying explanations, just that the same reckless individualism that had led me to Zimbabwe would take me away again.

"Sometimes you just have to do what's right for yourself," was about the best I could offer. Susan said she understood.

"You are American, in the end you guys always do what's best for yourselves." We both laughed, even though Susan had uttered an uncomfortable truth.

"*Zvaka pressa*," Lovelace said when I told him the news and we shared one of his uncomfortable giggles. This was the most difficult goodbye, because his was the future I could least predict. "Thank you, Jeel. I have gained much from you," he said, trying to be serious.

"Oh God, Lovelace, don't say that. You're the one who taught me. You've shown me your entire country, in all of its beauty." I stopped there, wanting to end in a beautiful reality. "Take care of yourself and your family, look after that little girl of yours." I leant in close to whisper, "I'm glad I got to know a real Zimbabwean leader while I was here." Lovelace just looked at me and giggled again.

Florence looked down at her hands when I said goodbye, her lips forming the familiar pout. She was always going to offer the perfectly correct farewell, a genuine "look after yourself" accompanied by a hug that lingered longer than usual.

There was no hug from Edward, just a phlegmatic, "Good luck, don't forget about us back here." I knew that for a little while my leaving would be yet another subject to be lamented over and laughed about over lunch. But I also knew that the staff would get on without me. Zimbabweans knew how to manage far, far better than I did.

A few days before I packed up my house, I gave Sarah some of my clothes, thinking she could sell them over time and earn some money. She came back to say goodbye, stuffed into one of my T-shirts, white with a studded star on the front, from Banana Republic. She looked like a superhero, like she could burst out of the T-shirt and go on to defend the world. Pathetic, endearing, enterprising – I wanted to take a picture of Sarah to remind myself of Zimbabwe when I got home.

Rutendo and Simon, the male staff whose lives took place outside my door, were probably the easiest ones to leave. I gave them each some money and we said our goodbyes through our shared fragments of English and Shona. The company would post Simon at someone else's home, maybe even a shorter bike distance from his own. And Rutendo would continue to serve as the caretaker of Snowhill Close, with each new white occupant offering more fragments of a discarded life with which he could keep building his own.

"Your husband," Rutendo said, "he never came."

"No, he didn't."

Then there was Shadrack. A few weeks earlier, when I'd only just begun to pack up books and label them in boxes, I had told him I was leaving. I set down his bread and his tea, took a deep breath and looked him straight in the eye.

"I'm going," I said. "I have to get back to America, my job, my job means I have to get back to America."

Shadrack stared at the ground. "Ah, madam, I am sorry."

"It's fine, it's fine, it's good for me to get home."

'Yes."

"So here, this," I said, holding up an envelope, "is for your studies. I've checked with various people and I think this should be enough, even with inflation, to pay for the rest of your studies. It's in US dollars, so make sure you wait to exchange it until the rate is the best."

"Thank you, madam."

"Now this," I held up a second envelope, "this is for your eye." Shadrack finally looked at me and gave an uncomfortable smile. "Again, this is US dollars. Inside the envelope is the name of the clinic and the doctor who can fix your eye, and this amount will pay for it." I handed him the envelope and looked into that cloudy glaze. "Now you use this money to fix your eye *soon*, do you understand? I know there are other things you need money for, but I *insist* you use this for your eye." Shadrack stood still. "You must get it fixed *now*, because the longer you wait the more difficult it becomes."

"Yes, madam."

"Do not use this money for anything else, okay?"

"Yes, madam." We stood there, Shadrack holding his two envelopes, me with no more offerings or instructions, the dogs barking in the background, moths ticking against the light.

"For more books you will have to use the library. I'm sorry I don't have any other solution. I know they're not as current, but you should still be able to find some good reading there."

"Yes, madam," he repeated. We stood together a few moments longer then I turned to go inside. "God bless you, madam. May God watch over you on all your journeys."

Inside, I crawled under the covers, my head buried in the pillow, knees pulled up to my chest, heart speeding. That was the last time I'd ever pay for someone's entire education with a thick wad of bills, the last time someone's health cover could be sealed in an envelope. It was the last time I'd ever feel compelled to try to secure someone's future; the last time I would ever dare to believe that I could. It was the last time I would ever feel all the power – and all the pain – that comes with possessing so much more than any other soul around you. I didn't know whether to laugh or to wet my pillow one final time with tears. So I just pulled my knees in tighter and closed my eyes.

I had finally let go of those feelings that had brought me to Africa in the first place, the ones that left me dreaming of greatness in front of my Zenith TV: the giddiness, the promise, the potential, theirs and mine, the power, oh yes, theirs and mine. The pure sense of rightness, of goodness. The simple, succulent belief that one day soon I would save a life.

SHAME

Soon I would climb into a business class seat that would take me away from Zimbabwe. I was absolutely clear that the only life I could save – the one I really needed to salvage – was my own.

Postscript

The ending of this book probably isn't what you were expecting. Because it goes something like this:

Small, grey country. I have a family of my own. Finally. Even two children. My husband is a white South African, born and bred in Benoni, just outside Johannesburg, whose idea of a struggle is playing eighteen holes of golf in the rain. And my sons would appear at home on the South African *platteland*, white-haired and blue eyed, their idea of make-believe to take a train or a fire engine or bus to "Souff Affrika" to visit Granny and Granddad. Maybe I really do have a little bit of Africa in my blood; at the very least I have made certain that Africa will always be a part of my life.

Not that creating this beautiful family was easy. It took years for me to embrace contentment, to release the notion that my life had to take place in service of a "struggle". But some form of acceptance is probably the final act of any coming-of-age story.

Needless to say, Susan was happy when I told her my news. I'd found that nice white man (finally!) and started a family with him soon after marriage, as any good African woman would. Gloria and Canaan and William would be happy too. But I don't speak to them anymore. They really are dead now, because I am resting in peace. And all the directors would probably be relieved to know that after leaving their lovely country, I'd focused on righting my own life rather than theirs. But I don't speak to the directors anymore; they are part of my life that is now dead.

I wrote so many endings for this book without mentioning my husband or sons. How could my mottled little story about African failures end with me in the arms of my little African family? Such a happy ending belied the rest of this troubled story; it felt like a betrayal to all the people I'd left behind in those troubled lands. Because more than ten years on, there would be no real happy ending for Zimbabweans. They're still struggling with their family, unable to find a way to rid themselves of their abusive father. In fact, Mugabe has cleverly managed to retain power in a "unity government" with the MDC that most people view as the opposition's ultimate capitulation, as well as the ultimate piece of savvy maneuvering on the part of wily old Bob. It appears Susan was right – the only way to get rid of your father is to wait for him to die.

And HIV/Aids? Zimbabwe hasn't managed to rid itself of that manly plague either – perhaps they're just waiting for a vaccine to keep them from dying. Of course there have been changes, even advances: many foreign donors actually like working with men now, treatment is more readily available, and ridiculous sums of money are pulsing through various pipelines thanks to the interventions of the beneficent billionaires Gates and Buffett. Periodically, a new intervention gets everyone excited – male circumcision! – because it promises that big change that might provide legitimacy, finally, to thirty years and billions of dollars of HIV/Aids work. Alas, such a big change remains elusive, and in private most of my friends in the business admit they have no idea if they're getting any closer to it.

Zvaka pressa. Or maybe not, maybe all over the place are little happy endings. Shadrack managed to get to school; Edward's wife had a baby. Maybe happy endings don't happen to whole countries or in relation to whole issues, maybe it's only when we locate the fight for change within our own lives, sensing the beauty of individual lives, that we will come close to something like profound change. Maybe it's only when we let go of the lofty ambitions that our lives really start to soar.

Maybe that will be the final act of another, bigger, coming-of-age story.

Thanks

So many friends have been supportive throughout this book writing process — and I'm grateful for all their interest and encouragement along the way. A special thanks to Jenny and Aasha, who read various iterations and gave meaningful comment. To Robert and Loraine, thank you for providing me rainy refuge when I needed to move this project forward. Claudette Sutherland was an early editor and an excellent teacher. I am so grateful to Julia Lord, who believed in my story when I needed someone to. And to Jacq Burns for her invaluable insights — she took this book to another level. Roxanne Reid provided superb editorial support – I read this book differently once she had worked on it. And Dominique le Roux literally brought my story to life, helping me put a public face to it. Finally, a special thank you to Christopher, who, perhaps without knowing it, ended my personal struggle.